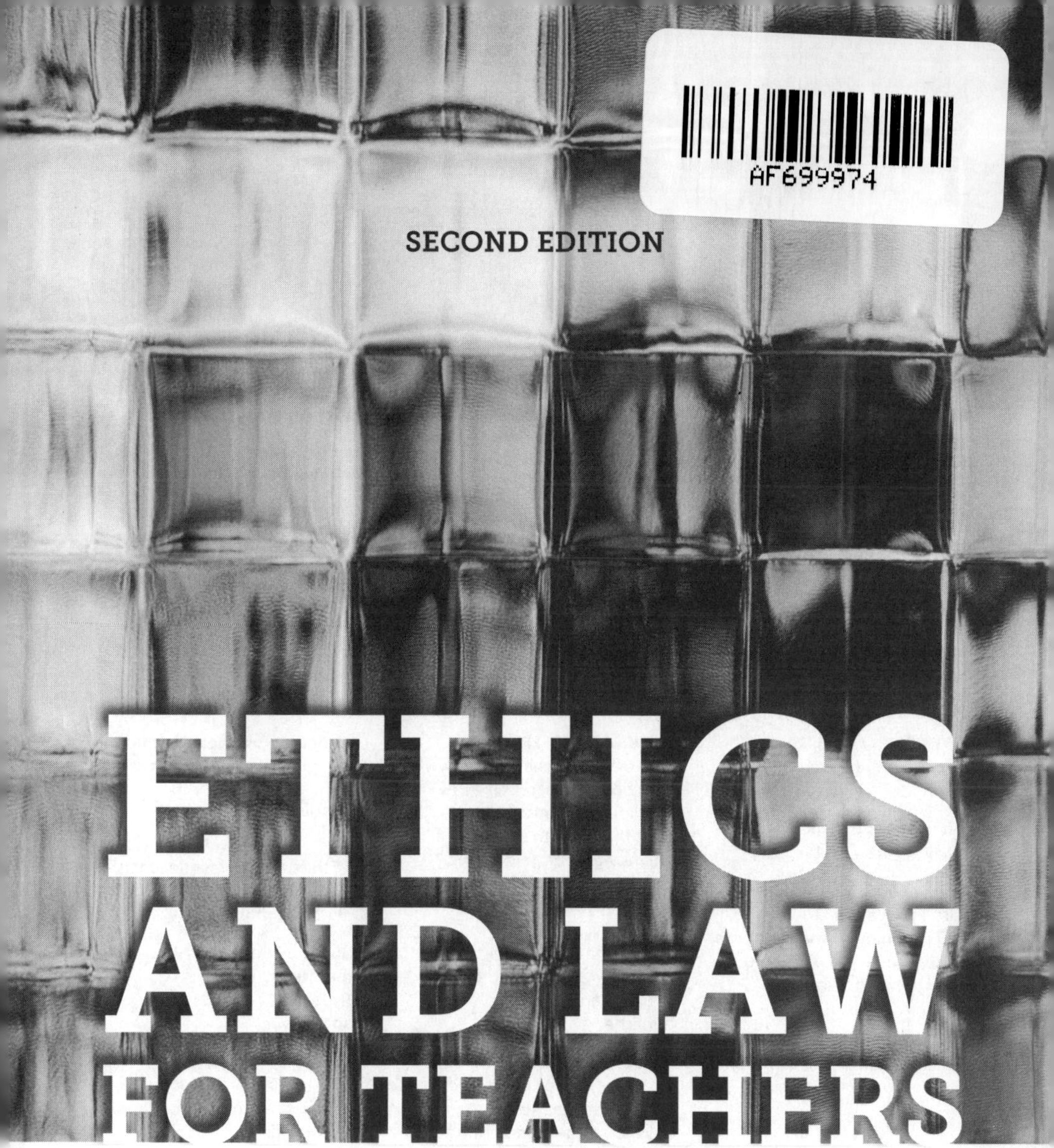

SECOND EDITION

ETHICS AND LAW FOR TEACHERS

DEREK TRUSCOTT
KENNETH CROOK

NELSON EDUCATION

NELSON EDUCATION

Ethics and Law for Teachers, Second Edition
by Derek Truscott, Kenneth Crook

VP, Product and Partnership Solutions:
Anne Williams

Publisher, Digital and Print Content:
Lenore Taylor-Atkins

Marketing Manager:
Terry Fedorkiw

Content Development Manager:
Roberta Osborne

Photo and Permissions Researcher:
Sandra Mark

Senior Production Project Manager:
Imoinda Romain

Production Service:
Cenveo Publisher Services

Copy Editor:
Matthew Kudelka

Proofreader:
Kavitha

Indexer:
Robert A. Saigh
Razorsharp Communications, Inc.

Design Director:
Ken Phipps

Managing Designer:
Franca Amore

Interior Design:
Sharon Lucas

Cover Design:
Sharon Lucas

Cover Image:
Ryan McVay/Getty Images

Compositor:
Cenveo Publisher Services

Printed and bound in the United States of America
1 2 3 4 18 17 16 15

For more information contact Nelson Education Ltd., 1120 Birchmount Road, Toronto, Ontario, M1K 5G4. Or you can visit our Internet site at http://www.nelson.com

Library and Archives Canada Cataloguing in Publication

Crook, Kenneth H., 1960–, author

Ethics and law for teachers / Derek Truscott, Kenneth Crook. — Second edition.

Includes bibliographical references and index.
ISBN 978-0-17-659031-4 (paperback)

1. Teachers—Professional ethics—Canada—Textbooks. 2. Teachers—Legal status, laws, etc.—Canada—Textbooks. 3. Teachers—Legal status, laws, etc.—Canada—Cases. I. Truscott, Derek, 1959–, author II. Title.

ISBN-13: 978-0-17-659031-4
ISBN-10: 0-17-659031-5

This book is dedicated to:

Raymond and Una Truscott—for instilling appreciation of the value of ethics and the power of the written word

and

Gerald A. Neely—lawyer, writer, educator, and good friend

ABOUT THE AUTHORS

Derek Truscott is a Professor in the Department of Educational Psychology, Faculty of Education, at the University of Alberta, and has been on faculty since 1997. He earned his doctorate in 1989 from the University of Windsor. He has taught, published, and presented widely on professional ethics and standards of practice and has served in numerous professional and collegial regulatory capacities.

Kenneth Crook was a partner in the Vancouver law firm of Alexander, Holburn, Beaudin and Lang. He earned his law degree from the University of Alberta in 1987. His practice consisted largely of trial work for insurance clients. He lectured and wrote extensively in the areas of insurance law, civil procedure, and medical malpractice.

TABLE OF CONTENTS

PREFACE

I had the honour of writing the first edition of *Ethics and Law for Teachers* with my dear friend Kenneth Crook, who died in 2008 after having fully lived every one of his forty-seven years. It was a privilege to have been best friends for most of that precious time as he taught me to live each day with love and purpose. He would have been pleased and proud that this second edition is being published. My part in its production represents but a small token of the tremendous debt of gratitude that I owe him.

When we wrote the first edition, we were motivated by our shared desire to write about the ethical and legal expectations of teachers in Canada so that we might provide guidance to those who perform such a vital function in our society. We began by surveying all of the teacher education programs in Canada, identifying the courses that dealt with ethics or law for teachers, and reviewing the course outlines of each. *Ethics and Law for Teachers* was and continues to be representative of the content covered by all of these courses, supplemented by other pertinent topics derived from legal cases, discipline decisions, and professional standards.

In doing this research, we came to learn that there are, broadly speaking, two divergent pedagogies for teaching ethics and law to teachers-in-training. Of the teacher training programs that offer courses on ethics, law, or ethics and law, roughly half provide guidance to professionals by exploring societal expectations of teachers. The remainder teach ethics and law in the context of courses on professional issues, promoting self-reflection as a guide to ethical actions.

In the first edition of *Ethics and Law for Teachers* we focused on the societal expectations for teaching professionals. However, when the draft manuscript of that edition was reviewed, some experts in the field felt that it was too prescriptive and would interfere with reflective learning. This criticism bothered us because it rang true. We didn't know how to address this limitation without writing another entirely different book, so we pressed ahead.

Since the publication of the first edition, I have continued to study the scholarly literature on law, ethics, and moral development. The issue of professional expectations versus reflective practice always threatened to disturb my calm. I learned that professional training across diverse fields such as medicine, law, and education is associated with an ethical deterioration that tends toward becoming more rule-bound. This unsettled me. I have taught ethics and consulted on matters of professional misconduct, and in my experience, unethical and unlawful actions rarely, if ever, result from ignorance of duties or the likely consequences of actions. Efforts to prevent or resolve unethical actions are largely ineffective without consideration of individual motivation and interpersonal circumstances.

These perturbations eventually jolted me out of a tendency to focus solely on the limited (yet important) role of reason and facts. I resolved to pay more attention to the powerful (yet irrational) role of intuitive processes and social forces. I was compelled to supplement my professional expectations approach to ethics with a more reflective one. I wanted to help teachers *be* ethical. So I abandoned my original plan to simply tidy and update the first edition of *Ethics and Law for Teachers*, and instead set out to significantly revise the second edition.

The biggest challenge I faced was how to engage readers in an authentic, personal consideration of the professional expectations placed on teachers in Canada. The objective, rational standards to which teachers are held accountable are not really all that difficult to understand (although they can be quite difficult to enact). What *is* difficult is to translate conscious knowledge of these standards into belief and action. The best way we know how to do so—to bring about true, transformational learning—is by honestly reflecting on the extent to which our *actions* align with our *personal beliefs* and with *societal expectations*.

This second edition thus includes many case studies and examples of the sorts of ethical and legal challenges teachers face. To encourage reflection on and engagement in ethical and lawful practice, I have included case studies and examples collected from teachers in the field, from discipline hearings, and from court cases. To encourage readers to consider these examples in a more reflective and less rote manner, ethical and legal expectations are presented in a descriptive rather than prescriptive manner. I invite readers to consider what they would do in each situation and then compare their personal predispositions with society's expectations.

I have also extended the first edition's ethics of duty and consequences with the ethics of intentions and relationships. I have incorporated all four of these systems of ethics into the completely revised chapters on ethical systems (Chapter 1) and ethical reasoning (Chapter 2) and integrated them into all of the other chapters. This expanded consideration of ethical systems is compatible with reflective learning and has the added benefit of promoting a more inclusive and flexible understanding of how ethics are enacted in real life.

Including reflective practice in my teaching has given me great satisfaction because it benefits students tremendously. Their experiences have provided invaluable feedback on how best to incorporate reflecting on societal expectations of teachers into learning how to be an ethical teacher. The lessons my students have taught me have informed this second edition of *Ethics and Law for Teachers* so that you, dear reader, might also benefit.

I thank the many students for sharing their ethical challenges, questions, and answers, and Jacqueline Leighton for providing a scholarly environment conducive to teaching and learning. Ken's thanks continue to go to the partners at Alexander, Holburn, Beaudin and Lang, and in particular to the late Michael P. Ragona, Q.C., Jo Ann Carmichael, Q.C., and Terry Vos, and to their law librarian Susan Daly. Lenore Taylor-Atkins and Roberta Osborne of Nelson Education provided much-needed and much-appreciated encouragement, guidance, and talent.

Thank you also to the following reviewers, who provided helpful suggestions:

Ken Brien, University of New Brunswick

Ginette Clarke, McGill University

Kent Donlevy, University of Calgary

Benjamin Kutsyuruba, Queen's University

Terry O'Brien, Lakehead University

Lynette Shultz, University of Alberta

I welcome any comments you might want to share about this book and how it relates to your experience of striving to be ethical. I can be reached at derek .truscott@ualberta.ca. I promise to consider your comments carefully and to incorporate as much feedback as I can if I am given the opportunity to write a third edition.

—Derek Truscott

CHAPTER 1

THE ETHICAL CONTEXT

CASE STUDY

JUSTIFICATIONS FOR CHEATING

A student in your class has been struggling in all of his subjects with a C average, and he is talking about dropping out as soon as he is old enough to do so. You know he has a very difficult home life and often looks tired and ill-prepared for his day. The only interest he has expressed about school is in taking Computer Studies as an elective, and he has shown some aptitude. You know that if he could experience success in one subject it could increase his confidence to master other subjects; that could really make a difference for his future. School policy, however, requires a B average in core subjects in order to take electives. You speak with him about the situation and he seems to respond to your encouragement to improve his grades. Sure enough, by the end of term his average has improved to the point that he is able to enroll in Computer Studies.

While you are finishing up after class a few days later, some of the student's classmates approach you and tell you that his girlfriend has been doing his homework and assignments for him.

1. What possible courses of action might you consider? Do you experience any conflict about what to do in this situation? Or does one course of action seem obviously correct?
2. What are your thoughts about why there could be more than one possible course of action? Why might some people think there isn't one course of action that is obviously correct?
3. What do you think the average person would expect a teacher to do in this situation? How important are these expectations to you when deciding what to do? Why?

The vast majority of teachers direct most of their energies toward providing their students with a high-quality education while relying on their own good intentions to stay out of trouble. Very few would ever intentionally do the wrong thing when dealing with a student, parent, or colleague. But good intentions are not always enough to ensure that we do the right thing. It is possible to do the wrong thing if we are unaware that an issue of right or wrong needs to be addressed, or are ignorant of what is expected of us, or don't know how to deal with the rightness or wrongness of a complex situation, or simply lack the fortitude to do what we know is right. And there are even times when we resist doing what we know is right because we very much want to do something else.

Most people who have read the Case Study at the beginning of this chapter realize that an issue of right and wrong is at stake, if only because it appears in an ethics textbook. Not all of us, though, know what we are expected to do in such a situation or how to deal with its complexities. And if we were actually faced with it in real life we would probably be reluctant to do anything other than nothing. Ethics is the study of how people should act toward one another in situations such as this and why people do and don't act toward others as they should. Learning about ethics helps us know how others expect us to behave and can help us do the right thing. That's why it is taught in most teacher education programs, and why books like this are written.

None of us come to the study of ethics completely ignorant. We all possess ethical intuitions—instinctive assumptions of right and wrong—that motivate our actions. Yet few of us consider then deeply or critically. This is because we rarely have to think about our personal ethical intuitions. They are the result of all the lessons learned over the course of our lives about how we ought to treat other people. They are so much a part of our understanding of the world that we just *feel* them. These intuitions arise very quickly and certainly much more quickly than conscious thoughts. When we hear about someone saving a student from a burning apartment, for example, we feel good because that person has done a good thing. Similarly, when we hear that the student's parents set the fire, we feel bad because they have done a bad thing. Such feelings serve as very efficient and mostly effective guides to most of our dealings with most of the people we encounter in most situations.

The catch is that ethical intuitions sometimes lead us astray. We have all done things that felt right at the time but later regret. We organize a picnic to celebrate the hero of the burning building only to learn that he was trying to kidnap his child because he had been denied parental visitation privileges. We organize a petition to imprison the arsonists and then find out that they were trying to keep their child warm because they had no money to pay the heating bill.

While such mistakes are understandable and even acceptable—albeit embarrassing—for the average person, teachers are expected to meet a higher standard. Teachers have expertise in the field of education and serve such an important role in society that they are granted an elevated status. With this status comes a corresponding expectation that they will be held more accountable for the things they do and say. Refer again to this chapter's opening case study. A teacher who looks the other way when a student cheats might reply, "It felt like the right thing to do." Most Canadians will not consider that an acceptable response. Teachers are expected to be able to justify their behaviour by referring to accepted ethical standards and reasoning.

Regrettably, there is no equivalent to medicine's Hippocratic Oath that summarizes the standards and reasoning teachers are expected to use. Each jurisdiction in Canada has its own unique ethical standards for teaching, and there is no complete agreement on specifics. This presents a challenge for teachers who want to do the right thing as well as for those who simply want to stay out of trouble. Fortunately, the situation is not entirely bleak. Society's ethical expectations of teachers are not particularly unique—rather, they are based on what we expect of everyone in society. Also, we can assemble some foundational ethical expectations for teachers from various codes of ethics and from legal decisions involving teaching. So no teacher need be completely uninformed.

But knowledge alone is not enough to make us ethical. For starters, new ethical expectations arise too quickly and in greater variety for codes, legal decisions, or textbooks to possibly address them all in a timely manner. So even if we did try to memorize all the rules and standards of teaching, we would still find ourselves unsure how to act in many situations. More significantly, while some teachers fail to meet their ethical obligations because they didn't know what was expected of them, most do so because their ethical intuitions are at odds with what society expects of them. People almost never deliberate carefully about what they should or shouldn't do in a situation involving matters of right and wrong. We do what we feel is right, and usually it is consistent with what others expect of us because our ethical intuitions have been shaped by a lifetime of learning about right and wrong. But just as knowledge is not always enough, sometimes what feels right is not the right thing to do. That's why teachers who understand the reasoning behind society's expectations of them and who heed their intuitions are better able to respond to the ethical demands of teaching in a manner that satisfies all concerned.

The purpose of this book, therefore, is to help you develop *knowledge* of Canadian ethical and legal expectations of teachers, personal *insight* into ethical intuitions, *awareness* of circumstances in which ethical and legal expectations and ethical intuitions are likely to become factors, and *skills* for making decisions based on accepted ethical standards and reasoning. These aims are addressed by presenting questions that are central to the enterprise of teaching but not always answerable by referring to facts, rules, and standards. Those questions include:

- What rights are owed students, their parents, and society in the context of teaching?
- What punishments are justifiable, if any, when a student misbehaves?
- What kinds of relationships are acceptable beyond teacher and student, such as friendships?
- What actions are considered to be those of a private citizen, and what ones are subject to the professional expectations placed on a teacher?
- How can students be treated fairly when they have differing advantages and disadvantages?

When you respond to these questions in real life by relying on personal whim, the risk of failing to meet society's expectations increases tremendously, as does the risk of having a complaint made against you. So in this book we will be inviting you to examine the degree to which societal expectations around such questions mesh with your ethical intuitions, and to consider how any conflicts between the two might be reconciled.

REFLECTIVE TASK

Establishing a Reflective Habit

Throughout each chapter in this book, you will be presented with reflective tasks related to the questions presented. These are prompts for thinking deeply and critically about being ethical. They provide an occasion to process the thoughts, emotions, questions, ideas, and life lessons that make up your ethical self. When you conscientiously reflect on your ethical intuitions in light of society's ethical expectations of teachers, you are creating an opportunity to foster a more harmonious ethical self. This will help you respond to the ethical expectations of teaching with greater integrity and confidence.

When it comes to reflective practice, the biggest challenge for most people is finding the time for it. Setting aside a regular time seems to be an important first step toward establishing a habit. Reflecting on events while they are still fresh is generally a good idea, but trying to do so every day can become burdensome. Many people find that once or twice a week is about right. Try experimenting until you find a routine that fits your schedule. Of course, if you are reading this book as a course requirement, you may have to reflect more often than you would otherwise.

Most people find that recording their reflective process is important to get the most benefit from it; experts usually recommend doing so. There is no one correct way to do it; what is important is that you record your thoughts. Don't worry if you misspell words or they come out in a jumble—that has no bearing on the effectiveness of your reflective process. Our thoughts are usually a mishmash of impressions, ideas, feelings, and images, so if we record them honestly they will not be particularly logical. Indeed, just transforming our experience into some semblance of language is probably an important part of what makes reflection helpful.

You can begin by thinking about how you can incorporate reflection into your schedule. You might ask yourself:

- What impediments do I foresee?
- What would help make it more achievable?
- Have I successfully undertaken something similar in the past? If so, what did I do that made it possible, and could I apply it to reflecting?

Take as much time as you need to think about these and other questions, and to develop a plan.

ETHICAL SYSTEMS

Some of the oldest writings in Western civilization, such as those of Plato and Aristotle, deal specifically with how we ought to treat one another. Western philosophers have always been deeply concerned about ethics and have proposed a variety of systems for determining the rightness and wrongness of actions. After literally thousands of years, no one system has emerged as clearly superior to the others. You have probably noticed that your sense of right and wrong is consistent with that of many people, and at odds with others. So it is with philosophers' ethical systems: each has its strengths and weaknesses, its champions and detractors, and none is universally acknowledged as the best. So it should not surprise you that the ethical expectations of teachers are not the product of any one system of ethics.

Happily for us, there are only four systems that inform those expectations. Each is built around an aspect of the human condition that is generally accepted as crucial to being ethical. Deontological systems of ethics concern themselves with duties; teleological systems, with consequences; virtue systems, with intentions; and relational systems, with relationships. The study of philosophy can bore some people to tears and terrify others, but have faith—a basic understanding of these systems will help you understand the ethical expectations placed on teachers as well as how to be more ethical.

Duties

Deontology (from the Greek *deont*, "duty," and *logia*, "reason"—therefore, "reasoning from duty") is a system of ethics that directs us to consider what duties ought to guide our actions. A deontological system calls upon us to *act as if the rationale that underlies our action were a universal duty.* This is why it is often referred to as *duty* ethics. It obligates us to treat others as rational beings worthy of respect. From a deontological point of view, the intention to bring about good results is irrelevant when assessing ethical rightness or wrongness, and so are the actual consequences of an act. Instead, deontology argues that an action should be judged on whether or not it was performed in accordance with accepted ethical duties such as honesty, respect, and care.

For example, the *Code of Ethics* (2006) of the Nunavut Teachers Association states that teachers "should at all times respect the individual rights, the ethnic traditions, and religious beliefs of his or her pupils and their parents."* Because every reasonable person would want to be treated similarly—who of us wants to have their rights, traditions, and beliefs disrespected?—the standard is, from a deontological point of view, ethical.

Consequences

Teleology (from the Greek *telos*, "end," *logia*, "reason"—therefore "reasoning from ends") focuses on the consequences of our actions. A teleological system considers right actions to be those that produce desired outcomes and wrong actions to be those that produce undesired outcomes. Its basic premise is: *An act is right if, all other things being equal, it produces or is likely to produce the greatest amount of good for the greatest number of people.* A pure teleological approach to teaching would require us to consider the likely impact on each person for each action in each situation we face. This would obviously be impractical, because we would be paralyzed by all the decisions we had to make. A more practical expression of this idea is: *We should behave in accordance with rules that, all other things being equal, produce or*

*Nunavut Teachers' Association

are likely to produce the greatest amount of good for the greatest number of people in most circumstances. Most professional codes of ethics contain such rules, and teachers then only have to know which rule to apply in a given situation.

The British Columbia Teacher's Federation *Code of Ethics* (2003), for example, states that teachers are expected to "review with colleagues, students, and their parents/guardians the quality of service rendered by the teacher and the practices employed in discharging professional duties."* This is a rule that is very likely to result in desired consequences for the colleagues, students, and parents/guardians of teachers who follow it and is therefore, from a teleological point of view, ethical.

Intentions

Virtue ethics assigns our intentions the central role when we consider the right thing to do. It focuses on our character rather than our duties, and on the motives behind our actions rather than on their consequences. Teleology and deontology address *what* is ethical; virtue deals with *who* is ethical. The right thing to do is therefore unique to the individual and cannot be arrived at solely by logic or prediction. After all, the virtue argument goes, we cannot and should not make the world conform to our will, so we are better off focusing on changing ourselves and our desires. Virtue ethics encourages us to ask: *How will my actions exemplify the type of person I want to be?* This obligates teachers to be ethical at all times rather than only when confronted with an ethical challenge, and to develop character traits that will result in their meeting ethical expectations.

To give an example, the *Code of Professional Ethics* (2000) of the Saskatchewan Teachers' Federation asks teachers to "respond unselfishly to colleagues seeking professional assistance." Obviously, being completely unselfish would leave us no time to satisfy our own needs and would encourage dependence in others. Yet most of us would certainly be better people if we were even a little more unselfish, so striving to be less selfish is, from a virtue ethics perspective, ethical.

Relationships

Relational ethics acknowledges that we are all members of social groups such as neighbourhoods, professions, religions, and nations, and that we have obligations to uphold our roles within these communities. It recognizes that our social roles give rise to ethical considerations of whether we are contributing the collective good. Relational ethics requires us to ask: *How will my actions manifest consideration of and concern for the social group?* Relational ethics is concerned with *how* we treat one another rather than *why* we treat one another that way. Motives and logic are not as important as service to the group. Ethical reasoning and actions are understood as being embedded in a complex interpersonal context that is never completely predictable. What is considered ethical is therefore open to reconsideration in response to changing relationships. Our actions can weaken or strengthen the ties that bind us together, and this encourages us to consider the welfare of the group as a whole as we seek to do the right thing.

---

*British Columbia Teacher's Federation

For example, the *Code of Professional Conduct* (2004) of the Alberta Teachers' Association requires that teachers "not undermine the confidence of pupils in other teachers." Although other teachers sometimes do things that we don't agree with and indeed may reflect bad teaching practice, supporting students' confidence in other teachers encourages them to respect the important role that teachers play in our society, and is, from a relational ethics perspective, ethical.

WHAT THE CODES SAY

Purpose of Ethical Standards

The purposes of the ethical standards for the teaching profession are:

- to inspire members to reflect and uphold the honour and dignity of the teaching profession
- to identify the ethical responsibilities and commitments in the teaching profession
- to guide ethical decisions and actions in the teaching profession
- to promote public trust and confidence in the teaching profession.

—Ontario College of Teachers' "Ethical Standards for the Teaching Profession"

FOUNDATIONAL EXPECTATIONS

While Canadian society's ethical expectations arise out of four ethical systems, our laws and standards are predominantly informed by deontology. Given that no system of ethics is able to guide us to a satisfactory course of action in every situation, when we encounter deontology's limitations, we enlist teleology. This means that, in essence, teachers are expected to act in accordance with agreed-upon duties *except* when doing so would obviously result in abhorrent consequences such as death or serious physical harm. When such an outcome seems inevitable, we are expected to do whatever is reasonable to prevent it even if doing so violates a duty. Such situations are rare, thank goodness, so it is safe to say that behaving in accordance with the accepted duties of Canadian society is indispensable if we are to avoid trouble and meet the expectations placed on us. The foundational expectations placed on teachers are these: to respect autonomy, provide care, maintain trust, and build community.

Respect Autonomy

The ethical duty of respecting autonomy deals with honouring the right of individuals to make their own choices and be free from the dominating control of others. We respect autonomy when we allow students to form their own judgments and when we involve parents and the school community in decisions about educational programs. Respecting autonomy is also reflected in acknowledging that each person has the right to decide who has access to their private information. Note that there is an important distinction between freedom of choice and freedom of action. While we respect people's freedom to make choices, their freedom of action is limited by the autonomy of others. So we accept an individual's right to hold bigoted views, for example, but not to distribute hate literature, because the latter would interfere with the autonomy of the people to whom the hatred is directed. The expectations and challenges of respecting autonomy are discussed in Chapters 6 and 7.

Provide Care

Teachers are expected to protect students from harms and to not inflict intentional or avoidable unintentional harms. Besides providing physical safety, teachers are responsible for protecting students from mental harms (such as fear) as well as from the thwarting of significant personal interests (such as obtaining an education). Consideration of care also requires teachers to establish and maintain minimum competence to meet the learning needs of students. Providing care can be viewed as involving a continuum from not causing harm at one end, to bringing about benefit at the other. Teachers are expected to balance the potentially harmful consequences of an action against the potential benefits. All considerations being equal, this balance is weighted more toward protecting and not harming students. This means, for example, that because of the harm it would do to their autonomy, we should not deceive students in order to have them learn an important lesson. Expectations and challenges around providing care are dealt with in Chapters 7 and 8.

Maintain Trust

Fairness, honesty, and dependability are at the core of the trust relationship between teachers and their students, parents, and society. Trust is particularly important for teachers because it is fundamental to the bond of social cooperation that makes teaching possible. Yet trust is continually threatened by the difference in social power between teachers and students. Maintaining trust involves considering the interests of students before our own, even when doing so is inconvenient or uncomfortable, and it extends to relationships with colleagues and the larger community. Teachers are expected to be open to reviewing with colleagues, students, and their guardians the quality of and practices employed in their teaching, for example. Teachers are also expected to abide by contracts with employers and to act in accordance with the rules of their professional associations. Expectations and challenges related to maintaining trust are discussed in Chapters 9 and 10.

Build Community

Allegiance, self-sacrifice, and respect for authority are central to the ethical duty of building community. Because a core function of teaching is preparing students to be good citizens, teachers are expected to be sensitive to the traditions and values of the society in which they live and work. We are expected to treat all students as valued members of society and to ensure that access to an education is fair and equitable. This means avoiding bias or discrimination based on social status, religious beliefs, sexual orientation, gender, physical appearance, age, ancestry, or any other attribute unrelated to a student's learning needs. It also means making accommodations so that students are able gain an education regardless of any disabilities that might make doing so difficult. Teachers are also expected to consider how controversial topics and practices impact the social fabric of which the school is a part and to balance the individual interests of students with those of the community. Expectations and challenges of building community are dealt with in Chapters 11 and 12.

REFLECTIVE TASK

An Ethical Value That Is Important to You

Select one of the following ethical values as the one you consider most important to you. It doesn't matter if more than one of them, or even all of them, are important to you. Just pick one for this task. You may want to pick the one that played a prominent role in an ethical challenge you recently faced.

- **Logic**—using analytical and critical thinking to decide right actions.
- **Experience**—using intuition and feelings to decide right actions.
- **Liberty**—allowing individuals to decide right actions for themselves.
- **Loyalty**—relying on the group to decide right actions.

Now take as much time as you need to reflect on and record why this value is important to you. Don't worry about what others might think about why it is important to them. Just write honestly for yourself.

ETHICS PROFESSIONAL AND PERSONAL

Personal ethics has a very long history; professional ethics is a much more recent development, one that involves applying ethical theory to the behaviour of groups, such as doctors, lawyers ... and teachers. In fact, the existence of a code of ethics has come to separate professionals from those who simply seek to earn a living. If a group of practitioners want to be acknowledged as a profession and allowed to practise independently and exclusively, their ethics must be based on ensuring that those who receive their services benefit from them and are protected from harm. In the case of teachers, such ethics include consideration for students and for the community in which they teach. A code of ethics thereby creates an implied social contract that balances professional privilege with commitment to public welfare.

To protect the public, professional codes of ethics are predominantly *prescriptive*—they state what members should and should not do. But ethics codes must also be at least partly *descriptive*—that is, they must state what members of the profession actually do—in order to take into account the compromises that real life requires. A purely prescriptive code based on the highest ideals of human conduct wouldn't reflect the reality of schools or teachers' personal ethics. Such a code risks being ignored or even rejected by most teachers. But balancing prescriptive with descriptive ethics is a delicate matter. If a professional code of ethics doesn't set a high enough standard, the public may worry that it is designed to protect professionals rather than them, and support for the profession can wane.

Codes of ethics serve an important function in that they articulate how members of a profession pledge themselves to meet society's expectations. However, codes are almost always developed by scholars, experts, and lawyers. People in these positions tend to view ethics from the high ground of philosophical rationality and to think in terms of principles that can be applied to solve practical problems. But the real world of teaching is such that we are rarely faced with obvious, well-formed ethical dilemmas in need of solutions. A teacher's typical day involves a succession of often messy, usually ill-defined situations in which ethics are embedded or implicated yet are seldom the central issue. This is where ethical intuitions serve us so well. They are much better than procedures and principles when dealing with the fuzzy, flowing nature of real life.

Our ethical intuitions are the product of our unique personal history and may or may not be congruent with the expectations placed on us as professionals. The communities in which we grew up and live our lives have ideas about what a good person is supposed to be and do. Through exposure to lessons about what actions and outcomes are regarded as the right and wrong things to do, we gradually adopt a variety of ethical beliefs. These beliefs are usually implicit, and are often contradictory, and the ones that are most influential are typically learned before we are old enough to question them. Many of our intuitions have therefore never been subjected to rational scrutiny and may be unsuited to the complex ethical demands of teaching.

Also, because our ethical intuitions arise without conscious effort, we rarely question their presence in our minds any more than we question whether something has a particular shape, texture, or taste. That is, we trust them as much as we do our perceptions. The *feeling* that something is the right (or wrong) thing to do is therefore usually experienced as a *fact* that we ought to do it (or not). This means we can act in ways that seem obviously to be the correct thing to do, yet may be inconsistent with society's expectations and our professional code of ethics. Even more problematically, our feeling of the right or wrong thing to do can just as easily be the product of sentiments other than ethical ones, such as self-interest. And when people confuse ethical and nonethical motives, their subjective experiences are often just as righteous as if they were acting from purely ethical intentions. Thus, when called to account for their actions, they usually respond with indignation, and the outcome is seldom satisfactory for anyone involved.

This is where awareness that we possess intuitions that feel like obligations can help us meet our professional expectations and refine our ethical selves. When we stop to reflect on our subjective experience, an opportunity is created to exercise at least some rational control over our intuitions. Intuitive reasoning tends to narrow the options for responding to a few—often very few—choices. This is what makes it so efficient for making all of the repetitive choices we face every moment of every day. Conscious reasoning, on the other hand, tends to expand our options. This is what makes it so effective for making complex and novel decisions. Knowing that just because something *feels* right doesn't mean it *is* the right thing to do can give us just enough pause to consider whether our intuitions match up with society's expectations of us.

WHAT THE CODES SAY

Character of Individual Members

The impact which the teaching profession has on our society is immeasurable and the quality and character of the individual members of the profession are prominent factors in the economic and moral levels of that society. Therefore, the profession must establish rules of conduct for all who are engaged therein to ensure the highest possible performance standards.

—From the Prince Edward Island Teachers' Federation

THE ETHICAL TEACHER

Perhaps more than in any other profession, ethics are essential to teaching. On a practical level, this is because teachers are faced with ethical choices every day. On a group level, this is because the acknowledgment of teaching as a profession, as opposed to mere employment, has been slow to be recognized and continues to be questioned. On a societal level, this is because teachers have such an immediate and indelible influence on the ethical lessons that students learn directly and indirectly.

The ethical teacher is therefore first and foremost an ethical person: someone for whom respect, kindness, honesty, and loyalty are established habits of intention and action manifested in all interactions with students, parents, and colleagues, and in the very way we teach. The tensions and complexities inherent in teaching are such that we routinely find ourselves caught between what we *feel* we should do and what we *think* we are expected to do. We may not even realize that we ought to be thinking about being ethical. The ethical teacher is aware of his or her own ethical intuitions and how they align (or not) with professional ethics. There are no guarantees or shortcuts to this ongoing refinement of our ethical selves. It is a part of the lifelong learning that is essential to the profession.

The ethical teacher knows that codes of ethics are but one aspect of this lifelong learning, partly because many are limited, partly because codified expectations are of limited usefulness in real life, and partly because ethical knowledge plays a limited role in our ethical consciousness. High-stakes situations that arouse strong feelings and that are not addressed by codes of ethics, laws, or books are common enough that we have to be able to rely on our ethical intuition *and* conscious reasoning. This requires a well-functioning ethical self.

The most potent influence on any habit—but especially our ethical habits—is the habits of those around us. The ethical examples of our colleagues and the ethical leadership of administrators can provide opportunity and encouragement for us to develop our ethical selves. Collaborative community building among teachers can foster a shared set of ethical values that can become part of the school's ethical culture and a positive influence on our ethical character.

Those around us can also *thwart* our attempts to be ethical, of course. Challenges, such as the pressure to give passing grades to underachieving students, to move students to different classes in order to accommodate parental intolerance, and to ignore crucial aspects of particular cases in order to enforce arbitrary policies, can undermine our sense of agency and foster cynicism. Belief in our ability to resolve ethical issues can falter, and we can become disillusioned, leaving us lacking the confidence to maintain a strong and adaptive ethical self. The ethical teacher recognizes the pernicious effects of such influences and takes steps to counter them.

It is also true that teachers are not expected to be perfect any more than anyone can possibly be. There may well be saints among us, but everyone else is expected to do their best. The ethical teacher knows that when we are too afraid to make an ethical misstep, we pull back from experimenting, taking risks, and challenging ourselves. In the same way that we want our students to make mistakes so they might learn from them, allowing ourselves to try and fail creates opportunities for growth. Failure is feedback. And feedback is the fuel that powers development of our ethical self.

Ethical teachers approach all professional activities with sensitivity to the ethical issues involved and are knowledgeable of and sensitive to society's ethical expectations of teachers; willing to strive to reconcile those expectations with their personal ethics; and prepared to reason and act in a manner consistent with professional ethics. The remainder of this book is devoted to providing incitements for achieving these challenging and rewarding goals.

REFLECTING ON THE CHAPTER

You might want to keep a pen and paper or other recording medium at the ready while you are reading this book so that you can make a note of your impressions while they are fresh, particularly with regard to the ethical case studies. Your immediate reactions can be a good source of information about your ethical self, so recording them before they are lost is a good strategy. You can later incorporate these impressions into your reflective journaling. Take some time now to go back through this chapter and make note of anything that struck you as important, confusing, or worth taking more time to think about. After you have done so, read through your notes and notice whether your sense of the material in the chapter has changed. If so, how? If not, why do you suppose that is?

■ SUMMARY

Ethics represent the core values of a profession that wants to be granted the right to practise independently. Teachers are expected to abide by a code of ethics that strives to ensure that students and the community at large are protected from harm. A professional code of ethics applies foundational ethical principles to activities characteristic of or unique to a given profession. The major ethical systems are deontological (duty-based), teleological (consequence-based), virtue (intention-based), and relational (relationship-based). Canadian society's foundational ethical expectations of teachers are that we respect autonomy, provide care, maintain trust, and build community. Being an ethical teacher requires knowledge of the Canadian ethical and legal expectations placed on teachers, awareness of the circumstances in which ethical and legal expectations and ethical intuitions are likely to come into play, skills for making decisions based on accepted ethical standards and reasoning, and personal insight into ethical intuitions.

■ QUESTIONS FOR DISCUSSION

1. Consider two people. One was motivated by an honourable purpose and brought about destructive results. The other was driven by selfish goals and achieved beneficial outcomes. Which individual would you consider to be more ethical? Why? Can you imagine how a reasonable person might disagree with you?
2. If ethical standards are objective, how can one avoid becoming rigid? If ethics are subjective, how can anyone be held accountable for his or her behaviour? Which do you tend to favour—objective or subjective standards? How would you justify your preference to others?
3. What should a teacher do if she or he does not accept the ethical expectations that society has of them? Can they still be a teacher? Why or why not?

CASE STUDY

■ UPGRADING CERTIFICATION

Over coffee a fellow teacher mentions that she has had her certification upgraded and is now earning an additional $7,000 a year in salary. Curious, you ask how and she tells you there's a loophole in the provincial certification regulation system, so she took some courses in sports coaching offered by an online university. When you point out that she doesn't teach physical education, she tells you "it's no big deal" and that she knows of a number of other teachers who have also taken advantage of the opportunity. You do some research and it's quite clear that this university has essentially no academic standards; anyone who pays the course fee is granted credit. While its educative value is highly suspect, you find the monetary value highly tempting. In fact, you feel a bit foolish for even having considered taking legitimate courses pertinent to your teaching.

1. Do you experience any conflict about what to do in this situation? Does one course of action seem obviously correct? What do you honestly think you would do if you actually had a chance to earn that much money with minimal effort? What does this tell you about your ethical self?
2. How compelling do you find the argument that teachers are so underpaid and overworked that they deserve a raise by whatever means are legally available to them? Can you formulate a counter-argument?
3. What do you think the average person would expect a teacher to do in this situation? Do you agree with these expectations? If so, how would you present them in a persuasive manner to a fellow teacher struggling with what to do in this situation? If not, how would you persuasively correct an average person's expectations?

CHAPTER 2

THE PERSONAL CONTEXT

CASE STUDY

DISCOMFORT WITH CURRICULUM

You have been experiencing some rather significant discomfort teaching Social Studies. You're new to teaching the course, but the curriculum is well enough laid-out that you have a good sense of how to proceed, which is reassuring. However, some of the students have been raising challenging and persuasive alternative interpretations of the course content. You have done your best to be respectful of the students' opinions without sacrificing the curriculum's learning goals. But because you agree with the students to a certain extent, you find yourself losing some faith in the course as you are expected to teach it. When you approach a colleague with your concerns, you are told to just finish out the term. "What are the odds that the next class will be as clever in quite the same way?" she says. You feel unsatisfied but can't quite put your finger on why.

1. What do you think your students would say about what you should do in this situation? What about their parents? What do you think most of your fellow teachers would say? Whose opinion is most central to your decision about what to do?
2. What feelings are aroused in you by this situation? What do they tell you about what you should or shouldn't do?
3. What ethical expectations of society at large do you think are relevant to this situation? Which are most important to you?

When people talk about being ethical, many say something to the effect that they learned in kindergarten all they really needed to know. The childhood wisdom of "play fair" and "don't take things that aren't yours" may indeed be good advice even for adults, but it doesn't really provide sufficient guidance for dealing with the complexities of teaching. Teachers regularly deal with situations that involve multiple conflicting expectations, expectations they do not personally agree with, and bewildering circumstances that make it difficult to discern what is expected of them. We need more than calming clichés if we are going to reliably do the right thing.

Many people will also say they "just know" what to do, and trust their ethical intuitions (see Chapter 1). Unfortunately, our intuitions are not often available to us for explaining to others why we prefer one particular course of action over another. Our actions may be founded on personal ethical values, but it is far easier to say what we believe than it is to explain what we did. As challenging as this may be, teachers are expected to be able to make explicit their reasons for choosing one course of action over another.

Others will say that every problem has only one right answer and that we would know the answer if we just used "common sense." But if that were true, we would not need as many laws as we do, nor would there be more than 5,000 years of conversation about the ethics of right actions. If the right answers were self-evident, surely we would have reached a consensus by now. Teachers are expected to be able to justify why they do what they do, or did what they did, using sound reasoning based on accepted ethical principles.

And of course every person knows *they* are ethical—just ask them. We often feel that others are ethically deficient while we are just fine. We are quick to judge the motives and actions of others but much more circumspect when it comes to our own. This leaves us with a question; Why, when so many of us feel we are above ethical reproach, do we so often do the wrong thing? It is tempting to conclude that the problem is the fallibility of human nature and that no one can claim to be ethical. But we know that some people do manage to be more consistently ethical than others. Teachers are expected to be more ethical than the average citizen.

The fact that teaching is a complex, fluid activity makes achieving any kind of consistency a challenge, let alone being consistently ethical. Teachers are required to make a series of judgments about what is going on, decide on an action, act, and then appraise the consequences of their actions. Over time, the choices we make culminate in a personal ethical approach or style. An underdeveloped ethical belief system increases the risk that our teaching style will be characterized by hypocrisy or outright unethical behaviour. Conversely, a well-developed, defensible ethical approach to teaching enables us to more consistently meet the expectations that society has of us. Those who have developed such an approach, did so by consciously reflecting on their circumstances, intentions, duties, and actions. The absence of ethical reflection increases the chances that we will fail to act in ways consistent with our ethical beliefs and expectations. Meeting the ethical expectations that society has of teachers thus requires our personal involvement. Self-knowledge from thoughtful reflection helps us consciously influence our actions and find the right words to justify them.

To say that teachers are expected to be able to defend their actions is not to say that we make excuses for them. Organizations and individuals routinely espouse ethical values that are not reflected in their actions. As professionals, we are expected to recognize and resolve any dissonance between our stated values and those manifested in our practice, as well as those endorsed by the organizations of which we are a part. This can be difficult, especially if our organization's practices are incongruent with our ethical expectations. Nonetheless, we are expected to take responsibility for our actions, as well as our share of responsibility for the organizational circumstances within which we live and work.

REFLECTIVE TASK

An Ethical Predicament

Think about a situation in which you had to make an ethical decision. Is there one that comes readily to mind? Or do you have to think long and hard to recall one? Does this tell you anything about how prominent ethics are in your life? Is it that your ethical values and actions are so congruent that you haven't experienced ethical distress? Or is it that you haven't attended to your ethical beliefs and actions as much as you could? During your ethical predicament, did your feelings and actions flow from your intuition, or was it more of a conscious, logical process? What were some of the personal impediments that made it difficult for you to do what you felt was right? Are those impediments still active in your life? How comfortable were you with your actions then? How comfortable are you with them now? What does your level of comfort tell you about your ethical self? Might you be inclined to act differently now? Why? Record these and any other reflections.

ETHICAL REASONING

Much of the time in our busy days, we are making decisions of an ethical nature without even being conscious of doing so. We take rapid stock of the information we have at hand and use what we believe about the nature of the world to understand what is going on, what is likely to happen, and what we should do. The process is usually so rapid that we don't experience having made a decision at all. This is our intuitive ethical reasoning. Such reasoning tends to be spontaneous and done with little if any awareness of having made a decision. For the majority of situations we encounter, this works remarkably well. Indeed, we would face what athletes call "paralysis by analysis" if we stopped to methodically consider every decision we had to make. Imagine having to decide every morning if you should brush your teeth or not, going through the evidence for and against doing so before even reaching for the toothpaste. We wouldn't get much done.

So it goes with our ethical decisions. Intuitive ethical reasoning is the basis for automatic reactions such as feeling outrage when a fellow teacher harms a student. Fortunately, this often leads to easy solutions for how to best behave ethically in a given situation. In ideal circumstances, our intuitions predispose us to make sound ethical choices and to act in ethically acceptable ways. This is particularly true when the ethical expectations are well-established and we are quite familiar with them, such as that we should not harm children. However, our intuitive ethical sense is based on a lifetime of learning about doing the right thing, and our training and experience in professional ethics may constitute only a very small part of this (especially so early in our professional training). When we encounter novel or ambiguous situations, our intuition can lead us astray. Even more importantly, when our personal values are in conflict with community, professional, or societal values, our intuition may lead us to indefensible or unethical actions.

Fortunately, we are all capable of using conscious reasoning to rigorously and rationally evaluate the conclusions we arrive at by intuition. Conscious reasoning is slow and inefficient, requiring more time and a lot more energy than intuition. Reasoning ethically in this way involves a methodical, logical, critical process that incorporates ethical duties and legal standards. This is the reasoning process by which teachers are expected to be able to justify their actions. However, given that intuitive reasoning is the raw material that conscious reasoning makes use of, good ethical decisions don't come from using one form of reasoning rather than the other, but of making the best use of both.

Ethical teachers are mindful of the conditional, context-dependent nature of the teaching encounter. They accept that there is both not *enough* data available to tell us what action is likely to result in how much of what type of outcome for what type of ethical situation, and *too much* data available in a single ethical situation for anyone to possibly process. As teachers, we realize that we must use our intuition *and* our rationality if we are to be truly ethical.

To grasp why this is so, think about how you have at least ten decisions to make in just one class: how to start the class, how to describe a learning task, et cetera. Now consider how each decision has at least ten possible options. Total it up, and that represents 10 *billion* possibilities. Then what to do next depends on the students' responses, how best to respond to their responses, and so on. The number of choices grows exponentially with the number of decisions to make. The result—a rather quick one—is informational overload.

The teaching encounter is therefore not the time to be weighing all possible combinations of actions and non-actions. We simply cannot compute all of the interrelations between all of the interdependent variables. Excessive conscious reasoning causes us to "choke" by focusing on discrete categories of our experience. This introduces so much inefficiency as we try to piece them back together that our ethical reasoning system crashes.

Skilled practitioners in all fields, including teaching, compress the informational load and avoid choking by making sense of their experience holistically. Highly ethical teachers are able to efficiently decide what to do by using knowledge derived from reflecting on previous experience to discern patterns invisible to the novice.

Especially when we are confronted with new situations, the best way to meet the ethical expectations placed on us is to proceed through a deliberate ethical reasoning process like the one described in detail in the next section of this chapter. As we encounter more and more new situations and repeat this process, our personal ethical values will become increasingly congruent with professional ethical values. In this way—that is through deliberate reflection on experience—ethical decisions that are justifiable and professionally appropriate will become more intuitive for us.

WHAT THE CODES SAY

Reflect and Adapt

These are the ethical ideals for Saskatchewan teachers . . .

. . . To reflect upon the goals and experience of professional practice, and adapt one's teaching accordingly.

—From the Saskatchewan Teachers' Federation Code of Professional Competence

REASONING FROM EXPERIENCE

Despite being expected to justify any actions we take that have ethical implications (which is most of them), teachers are not always motivated by conscious beliefs about what constitutes ethically proper behaviour. As often as not, they are motivated by unconscious ethical intuitions. And while our intuitions are often congruent with accepted ethical standards for teaching, when they are not the discrepancy hinders our ability to meet our ethical expectations.

Reflective practice is considered a basic skill for all teachers because it enables us to explore the ethical assumptions and beliefs that motivate our actions. Through deliberate and sustained reflection, we can clarify our ethical intuitions and translate them into the language of ethical principles. In this way any differences between what we believe and what is expected of us can become apparent and be addressed.

Reflective practice entails a type of "self-research" for fostering greater awareness of our ethical intuitions. Reflective teaching practices enable us to consider our actions and intentions carefully and identify opportunities to make them more congruent. However, not all congruence between our intentions and our actions is desirable. The kind of congruence that enables us to meet our ethical expectations is based on the ethical principles contained within our professional codes of ethics. Congruent but undesired ethical actions and intuitions are based on beliefs that are inconsistent with societal expectations. These can be the most pernicious and intractable of all.

The intuitive explanations by which we understand the ethics of teaching and feel good about that understanding—even when we are mistaken—are difficult to modify *because* they are unconscious. We do not have direct access to them, so they can't easily be revised. Our intuitions are therefore best refined through purposeful reflection on what we actually do, not what we *think* we do. By deliberately and critically reflecting on our actions, we can deduce the otherwise inaccessible nature of our ethical intuitions and intentions.

In particular, our learning progresses more rapidly when flaws in our ethical beliefs are revealed. When things don't turn out as expected, we have an opportunity to improve our understanding of how to be a more ethical teacher. We need to know what we are doing wrong in order to know what we are doing right. Conscious identification of errors and monitoring of outcomes drives improvement. New or revised beliefs can be tested to see if they reduce our mistakes and improve our ethical integrity.

The process presented here incorporates the four ethical systems and four foundational expectations outlined in Chapter 1. Given that they all have something important to say about being ethical, we are much more likely to arrive at an ethically acceptable and congruent decision if we incorporate all of them into our deliberations. This can be done by using simple heuristic of *listen, feel, think, act.*

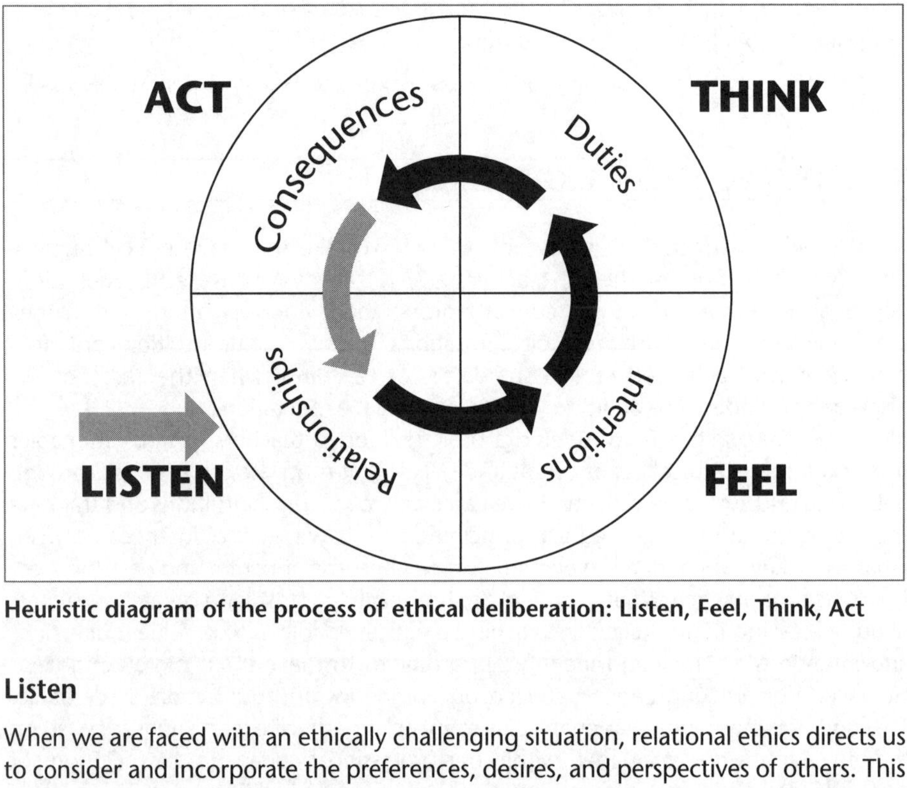

Heuristic diagram of the process of ethical deliberation: Listen, Feel, Think, Act

Listen

When we are faced with an ethically challenging situation, relational ethics directs us to consider and incorporate the preferences, desires, and perspectives of others. This means taking as much time as is necessary to understand the social circumstances of our decisions and actions. How often have we rushed to a decision based on limited information, only to later find out that the situation was more—or less—complicated than we first thought? By stopping to ask questions and listen to others with respect and compassion, we can better appreciate the interpersonal context of the problem we are faced with. A guiding question that is often useful is, "Why now; why has this problem manifested itself today and not yesterday or tomorrow?" Sometimes we even have the good fortune of bringing to light a misunderstanding that, once clarified, enables us to resolve the conflict without having to do anything more.

Feel

Once we have listened carefully to others in order to understand the interpersonal circumstances, virtue ethics prompts us consider how we feel about them. That is, it encourages us to look inward and honestly take stock of our true intentions. We almost always have strong feelings about an ethical dilemma—that's usually how we first become aware that something needs addressing. Rather than ignoring our feelings or trying to hold them in abeyance, we can treat them as guides to our motives. By intentionally incorporating our emotions into our ethical reasoning, we harness their power to motivate us toward right action. After all, doing the right thing is often arduous, and knowing it's the right thing to do doesn't mean we will be able to see it through to its resolution. We need the energy of our emotions to power our virtuous intentions.

Think

After taking into account the interpersonal circumstances and our personal intentions, deontological ethics obligates us to ask, "Does a relevant professional ethical duty, guideline, or legal standard exist?" This question directs us to review relevant professional documents, starting with practice standards, then codes of ethics, professional guidelines, and occasionally even legal case law. Canadian society operates within a normative framework for ethical behaviour that is based on ethical principles. That framework constitutes a common ethical language whose grammar is abstract, universal, objective, and defensible. By comparing and contrasting our personal beliefs with what is expected of us, we can identify any incongruence. If we decide to act in a manner inconsistent with our ethical expectations, we should think long and hard before acting and be prepared to thoroughly justify our decision. When we review the codes and guidelines of our profession, we are often prompted to consider our intentions in a new light; we may even experience a shift in our personal ethics so that we feel differently about what we prefer to do. In situations where no ethical or legal duty clearly implicates one course of action, the number of acceptable avenues will at least be lessened.

Act

Once we have identified the possible courses of action that are congruent with our professional expectations in an ethically challenging situation, teleological ethics directs us to take stock of the likely consequences of each alternative. All other things being equal, we are expected to choose the alternative that is likely to cause the least amount of harm and the most benefit (in that order). Having identified the best course of action, we are then expected to carry it out. Often, our actions bring to light additional dimensions of the situation that may lead to a redefinition of the problem, or change the circumstances in significant ways, necessitating consideration of further alternatives that have consequences we must deal with, and so on. This is why the model is presented in a circular, iterative form.

■ REFLECTIVE TASK

Autobiographical Sketch of Your Ethical Self

This might be a good time to record an autobiographical sketch of your ethical self. You might begin by thinking about what have been the pivotal events in your life whereby you became aware that there are right and wrong ways to behave. Perhaps you did something at a young age about which you still feel embarrassed to think about even now. Or perhaps you were accused of doing something that you didn't think was wrong. Maybe you still don't. Or you may remember something you did for which you felt proud.

You could also consider some of the people who influenced your sense of right and wrong: Family, friends, teachers? Were they a positive influence whereby your sense of being able to be a good person was enhanced? Were they a negative influence whereby you felt diminished or bad about yourself? Or perhaps they set a good or bad example that remains relevant. What is most salient about these people for you? Are there other significant influences that have continued from your childhood? Or have new people and circumstances come to be more potent? What is your sense of who you are ethically today?

Take as much time as you need to reflect on those formative events and how they are a part of how you think about yourself.

RESPONDING TO AN ETHICAL PREDICAMENT

Consider a hypothetical situation in which you are teaching English in an urban high school. One of your students, Ed, whom you don't particularly like yet is clearly a very clever student, comes to class wearing a T-shirt emblazoned with the words "White Power" across a clenched fist. You find the slogan and what it appears to represent distasteful, and a few other students have complained that it makes them uncomfortable. An ongoing problem in your school has been that Aboriginal and non-Aboriginal students rarely socialize with one another. There have been instances of racial tension in the school and the surrounding community.

You ask Ed not to wear the T-shirt to school again, and he objects. The following day, your principal tells you about an irate phone call from Ed's father, who says that either his son is allowed to wear the shirt or he will be kept home from school. The father is adamant that the shirt is "free speech" and accuses you of being hypocritical because you have allowed, without comment, other students to wear T-shirts endorsing gay marriage. While the administration supports your decision in general terms, you are asked to justify your position, especially in light of the fact that the school does not have a dress code.

One possible line of ethical reasoning using the model presented in this chapter is as follows.

Listen

An identification of individuals and groups involved in or likely to be affected by our actions obviously includes Ed and his father. The other students feeling uncomfortable with the T-shirt should also be considered. It follows that the school administration has an interest because the educative environment is affected. Finally, schools exist within the larger community, which will always have a stake in the moral climate of the school and its influence on the next generation of citizens.

In the best possible scenario, a conversation with Ed would result in him coming to understand the impact that his T-shirt's slogan has on others, and deciding that he wants to have a more tolerant and respectful relationship with his fellow students and the broader community. This would promote all of our foundational ethical expectations of respecting autonomy, providing care, maintaining trust, and building community without compromising any of them. Of course, such a conversation could also uncover that he wants to express intolerant views and does not want to explore other points of view, or that he is unwilling to compromise his desire for unfettered choice of clothing.

By expanding the conversation to include Ed's father, you are respecting his right to be involved, and his involvement may help resolve the matter. His objection to your position that his son ought not to wear the T-shirt to school may be based on a misunderstanding of the broader implications of doing so. He may then be able to positively influence his son. There may also be some other, unstated reason or concern underlying his position that is amenable to an open and respectful conversation with you. On the other hand, the meeting may be acrimonious and unproductive, leaving the issue unresolved.

In our hypothetical situation, we aren't able to have a conversation with the people involved. Ed and his father appear to be entrenched in their views, and many people appear to be sensitized to and troubled by the issue of racism. Ed's T-shirt may constitute a flash point incident around this issue, and we are expected to respond.

Feel

Considering our own values, biases, stresses, and self-interest in this matter, the fact that you do not personally like Ed very much is a potential source of bias. Would you have the same reaction to the T-shirt if it was worn by a student you liked better? Or might you be able to generate more agreeable alternatives if you and Ed had a friendlier relationship? Our feelings might also be a source of information. For example, is the fact you don't particularly like Ed a reflection of his tendency to be rather nasty to others? If so, your response to the situation will be different than if Ed generally behaves kindly. Or are your feelings toward him a reflection of the fact that Ed is socially awkward and as unliked by his peers as he is by you?

You also recognize that you support (or at least do not openly condone) students who engage in free speech in support of alternative marriage. Your reaction to Ed's T-shirt might reflect your bias toward opinions you share. So you might wonder: If an Aboriginal student wore a T-shirt with a slogan in support of Native rights, would you feel the same way you do toward Ed's T-shirt?

Your personal ethical opinion is that the T-shirt slogan shows a lack of tolerance and a disrespect of others and suggests a sinister agenda of white racial supremacy. While you agree in principle with the value of respecting Ed's autonomy, you feel a responsibility to resolve this situation in a manner that provides care, promotes trust, and builds community for everyone connected with the school.

Think

From the point of view of Ed and his father, the ethical value of respecting his autonomy—Ed's right to freedom from control by others—is central in this situation. Ed chose to wear a T-shirt with a controversial slogan on it. Ed's father states that he wants his son to be able to wear the shirt in school—again, an expression of desire for respecting autonomy. From the perspective of providing care, you want to help Ed learn how freedom of choice is limited by the degree to which our choices threaten the autonomy of others. For example, in common with other codes, the Yukon Teachers' Association *Code of Ethics* states that teachers are expected to "deal justly, considerately and appropriately with each student." The message conveyed by Ed's T-shirt is not one of compassion and tolerance for others, and you are concerned that he may not understand how his choice of clothing is a moral position.

Providing care for the other students is at issue in this situation given that they feel uncomfortable and there is an underlying threat inherent in Ed's T-shirt slogan that may cause students to feel personally afraid. The school has an interest in respecting the autonomy of students through free speech; it also obliged to provide care in the form of an inclusive, safe environment for learning. You are concerned that the other students' feelings of discomfort suggest that the school environment is being imperilled. Referring to the Saskatchewan Teachers' Federation *Code of Ethics*, teachers are expected to "develop teaching practices that recognize and accommodate diversity within the classroom, the school and the community."* How you handle this situation has implications for the lessons that other students will learn about accommodating diversity.

Using the Prince Edward Island Teachers' Federation *Code of Ethics* as an example, a teacher is expected to "endeavour to develop in his/her pupils an appreciation of the principles of democracy." The community at large always has an interest in how children are taught to become good members of society. Tolerance and freedom of expression are important—though often controversial—societal values. You and the school administration will be expected to deal with this situation in a democratic manner that builds community.

Act

In considering viable courses of action in this situation, simply ignoring the matter and allowing the T-shirt to be worn does not respect the views of the other students; nor does it strengthen the safety and moral climate of the school; nor does it promote Ed's betterment, although it does respect his personal autonomy. Banning the shirt against Ed's and his father's wishes does not respect Ed's autonomy; moreover,

*Saskatchewan Teachers' Federation

it would not have any substantive educative value for him and would likely compromise the moral climate in the school. It would, however, provide care with regard to the safety of the other students.

You could use this situation as an opportunity for learning about the limits of freedom of expression in society vis-à-vis tolerance and respect for others. You might also initiate a classroom project to facilitate a dialogue among the students—Ed included—that would promote their learning about the issues and the development of a more tolerant climate in the school. However, this could isolate Ed from some of his classmates and has a high risk of shaming him. And, realistically, our confidence in being able to design and deliver an assignment that would draw out and resolve the issues involved is not particularly high, given how time sensitive and controversial the situation is.

The most straightforward course of action, in light of all of the above, would be to recommend to the school administration that a discussion about the T-shirt be held between Ed and his father and the principal and yourself. Ideally, before that meeting you would gather some information from the other students on what the slogan represents and what it means to them, as well as from the principal. During the meeting, you would want to find out whether Ed is, in fact, making an expression. If, for example, Ed indicates that he wants to wear the shirt in an effort to promote constructive controversy, then how you proceed will be different than if he honestly intended to express racial pride.

If Ed and his father are intractable, you will ultimately have to "lay down the law" and require Ed to refrain from wearing the T-shirt to school. The threats it represents to the autonomy of the entire school, the moral education of the other students, and the bonds of the community, when weighed against his personal autonomy, are simply too great to allow him to continue wearing it there. You will be expected to tell him so in an open and honest way, explaining your reasoning respectfully and in a manner designed to make it a learning experience for Ed.

WHAT THE CODES SAY

Integrity and Diligence

A Member acts with integrity and diligence in carrying out professional responsibilities.

—From the Manitoba Teachers' Society Code of Professional Practice

BEING AN ETHICAL TEACHER

Making an ethically justifiable decision involves incorporating the point of view of the individuals involved, appreciating how our personal ethical intuitions shape our appraisal of the situation, considering how professional expectations limit the acceptable choices of action, and then weighing the harms and benefits of each. It ought not involve simply following our intuition; nor should we slavishly follow rules. When confronted with ethical dilemmas that are new or particularly challenging, we should pause and proceed through a deliberate decision-making process so that we might *discover* what course of action is best, rather than *justify* what we want to do or feel we have to do. The resolution of an ethical conflict by this process can be both difficult and potentially unpleasant. We risk discovering that some of our deeply held beliefs—sometimes so deeply held that we are not conscious of them—are incongruent with what society expects of us. Or that we do not consistently act in accordance with our own espoused beliefs.

Being an ethical teacher requires us to allow the knowledge, skills, and attitudes developed and refined through reflective practice to be expressed organically in relation to our students. It requires us to let our tried and tested ethical beliefs guide our actions without dictating fixed responses. And it requires us to submerge our knowledge and skills in a context-sensitive manner so that our influence can be implicit while we explicitly attend to the present moment.

In order to do so, we must paradoxically trust that we know how to be ethical. The classroom is not the place to throw out our established ethical beliefs and start from scratch. Indeed, if we have been working hard at being ethical, it would be ludicrous to ignore what we've learned. We ought to be applying what we have good reason to believe is ethical. This obliges us to continuously entertain the possibility of new ways to understand the complexity of each teaching encounter. Once we have learned what is expected of us, we do well to pay particular attention to information that does not fit with our understandings, no matter how sure we may be about them.

By conscientiously working through ethical conundrums in a deliberate reflective manner, we often achieve a greater appreciation of the nuances of ethical issues, the true nature of our values, and the usefulness of ethical codes. As we encounter more and more ethically challenging situations and repeat this process, our intuitive ethical values become more congruent with the explicit ethical expectations of our profession through greater awareness of ethical circumstances, enhanced ability to incorporate our personal intentions into our ethical reasoning, repeated exposure to our ethical duties, and experience with the consequences of our actions. In this manner we can develop a more "informed intuition," and ethical decisions that are congruent with professional ethical values become more reflexive. This also helps us become more internally motivated, resulting in higher engagement in ethical tasks, better quality decision making, more persistence, and assumption of greater responsibility for the consequences of our actions.

Ethical inconsistencies can be the result of never having subjected our ethical assumptions and beliefs to critical reflection, or of possessing incomplete or underdeveloped ethical beliefs. If ethical inconsistencies are not identified and minimized, we are unlikely to develop a cohesive, congruent ethical approach to teaching. In particular, congruent ethical intuitions enable us to behave in a manner consistent with the ethical expectations of us, or at least to diverge from those expectations intentionally. Teachers who possess incongruent ethical intuitions risk failing to "practise what they preach," espousing an ethical standard but acting in a manner inconsistent with it. An unexamined ethical intuition reflects a lack of intentionality and purpose.

Discovering areas of incongruence within our ethical assumptions can prompt thoughtful reflection on the underlying cause(s). Do my areas of incongruence result from poorly developed ethical beliefs? Have I simply failed to behave in a manner that consistently supports my ethical beliefs? Have external factors prompted me to compromise the integrity of my personal ethics? Identifying the underlying causes of incongruence enables us to respond in ways that minimize or eliminate them from our teaching. Responding to ethical incongruence thus requires us to either revise our ethical beliefs or change our behaviour. Changing ethical beliefs can be a difficult and slow process. However, it can also be the source of profound professional and personal growth.

The process of reflective ethical reasoning presented in this chapter provides a framework for considering how our ethical intuitions align with the ethical expectations of teachers. The language of principles and rules can feel somewhat abstract and devoid of inspirational values and virtues. In practice, however, it can serve as a very helpful guide for applying ethical concepts and expectations to the problem of deciding how to act in specific situations. Especially in those situations where the stakes are high, a deliberate process of arriving at a defensible course of action is in the best interests of you, the profession, and the public you serve.

REFLECTING ON THE CHAPTER

Take some time now to think about the chapter you have just read. You may want to go back and reread some portions or, if you have been making notes, review them. What ideas or questions stand out for you as most important to your development as an ethical teacher? What aspects of the chapter strike you as less important? After thinking about this, go back and read the less important sections and ask yourself why they might be important to others and how they might be important for you. If they still seem less important, make a note to return to them later. As for the important ideas in the chapter, take some time to make a plan to incorporate those lessons into your personal and professional development. How might you do so? What impediments do you foresee, and how might you address them? Take as much time as you need to make a plan to fortify your ethical development.

SUMMARY

Teachers are expected to be able to justify their actions with reference to accepted ethical values. Doing so is made difficult by our tendency to act according to our intuitions, which are not readily available for conscious consideration. We can access our intuitions and reason from experience if we *listen, feel, think,* then *act*. This involves speaking to those involved and listening respectfully to what they have to say. Then we reflect on our personal feelings and intentions, including our values, biases, stresses, and self-interest. Next we think about the relevant ethical expectations and how they narrow the acceptable alternative courses of action. Finally, we analyze the likely consequences of each course of action and choose the one that causes the least harm and provides the most benefit. Having done so, we are expected to evaluate the results of our actions and take appropriate action to address any untoward consequences by repeating the four steps in light of the new circumstances brought about by our actions.

QUESTIONS FOR DISCUSSION

1. In your experience, why do teachers not always behave as ethically as they ought to? Are these reasons different from the reasons why nonteachers do not always behave ethically?
2. You may have heard people say (and may have thought so yourself) that the right thing to do depends on the situation and cannot be reduced to "rules" or "standards." How would you respond to this point of view after having read this chapter?
3. Under what circumstances would you feel tempted to disregard the ethical expectations that society has of teachers in favour of your intuitive judgment? Under what circumstances would you feel justified in doing so?

CASE STUDY

NO ZERO POLICY

Your school has a "no zero" policy whereby students who have not completed an assignment are to be given a mark of incomplete. That mark is not included when final grades are calculated. During a parent–teacher meeting, the father of one of your students asks about his daughter's low grade in another class. He tells you she missed a number of assignments when they took an extended holiday and that her teacher awarded zeros instead of incompletes. You know of the teacher's opinions and actions. You feel annoyed that you have been complying with the policy even when students fail to complete assignments for voluntary reasons, such as family vacations, while your colleague is flaunting the rules and doing what most teachers think is right. The father says to you, "If that teacher wants to hand out zeros, he should be doing some other job—not teaching. What are you going to do about it?"

1. How would you describe the interests of the key people involved in this situation? That is, what does the parent want? The student? Other students? Fellow teachers? The school administration?

2. What ethical principles from Chapter 1 are at play in this situation? How would you prioritize them? Does your list vary from your consideration of the first question?

3. How do you weigh your personal opinions about best teaching practice against school policies that contradict them? Explain.

CHAPTER 3

THE LEGAL CONTEXT

CASE STUDY

AFFECTIONATE TEACHING STYLE

A teacher is well-known for his physically demonstrative interpersonal style, which includes rubbing, patting, and slapping students' buttocks. He does not do so in a sexual way, and most students take it in the affectionate manner in which it is intended. Even those students who don't particularly like him or his style accept that it is "just the way he is," and neither they nor their parents seem to give it a second thought. Most of his colleagues feel that his behaviour is perfectly acceptable, and he is, in fact, quite popular with them. However, last year a female grade six student charged him with having touched her in a manner that she perceived as sexual and made her uncomfortable.

Numerous character references from respected members of the community were presented at his trial and no evidence of sexual intent was established. Nonetheless, he was found guilty of child sex assault and given a conditional discharge.

1. How do you feel about the verdict? Do you think it was fair? Why or why not?
2. This teacher was required to give a DNA sample and was placed on the sexual offenders registry. Do you think it's appropriate that he was treated as a sexual offender? Explain.
3. What role do you think community opinion should play in legal decisions? What about the opinions of other teachers? Can you justify your position?

Canada's legal system has a much more significant influence on how teaching is practised than it does on most other professions. The law can be understood as giving form to the social forces that bear on education. Laws permit and limit such essential aspects as who will be taught, what can be taught, who can teach, and how those involved in education ought to treat one another. At the most basic level, teachers can be sued or prosecuted for failing to meet the expectations the law places on them. More broadly, the law has long been one of the primary determinants of the *form* of Canadian education. Society's attitudes toward human rights, for instance, are reflected in the *Canadian Charter of Rights and Freedoms* and the *Youth Criminal Justice Act*, which also articulate expectations for teachers and schooling.

In the province of British Columbia alone, as one example, there are more than forty statutes and regulations relating to education. It would be a monumental task for any teacher to become familiar with the laws concerning education in their jurisdiction and the literally thousands of legal cases that have a bearing on the practice of teaching. Even if one were to accomplish such an undertaking, keeping abreast of relevant new legal developments would leave precious little time to teach. How can teachers stay focused on being a good teacher while avoiding running afoul of the law?

The key to doing the right thing as a teacher in the eyes of the law is to learn the basics of the Canadian legal system and how it perceives the profession and practice of teaching. This will make you aware of how the courts are likely to judge you if your actions are brought before them. Armed with this knowledge, you can avoid behaving in ways that prompt others to seek legal recourse; perhaps you can even incorporate practices that exemplify the highest expectations that society has of teachers.

The first thing to know about Canada's legal system is that it is primarily concerned with disagreements. If we all agreed completely on what people—including teachers—ought to do, our legal system would hardly be necessary. Of course, even reasonable people can have quite different ideas as to what kinds of actions are right or wrong. This is why some system for settling disagreements about important matters such as educating children is a feature of every human society. In Canada that function is handled by our legal system. Thus conflict is part of every aspect of law, and the laws relating to education are no exception.

In fact, many aspects of education that seem obvious to us now were subject to considerable disagreement when the laws that compel these practices were enacted. That students begin schooling around age six, that the school year runs from fall to spring, and that school boards are locally elected are all conventions not usually questioned today. But even the basic notion that school attendance should be compulsory was argued both for and against in Manitoba before laws stating as much were passed in the 1910s. Changes in language requirements in Quebec schools in the 1970s and the secularization of Newfoundland religious schools in the 1990s were hotly debated at the time; so has been the presence of Gay–Straight Alliance clubs in Alberta schools in the 2010s. Many other ideas about the essential nature of education have been a source of discord for much of Canada's history; none of these ideas are likely to be taken for granted any time soon.

When any law is enacted, some people's views about how society should function are usually promoted at the expense of other people's views. A law that creates school boards with certain powers, for example, at the same time limits the influence of teachers or parents. Under a different law, the role that each plays in how schools function might be quite different. Such decisions can spawn lingering resentments that take considerable time to settle and that can flare up years later when circumstances change.

To keep disagreements and resentments from disturbing peaceful social relationships, our legal system is therefore also intended to compel people to behave in certain ways. Anyone who has spent time in a part of the world without an effective legal system has probably had the uncomfortable experience of not feeling particularly safe. To ensure greater compliance with societal expectations for interpersonal harmony than might otherwise occur, laws prohibit or regulate certain actions or make them compulsory. Law, then, involves imposing some view of the world on people who do not necessarily share that view. More specifically, laws are almost always based on some view of how people ought to behave toward one another.

The fact that even within Canada the delivery of education varies across jurisdictions and over time highlights that there is no single agreed-upon way to deliver it. Changes in social conditions and beliefs, as well as changes in who has the power to influence the social-political agenda, generate demands for new or different laws. This can effect how children are expected to be educated and how teachers are expected to behave. For example, as the notion of what legally constitutes a "family" has changed, marriage laws have been revised to recognize same-sex unions. This has required changes in how schools are expected to respond to parental rights and responsibilities. Clearly, the law is shaped as much by shifting values as it is by fixed truths. And nowhere are society's values more pertinent than in the teaching of its children. A fair and dependable system of laws dampens

■ REFLECTIVE TASK

Experience with the Law

What has been your experience with the law? Have you been issued a lot of speeding or parking tickets, for example? Perhaps you or someone close to you has had a more serious involvement with the law. Have you ever broken the law and not been caught? Or are you an especially law-abiding person? How do you think your experiences have influenced your relationship with our laws and law enforcement system? How have they influenced your relationship with others who are more or less law-abiding than you? Do you think that your stance on how leniently or severely Canadian society enforces its laws is typical of most Canadians? How does this impact your ability to fulfill your role as a teacher? Take some time to reflect on these and any other related matters you wish to consider.

sudden and destabilizing social changes so that people can more easily cooperate in the tasks that are necessary for the building of community, such as educating the next generation of citizens.

CANADA'S LEGAL SYSTEM

The fundamental purpose of Canada's legal system is to make explicit society's expectations of its members and thereby reduce conflicts between people. Laws (statutes) passed by the federal, provincial, or territorial governments, and the regulations that relate to them, are the most visible expressions of that purpose. The various Education Acts are statutes; the details of teacher certification are set by regulation. Most laws can be readily changed by the presiding government and thus are susceptible to political whims and fancies. Some, however, notably the *Charter of Rights and Freedoms* (see below), have protections that make them more difficult to change, for they are meant to enunciate the nation's basic values.

A second purpose of our legal system is to resolve conflicts as they arise by being *visible, remedial,* and *predictable* so as to promote, restore, and maintain the social order.

Visible

The courts are highly bound by tradition and rules of procedure. This is to preserve the dignity and decorum of the institution so that society can benefit from its authority, as well as to promote stability. So that this can impact the community at large, and not just those directly involved in the proceedings, courtrooms are open to the public. That is why it is said that "justice must be seen to be done." While a court may in certain situations ban the publication of information about a case or exclude the public entirely from the courtroom in order to protect the people involved (as in the case of children who are victims of sexual abuse), openness is generally considered essential to a court's function. Courts also have many rules and procedures for ensuring that everyone involved is treated fairly and with respect, both of which are valuable in their own right, in order for citizens to see that social order is possible.

Remedial

Our legal system seeks to restore the social order by providing remedies when settling a conflict or correcting a wrong. In particular, and contrary to what many people believe, lawyers have a duty to try and resolve their clients' disputes by agreement before resorting to court action. More and more cases are being dealt with through alternative dispute resolution mechanisms such as mediation or arbitration, both of which are usually more timely and less expensive. Whether a case is resolved outside or within the courtroom, remedies are sought. When the accused in a criminal case (see below) is found guilty, for example, the sentence handed down can have a variety of objectives, including to denounce unlawful behaviour, to deter the offender, to separate the offender from society, to rehabilitate the offender, to promote a sense of responsibility in the offender, and to provide reparations for harm done to the victims. Similarly, when someone is found to be at fault in a civil dispute (see below), an appropriate remedy to rectify the injury or damage will be imposed, such as payment of money to compensate for damages or punish the wrongdoer, and performance or discontinuance of specific activities.

Predictable

Our legal system is committed to maintaining social order by being predictable. When the dispute is between individuals, this is accomplished through the process of common law (also referred to as case law), which originated centuries ago in Britain. It is a way of ensuring that cases that raise similar legal issues will be resolved in a similar fashion. When deciding a case, judges review the rulings of other judges for principles of law applicable to the situation in dispute. They may also add refinements of their own based on the specific facts of the case at hand, and in this way the common law evolves in a measured and expectable way.

Decisions in individual cases thus become part of the larger case law in Canada and have *precedent* value, meaning that judges will be guided by that court's reasoning. The doctrine of precedent requires that cases must be decided the same way when their material, or pertinent, facts are the same. Obviously, it is not required that all the facts be identical—in the flux of life, all of the facts of a given case will never be repeated. The legally material facts may recur, however, and it is with these that the doctrine is concerned.

Also, judges are obligated to follow a precedent set by a higher court. In fact, the decision of a higher court acts as a binding authority on a lower court within the same provincial or territorial jurisdiction. Judges are required to follow the reasoning of a higher court's decision except when the facts in the case they are deciding are significantly different from those of the case in the higher court. In practice, however, this is only a general rule, because each case is different on the facts and all judges strive to achieve a just result.

If a novel issue arises and there is no precedent to follow, judges must craft a decision that breaks new ground while still being consistent with the principles and precedents laid down in common law. Judges may also consider common law precedents from other jurisdictions and countries; these are not binding, but they can offer guidance as to the best way to resolve a dispute.

The province of Quebec is unique among Canadian jurisdictions by virtue of using a codified system of law rather than common law. The legal principles set out in Quebec's Civil Code and provincial statutes are to be applied when settling a dispute. Judges may refer to the legal principles of common law precedents as a secondary source to help them apply the Civil Code in a particular case. So even here, despite being based on a different system of law, predictability and fairness and maintained for the social good.

The most important implication of our legal system's reliance on common or civil law is that it is not necessary for teachers—or anyone else, for that matter—to be overly concerned with having to learn about every new legal decision. The principle of precedent or the use of a civil code ensures that legal expectations affecting teachers are very unlikely to abruptly change in any significant way. Minor refinements are always occurring, of course, and any changes to teachers' legal expectations are incorporated into legislation and professional standards, which are then made available through a variety of means to ensure that all teachers are aware of them.

WHAT THE CODES SAY

Unethical to Behave Criminally

It shall be unethical for a teacher to conduct himself/herself in such a way as to be convicted in a court of competent jurisdiction of a criminal offense which, in the opinion of the Provincial Committee, represents serious misconduct which is relevant to the teacher's suitability as a member of the profession.

—From the New Brunswick Teachers' Association Code of Professional Conduct

THE *CHARTER OF RIGHTS AND FREEDOMS*

When the Canadian Constitution was repatriated in 1982, the *Canadian Charter of Rights and Freedoms* was also enacted. The *Charter* sets out four categories of fundamental freedoms: freedom of conscience and religion; freedom of thought, belief, opinion, and expression; freedom of peaceful assembly; and freedom of association. It then outlines a series of rights: to life, liberty, and security of the person; to be secure from unreasonable search or seizure; not to be arbitrarily detained or imprisoned; to be told upon detention the reasons for such and the right to retain counsel; and to equal protection before and under the law without discrimination, in particular based on race, national origin, ethnic origin, colour, religion, sex, age, or disability.

Unlike any other laws enacted by the federal, provincial, or territorial governments, the *Charter* is the "Supreme Law of Canada" in that all other laws and regulations are subordinate to it and any that are inconsistent with it are invalid. Also, the mechanism for amending it is much more difficult than for other laws; doing so requires a resolution of both the House of Commons and the Senate, or of the legislative assemblies of at least two-thirds of the provinces representing at least 50 percent of the population.

The *Charter* was written primarily to shield Canadians from the actions or inactions of the government that might threaten our rights and freedoms. It was not intended to interfere with private individuals, businesses, and institutions. However, a number of legal decisions have established that the *Charter* does regulate them if they are under governmental control or if they function as an aspect of government. Because education is established by provincial statute, funded by public money, and compulsory for all children and youth, the *Charter's* goals and reach apply to the actions, policies, and decisions of departments of education, school boards, school administrators, and teachers. Independent and private schools operating under delegated government policy are also bound by the *Charter*.

Prior to the *Charter*, Section 93 of the *Constitution Act, 1867*, gave provincial and territorial governments essentially complete jurisdiction over matters of education, except when it came to the rights of religious minorities in denominational schools (see Chapter 4). Since the *Charter*, however, the laws, policies, and practices relating to education have been expected to abide by the rights and freedoms detailed within it. This means that teachers and schools are expected to protect the rights and freedoms of students and staff and may be subject to a *Charter* challenge if they fail to do so or if they infringe on those rights and freedoms.

The remedies available under the *Charter* are diverse. Section 24 allows a person whose rights or freedoms have been interfered with to apply to the courts for whatever remedy is appropriate and just in the circumstances, such as excluding evidence entered in a legal proceeding that was obtained in a manner that denied or restricted the accused's rights or freedoms. *Schachter v. Canada et al.* (1992) further established that all or part of a law or regulation can be struck down or supplemented in order to enforce the *Charter's* goal. In addition, *Doe v. Metropolitan Toronto (Municipality) Commissioners of Police* (1998) established the prerogative to sue for the loss of one's constitutional rights.

The *Charter* is the supreme law of Canada; however, the fundamental rights and freedoms it enumerates are not absolute. Rather, they are subject to reasonable limits as prescribed by law and justified in a free and democratic society. The purpose of this limitation can easily be demonstrated using the timeworn example of someone who mischievously shouts "fire" in a crowded theatre. The individual's freedom of speech rightly ought to be limited for the greater good of the others in the theatre, who might be harmed in the resulting needless mayhem. The mechanism for determining whether a limit is reasonable was established in *R. v. Oakes* (1986), which requires that the end result sought be sufficiently important and the means to this end be reasonable and demonstrably justified. In establishing reasonableness and justification, the government must provide clear and persuasive evidence that the method chosen is designed to reach the objective, that it impairs as little as possible the rights and freedoms of the individual, and that the harmful effect of the measures is proportional to their beneficial effect.

The *Charter* is also meant to promote and protect the two official languages by providing via Section 23 that Canadian citizens whose first language is English or French and who reside in a linguistic minority community are entitled to have their children educated in the language of the minority. This section was a political compromise to remedy a number of defects in existing provincial legislation by not only allowing a choice of language instruction but also requiring that facilities be provided for teaching it.

In many respects, the issue of language rights has supplanted that of religious instruction in the school system as one of the most troubling areas for provinces. Some provincial governments have tried to avoid making controversial and thus potentially politically damaging decisions on this issue by seeking rulings from the courts. However, Section 23 of the *Charter* is intentionally vague. The Supreme Court of Canada, in *Mahe v. Alberta* (1990), ruled that while Section 23 was intended to promote the concept of an "equal partnership" between the two languages, there was no requirement that the services be identical. Thus, where the numbers of linguistic minority residents did not warrant establishing a separate school board, it may be necessary to provide representation within the existing school board in proportion to the numbers of minority language students in the district. These representatives have the responsibility of determining how funds are used for the teaching of the minority language and the hiring of appropriate teachers.

The Supreme Court has made it clear that the *Charter* will be given a broad interpretation when applied to any dispute under review. Compared to other laws that are specific and may be limited by precedent, interpretation of the *Charter* is to be comprehensive enough such that changing circumstances will not restrict its protection of Canadians' fundamental rights and freedoms.

■ REFLECTIVE TASK

Save a Copy of the *Charter*

Go online and search for the *Canadian Charter of Rights and Freedoms*. Download it and save it somewhere on your computer where you can find it easily next time you want to refer to it. Once you have done so, read it. After you have read it, take some time to reflect on your reactions. Did the content surprise you? Or was it familiar? Are there aspects of it you disagree with? Did anything strike you as peculiar or out of place? Or were you generally pleased with the content? Take some time to reflect on these and any other questions that occur to you.

CRIMINAL AND CIVIL LAW

The legal system of any nation, including Canada, can be understood as being made up of public law and private law. Public law deals with relationships between individuals or institutions and the state, which in Canada is referred to as the Crown (a vestige of our British colonial roots). One type of public law is constitutional law, which establishes our system of government and its administrative processes, including education; the other is criminal law, which deals with offences by individuals against society. Private law deals with relationships between individuals and is referred to as civil law to distinguish it from criminal law. Both public criminal law and private civil law have important implications for teachers and schools.

Criminal

Criminal law deals with offences as set out in the *Criminal Code of Canada* (1985) and related federal statutes. The role of the Crown is to prove beyond a reasonable doubt that the accused committed the offence with which he or she was charged. The role of the court is to adjudicate between the Crown and the accused. Elaborate and detailed procedural rules exist to protect the rights of the accused, given the vast discrepancy in power and the potential for loss of liberty.

The welfare of children has long been an area of concern of the criminal law, so the *Criminal Code* contains a number of provisions that impact directly on teachers. In particular, Section 161(b) allows that when a person has been found guilty of certain sexual offences against children under the age of fourteen, the sentencing judge can prohibit the accused from obtaining or continuing in a position of trust or authority, such as being a teacher, that involves children under that age. In addition, Section 153 makes it an offence for persons in authority (such as teachers) to make sexual advances to children between the ages of fourteen and eighteen. The *Code* also has sections pertaining to sex with minors and sexual assault.

The treatment of youth under public law has changed significantly over the past decades and remains a matter of some controversy. Public law now has three levels of culpability: no criminal accountability up to age 11; limited accountability from 11 to 18; and full accountability under the criminal law from 18 onward. The *Young Offenders Act*, passed in 1985, was a significant change from its predecessor, the *Juvenile Delinquents Act* of 1905, in that it adopted less of a child welfare approach and stressed increased responsibility on the part of youths, increased attention to the rights of youths, and greater protection of society. During the 1990s there was a public outcry for "tougher" laws for youth crimes, which resulted in a series of amendments to the *Young Offenders Act*. The *YOA* was replaced in 2002 with the *Youth Criminal Justice Act*, which, while not as significant a change as its predecessor was from the *JDA*, nevertheless constituted serious reform. For example, it made available a wide variety of alternatives to custody.

Civil

Civil law involves the regulation of relationships and the resolution of disputes between parties. It can compensate the wronged party by awarding damages, establish standards for the limits of behaviour, educate the public, and provide a means for parties to address their differences in a controlled setting. In civil law the complaining party is called the *plaintiff,* while the party responding to the complaint is the *defendant*. It is the plaintiff's burden to demonstrate a valid basis for his or her complaint. If this cannot be done, the court will refuse to hear the case. Many complaints fail at this point. Even among complaints that do pass this test, many if not most are settled by the parties without ever going to court.

The courts recognize that wrongs perpetrated by one person against another can be intentional or unintentional. Intentional wrongs involve deliberate interference with another person through battery, trespass, invasion of privacy, assault, false imprisonment, or infliction of mental suffering. In the case of battery, assault, and false imprisonment, it is not necessary for the plaintiff to prove that any loss or injury occurred in order to recover damages—only that the defendant's conduct was intentional. In the case of mental suffering, however, the plaintiff must establish that it is a result of the defendant's intentional conduct. The primary form of unintentional wrong is that of negligence, where the defendant's conduct fails to meet the standards expected of society.

To successfully bring an action in negligence, a plaintiff must establish five elements. First the plaintiff must show that the defendant owed him or her a duty of care. In the case of teachers, this duty typically arises because the teacher has a delegated authority over the student coming from the parents or guardian of the child, or because as teachers they act as an arm of the state in fulfilling the latter's interest in the child's education. A teacher's duty of care might also arise from undertaking responsibility for an extracurricular activity, or from undertaking a task outside of the normal activities of teaching, such as offering medical aid to an injured student.

The second requirement is that the plaintiff must establish that the defendant failed to use reasonable care. The expectation is that a teacher brings a reasonable degree of skill and knowledge and exercises a reasonable degree of care. The degree of skill and care that teachers are expected to exercise is what could reasonably be expected of a typical, prudent teacher of the same experience and standing. This is not a standard of perfection, and the law recognizes that mistakes can and will occur without there necessarily being negligence.

The third requirement is that there be, in fact, an injury suffered by the plaintiff. In cases where the harm is very slight, the court can order that no damages be awarded.

The fourth requirement is that the defendant's conduct caused the injury. The question of causation is one of the most difficult issues to be resolved in civil cases and is often the basis for plaintiffs being unsuccessful. Legal causation can be factual or proximate. The classic description of factual causation is that if not for the defendant's negligence the plaintiff would be uninjured. However, in the real world there are often multiple causes for events, or the causes may be suspected but not certain. This is why in *Snell v. Farrell* (1990), the Supreme Court reiterated that the civil law standard is a balance of probabilities, not that causation be proven with scientific precision.

Proximate causation recognizes the general societal expectation that defendants should not be responsible for damages that have almost nothing to do with their conduct. The legal test is whether the damage is foreseeable by a reasonable person in the defendant's situation. A teacher who taught a lesson on probabilities would not be liable for a student refusing to purchase a lottery ticket with her friends that turned out to be a winning one, for example.

If there are multiple causes of an injury, defendants are responsible only for that portion of the harm attributable to their conduct. Similarly, where there are multiple defendants, each will be adjudged at fault to the extent of his or her own contribution to the plaintiff's injury.

Finally, there must be no conduct on the part of the plaintiff that would preclude him or her from recovery. The most common example here involves a plaintiff who was engaged in a criminal act at the time of the injury. Usually, however, the courts will address this issue by apportioning some degree of causation to the plaintiff's conduct, rather than dismissing the claim entirely.

WHAT THE CODES SAY

Respect for Law

A member should show respect for law, authority and codes of conduct acceptable both within the profession and society as a whole.

—From the Prince Edward Island Teachers' Federation Code of Ethics

EDUCATIONAL MALPRACTICE

Malpractice is a legal accusation made against a professional. The claim is that the defendant was expected to act (or refrain from acting) in a particular manner but failed to do so according to accepted professional standards, and that an injury resulted. As an obvious example of malpractice, most of us can rather easily think of a surgeon who performs an operation negligently and harms or kills a patient. Educational malpractice involves a student claiming that a teacher or school was negligent in the way they taught and that as a result the student was prevented from reaching his or her full scholastic potential.

Even though teachers can significantly influence students for better or worse, malpractice has never been applied to an educator in Canada. Teachers and schools are expected to protect the physical well-being of students under their supervision (see Chapter 8), but this form of liability is not unique to the teaching profession. Educational malpractice refers to a distinct type of negligence relating to the essential function of teaching. The issue of whether teachers are expected to protect the educational well-being of the students they teach has not been entirely settled.

Many students at every educational level complain about their teachers, but there is, and should be, a world of difference between being dissatisfied with a teacher's style or level of effort, and having the right to sue that teacher or the school for those qualities. In theory, grounds for claiming educational malpractice might include that a teacher was unqualified to teach a particular subject, or failed to advise the student on how performance would be evaluated, or used a marking system that was unfair or invalid, or did not adequately cover the curriculum, or used flawed educational material.

In *Hozaima v. Perry et al.* (2008), however, the court noted that American courts have so far rejected all educational malpractice cases. Decisions in many Canadian cases have been based on two leading American decisions: *Peter W. v. San Francisco Unified School District* (1976), and *Donohue v. Copiague Union Free School District* (1979). These cases involved students claiming, among other things, that the school failed to detect their unique learning impediments, advanced them to higher grades without acknowledging that they hadn't mastered the material, and allowed them to graduate despite not having achieved minimum proficiency. In both cases the court rejected the claim, arguing that it is too difficult to demonstrate precisely what a teacher should have done differently or what injury the student suffered as a result. These courts also reasoned that society would suffer because schools would constantly be defending themselves against such claims, or be worried about doing so, if every student who didn't understand a subject could sue their teacher.

Both these cases were decided in the late 1970s. Since then, courts in both the United States and Canada have rejected claims against schools and teachers based on the quality of education. As a result, whenever a claim is launched that is conceptually similar to educational malpractice, one of the defences is that the claim should not be allowed to proceed because educational malpractice cannot be the basis of a lawsuit.

Nonetheless, there is some possibility of Canadian courts accepting educational malpractice in the future. For example, in *Gould v. Regina (East) School Division No. 77* (1996), the Court commented:

> It is surely not the function of the courts to establish standards of conduct for teachers in their classrooms, and to supervise the maintenance of such standards. Only if the conduct is sufficiently egregious and offensive to community standards of acceptable fair play should the courts even consider entertaining any type of claim in the nature of educational malpractice.

As well, there have been several cases in which a court refused to dismiss a claim involving educational malpractice where the allegation involved the failure of a post-secondary school to deliver what it had promised. For example, if a school advertises that a degree can be obtained in two years, a student could probably sue if it actually cannot be done in less than three years (see *McKay v. CDI Career Development Institutes Ltd.* [1999] and *Smart v. College of the Rockies* [2002]). Note that these decisions dealt with a court refusing to dismiss a claim, not whether the claim was true. Allowing a lawsuit to proceed to court because it may not be a waste of the court's time is a much lower standard than deciding in favour of the student's claim.

The response of courts in the United Kingdom regarding educational negligence cases has been somewhat more open than in the United States and Canada, and their reasoning could be followed in a Canadian court if the material facts were sufficiently similar. The most significant of these cases is *Phelps v. Hillingdon London Borough Council et al.* (2000), which involved an educational psychologist who allegedly failed to diagnose a learning disability. The court stated:

> It is long and well-established, now elementary, that persons exercising a particular skill or profession may owe a duty of care in the performance to people who it can be foreseen will be injured if due skill and care are not exercised, and if injury or damage can be shown to have been caused by the lack of care ... A doctor, an accountant and an engineer are plainly such a person. So in my view is ... a teacher.
>
> A teacher must exercise due skill and care to respond appropriately to the manifest problems of such a child ... If he does not do so, he will be in breach of the duty he owes to the child, as well as being in breach of the duties he owes his employer, and his employer will be vicariously liable accordingly.*

The lessons that can be drawn from legal decisions involving educational malpractice are limited since, to date, there have been no cases in Canada where a teacher has been successfully sued for failing to educate a student. In fact, no

---

*Phelps v London Borough of Hillington (2000)

such claim has ever been allowed to proceed to court in North America. Even so, the possibility remains. Flagrantly offensive conduct on the part of a teacher that hinders a student's education could—and most would agree probably should—be grounds for educational malpractice. Also, there does appear to be some willingness on the part of the courts to consider claims involving contracts and misrepresentation by an educational institution. This suggests that schools and teachers are expected to review any representations they make to ensure that they can deliver on what they promise.

REFLECTING ON THE CHAPTER

Set aside some time to reflect on the chapter you have just read. Are there ideas that remain uncertain or confusing for you? How might you resolve your doubt or puzzlement? Does any information or idea strike you as disagreeable? After reflecting on these, go back and read the sections or passages you found controversial or that you think others might, and consider how the controversy might be resolved. Might they have to remain unsettled? If so, why? What are the highlights of the chapter for you—what knowledge did you find enlightening or uplifting? Take some time to think about how you might incorporate these edifying ideas into your evolving professional self.

■ SUMMARY

A basic understanding of the Canadian legal system's expectations of teachers can serve as a guide to how the courts would likely judge them. The *Charter of Rights and Freedoms* supersedes all other laws in order to shield Canadians from the actions or inactions of the government—including with regard to education—that might infringe upon their rights and freedoms. Canada's legal system is visible, remedial, and predictable in order to promote and maintain social order. Public law deals with relationships between individuals or institutions and the state. It includes constitutional law, which establishes our system of government and its administrative processes, including education, and criminal law, which deals with offences by individuals against society. Civil law deals with relationships between individuals. Negligence has five elements: a duty of care, a failure to provide reasonable care, an injury, causation between the failure and the injury, and an absence of factors on the part of the injured party that would preclude recovery. Although no Canadian teacher has ever been sued for failing to educate a student, the possibility remains.

■ QUESTIONS FOR DISCUSSION

1. Is a teacher ever justified in breaking the law? If so, under what circumstances? What system of ethics does your answer represent?
2. Why might legal decisions not always be a good guide for teachers' behaviour?
3. Should a teacher who has broken a serious law unrelated to teaching practice, such as embezzling a charitable organization, be prohibited from teaching? Why or why not?

CASE STUDY

■ TEACHERS' ASSOCIATION SUSPENDS PRESIDENT

During tense contract negotiations between your teachers' association and the government, you receive a group e-mail from the association. It states that the president has been removed from her duties and barred from contacting members regarding matters relating to the association. The e-mail goes on to say that the removal "did not arise out of anything illegal, unethical, or immoral but only as a result of her conduct." Soon afterwards you receive a group e-mail from the (former) president stating that her removal was an unjust response to an anonymous website posting. The posting detailed a twenty-year-old legal matter in which she was found guilty of stealing alcohol from a bar, inappropriate conduct, and causing a disturbance while supervising high school students on an overseas trip. She says that she no longer has a criminal record, has successfully recovered from the "medical issues" she was battling at the time, and has "gone on to a stellar teaching career."

1. What feelings are aroused in you upon reading this case? What do those feelings tell you about what you believe to be important about this situation?
2. If an acquaintance who isn't a teacher were to ask you what all the fuss was about, what would you say? How would your explanation differ if you were talking to a fellow teacher? What do the differences between your two accounts tell you about the ethical values implicated in this situation?
3. What do you think the average person would expect the association and the president to do in this situation? Do you agree with these expectations? If not, how would you persuasively correct these expectations?

CHAPTER 4

THE SOCIETAL CONTEXT

CASE STUDY

STUDENT DESERVES TO BE INCLUDED

You are under pressure from your principal to exclude a visiting student from being part of a school delegation to a Model United Nations convention, ostensibly because of unpaid school fees. Her family is in Canada on a student visa while her father completes a training program. The local media have publicized the bombing of the office of the company in their home country that had been paying her student fees, and her family's being without financial support of any kind. Her plight, combined with the fact that she is Muslim, has become a controversial issue in the school community because an application has been made to establish a Muslim school in the district. You are concerned that including her will jeopardize the entire trip. Yet the other students value her for embodying the unity of nations by virtue of being from another country, and you worry that they will be disillusioned and demoralized.

1. Do you think this is dilemma you should be expected to resolve? Why or why not? If not you, who?
2. What do you think are the likely consequences of not allowing the international student to participate in the Model UN convention? What would be the likely consequences of going against the wishes of the principal, assuming you were somehow able to do so?
3. How would you respond to this challenging situation if you were to do so? If you don't know what to do, how might you go about developing an appropriate response?

Canada's education system was shaped by a series of political and religious accommodations intended to protect the interests of French and English colonists, including the Catholic and Protestant school systems they had established prior to Confederation, and to honour promises made to the original inhabitants, who had been colonized. An appreciation of these social processes is central to understanding the ethical and legal expectations that Canadian society has of teachers.

The Roman Catholic Church established the first European system of education in Canada during the early 1600s for French colonists living in the regions now known as Nova Scotia and Quebec. This system was under Church control and sponsorship in the same manner as it was in France at that time: local priests provided education to the children of the colonists in settlements with a parish. By 1756 there were some eighty-eight established parish schools offering instruction in religious doctrine, reading, writing, and arithmetic. While there was no public support for education in the form of taxes, the Church provided priests to do the teaching and the French king provided cash and land grants to the Church to fund education.

In the British-controlled regions now known as Ontario, schooling developed in a more haphazard manner than this. Anglophone immigrants from England, Scotland, Ireland, and the United States did not prioritize cooperative undertakings such as education to the same extent as the French. Their first schools were established in the late 1700s without government or church assistance, basically by anyone who felt so inclined. Over the next century a system of education gradually evolved that was supported partly by government grants but primarily by tuition fees. Although these schools were not church-run, most parents did expect that their children's education would stress the importance of the Bible and God, in accordance with the Protestant Church of England.

In 1763 the British conquered the French-controlled regions of Canada and brought with them their secular system of education. Over the next hundred years, they passed a variety of acts in an effort to establish a centralized government—and corresponding educational system—consistent with the British way of life that would also appease French Canadians. This compromise dealt primarily with religious freedom. Under the French system, religion and education had been inseparable, and the British accepted that the state had a responsibility to foster a harmonious relationship between French and English wherever possible. Religion in education was important, even essential, to both British and French, Protestants and Catholics.

The Church of England was the majority religion in Upper Canada (now Ontario), and French Catholics were the majority in Lower Canada (now Quebec). Thus, French Catholics had to fight for their legitimate rights in Upper Canada while English Protestants fought for theirs in Lower Canada. This tension impelled the state to establish denominationally based schooling. Denominational schools were also a response to fears that religious factionalism might render the colonies vulnerable to American republican influence and thereby scuttle nation-building efforts. So, despite the risk that they could be socially divisive, separate religious schools were legally recognized as a way to maintain state control over schooling while also ameliorating national, religious, and linguistic conflicts.

In 1829, Lower Canada was given authority over education, but their schools were placed under the control of locally elected boards rather than the Church, and money to support them came from government grants. Also, non-Catholic schools were established for the children of residents who were not of French origin. This resulted in two distinct educational systems in Quebec based on nationality but inseparable from language and religion: francophone Catholic and anglophone Protestant.

When Upper and Lower Canada were merged in 1840, one of the first acts of the new government was the *Common School Act, 1841*. It established three types of schools—common, grammar, and separate—to cater to the needs of three types of people as they were then understood. Common schools were intended to provide schooling for the "common" person in the sense of "average," but also in the sense of lower socioeconomic status. Local trustees were given the authority to hire and fire teachers and to create rules for the proper administration of the school. Boards of education were also established to apportion government monies and approve the curriculum. The teachers in this system were typically barely educated themselves. Their occupational status was more that of a skilled labourer such as a farmhand or lumberjack, rather than that of a professional such as a banker or lawyer. This was reflected in the widespread practice of parents taking turns boarding the local teacher in lieu of pay, for example.

Grammar schools were established to give students the opportunity to learn the classical languages and literatures of ancient Greece and Rome. They were intended to prepare the children of privileged families for university studies. As might be expected, the quality of teachers was much higher than in common schools. Grammar schools were not originally designed to provide post–common school education. They were distinguished from common schools by the subjects they taught rather than the age of the students. Today's system of elementary

REFLECTIVE TASK

Knew You Wanted to Be a Teacher

This might be a good point to record an autobiographical sketch of how you came to pursue teaching as your career. When did you decide that you wanted to become a teacher? What ideas did you have at that time about what a teacher is and does? How did you come to form these ideas? You might want to consider some of the influences on your choice. Were they familial, personal, or some other influence? Think about the turning points in your career as a teacher to date, even if you see yourself as "just a student." What pivotal events have occurred in your life on your way to becoming a teacher? What important choices have you made? You may also consider some of your formative experiences as a teacher. What is most salient about these experiences for you? Take some time to write down your responses to these and any other questions that occur to you.

schooling, in which younger children progress to secondary schooling, where they receive an education broader than the "Three R's," was developed in the latter decades of the last century.

Separate schools were recognized under the 1841 *Act* to enshrine the right of parents professing a minority religious faith to establish their own school in a community. Separate school boards were granted the same powers as those of common schools to regulate the curriculum and appoint teachers, but they were required to report to the District Superintendent of Common Schools. Thus, by the time of Confederation (1867), the protection of a separate school system, based primarily on religious affiliation but with roots in national origin and language, was already well established in law.

THE *CONSTITUTION ACT, 1867*

With the formation of Canada through the passing of the *British North America Act, 1867* (re-enacted and retitled the *Constitution Act, 1867,* by the *Constitution Act, 1982*), a national framework for providing of education was established. Schooling was not a prominent issue in the negotiations around Confederation, however, and only Section 93 of the *Act* deals with education. It granted the provinces (as we now know them) exclusive legislative authority to make laws in relation to education; schools "as they existed at the time of Union" would be allowed to continue. Section 93 was written to protect the two dominant religious groups:

> 93 (1) Nothing in any such Law shall prejudicially affect any Right or Privilege with respect to Denominational Schools which any Class of Persons have by Law in the Province at the Union:
>
> (2) All the Powers, Privileges, and Duties at the Union by Law conferred and imposed in Upper Canada on the Separate Schools and School Trustees of the Queen's Roman Catholic Subjects shall be and the same are hereby extended to the Dissentient Schools of the Queen's Protestant and Roman Catholic Subjects in Quebec;
>
> (3) Where in any Province a System of Separate or Dissentient Schools exists by Law at the Union or is thereafter established by the Legislature of the Province, an Appeal shall lie to the Governor General in Council from any Act or Decision of any Provincial Authority affecting any Right or Privilege of the Protestant or Roman Catholic Minority of the Queen's Subjects in relation to Education:
>
> (4) In case any such Provincial Law as from Time to Time seems to the Governor General in Council requisite for the due Execution of the Provisions of this Section is not made, or in case any Decision of the Governor General in Council on any Appeal under this Section is not duly executed by the proper Provincial Authority

> in that Behalf, then and in every such Case, and as far only as the Circumstances of each Case require, the Parliament of Canada may make remedial Laws for the due Execution of the Provisions of this Section and of any Decision of the Governor General in Council under this Section.

This protection of the Catholic minorities in Ontario, Nova Scotia, and New Brunswick and the Protestant minority in Quebec was essential to achieving Confederation. The importance of this "Great Compromise" cannot be overstated. It not only allowed for Confederation but also shaped education in Canada in ways very different than in England, France, or the United States. In particular, because it placed education under provincial control, there is no explicit constitutional guarantee of an education in Canada, apart from the religious minority provisions, nor are there national educational standards.

As more regions became part of the Dominion of Canada over the next four decades, public funding of Catholic separate schools was made a legal condition of joining Confederation. These conditions did not specify members of other religious minorities because there was no perceived need to guarantee the rights of English-speaking Protestants, who were in the majority everywhere outside of Lower Canada. "Public" schools were by default Protestant schools. At that time, there was no political consideration of accommodating the religious beliefs of non-Christians.

Public and separate schools and school boards now exist in a variety of forms across Canada that reflect the status of denominational schools in the provinces prior to entry into Confederation, as well the outcome of legal and political challenges since entry. The most significant challenge to Section 93 of the *Act* arose in Manitoba in 1890 when the legislature abolished the Catholic and Protestant systems in favour of a nondenominational system in which religious exercises would be subject to regulation by an advisory board. Despite a series of court cases and attempts by the federal government in 1896–97 to introduce legislation that would overturn their abolition, Manitoba remains a strictly nondenominational education system.

Section 93 protected the rights of separate schools, but it did not "freeze" those rights. Provinces were free to make new laws concerning education, subject to a right of review to ensure that such legislation did not degrade the privileges enjoyed up to that point by the denominational schools. In recent times, objections to the discriminatory impact of these Section 93 guarantees has most often been based on the *Charter of Rights and Freedoms* (see Chapter 3). Provincial legislation that does not conform to the provisions of the *Charter* may be declared by the courts to be of no force or effect.

In response to these objections, Quebec and Newfoundland have made constitutional amendments eliminating their denominational school systems. Other provinces have resolved the discriminatory favouritism towards Catholic schools by providing equal funding for religious and nonreligious separate schools. The only exception remains Ontario, which continues to recognize Catholic denominational separate schools.

Today, schooling in Canada continues to be shaped by a cultural and legislated belief that education should reflect the values of the community in which it is offered. The public school system makes education available to all who fall within a certain age group, and the state administers that education. The system is funded largely by the state, although current political exigencies are such that schools are increasingly having to raise additional monies on their own.

The accommodation of minority separate schools within the public system reflects a consensus that education should be responsive to parental demands in matters relating to morality and religion. Minority schools receive equivalent public funding and are subject to provincial control over their curricula. Also, to qualify as denominational separate schools, they must offer religious instruction. This concept of church and state as partners has also made possible Jewish schools in Quebec, Amish schools in Ontario, Salvation Army schools in Newfoundland, and Hutterite schools in Alberta, Saskatchewan, and Manitoba.

Private schools, which receive some public funds in some jurisdictions, are largely self-supporting and are managed by boards or individuals, sometimes as corporations (either for-profit or not). They exist because Canadians respect the right of parents to emphasize certain aspects of their children's education—such as religious tenets or academic rigour—to a greater degree than what is provided in the public school system. The curricula of private schools are governed to some extent by provincial legislation (e.g., British Columbia's *Independent School Act*) but are not as tightly controlled as in public schools.

WHAT THE CODES SAY

Improve Quality of Education

Members of the Association use their best efforts to broaden educational opportunities and improve the quality of education in the Northwest Territories.

—From the Northwest Territories Teachers' Association Code of Conduct

ABORIGINAL EDUCATION

A very important exception in Section 93 of the *Constitution Act, 1867*, was that it kept the education of Aboriginal people a federal responsibility. This authority is regulated by the *Indian Act*, first introduced in 1876 and revised several times since. However, the federal government is responsible only for the education of Aboriginal Canadians whose names are included on a federal register (i.e., registered or "Status Indians") and who are living on reserves. The education of non-Status Aboriginal people and of those not living on reserves has always been a provincial responsibility.

The *Indian Act* empowers the appropriate federal minister to operate schools and to enter into agreements with provincial governments, territorial commissioners, school boards, and religious and charitable organizations for the education of Status Aboriginal children. Under the *Act*, that minister is accountable to Parliament for the expenditure of public monies and the educational results achieved.

The federal government first implemented its responsibility for Aboriginal education by enlisting the churches to operate schools. A number of different forms were tried, including community day schools similar to non-Aboriginal schools, before the now-notorious residential schools became the dominant model. The general goals of residential schools were to convert Canada's Aboriginal peoples to Christianity and to assimilate them into Euro-Canadian culture. The assumption in all of this was that they were godless savages. Children were taken from their families and communities and placed in residential schools at a young, impressionable age so that they would be isolated from the influence of what was assumed to be their inferior traditional way of life. They were forbidden to acknowledge their Aboriginal heritage and culture or to speak their own languages. Students were usually severely punished if these, among other, strict rules were broken.

Residential schools were established in every province and territory except Newfoundland, New Brunswick, and Prince Edward Island. At their peak in the mid-1900s, there were 132 residential schools in Canada; the last one did not close until 1996. By every measure they were a tragic failure. The education offered was deficient, often progressing only up to grade five. Also, they focused mainly on training students for manual labour in agriculture, light industry (such as woodworking), and domestic work (such as laundry and sewing).

Their failure struck at a deeper level than just education. Because the children had been removed from their families at an age when they still required parenting, many grew up without experiencing a nurturing family life and were deprived of the knowledge and skills to raise their own families. Even more blatantly egregious, students were subjected to physical, emotional, sexual, and cultural abuses at terribly high rates. On 11 June 2008, Prime Minister Stephen Harper offered a full apology on behalf of non-Aboriginal Canadians for the residential school system. The Anglican, Presbyterian, Roman Catholic, and United churches have also publicly apologized.

By the 1960s the federal government had begun to rely less on churches and to take a more direct role in Aboriginal education. It did so by implementing programs to integrate Status Aboriginal children into provincial school systems through transfer payments, as well as by operating federal schools. In the 1970s and 1980s, moves were made to develop an Aboriginal educational system in which authority and administrative control would be held by individual First Nations. These actions were an acknowledgment that the Canadian value of being responsive to local values should apply to Aboriginal communities as much as it does to non-Aboriginal ones.

Presently, there are some 119,000 Aboriginal elementary and secondary students living on reserves across Canada. Around 60 percent of them attend one of 515 First Nations–managed schools. After an initial improvement in educational outcomes for students attending these schools, gains have stagnated. By 2011, 45 percent of on-reserve students had graduated from high school, compared to 70 percent who attended off-reserve schools. Almost nine out of ten students in

First Nations schools are two or more years behind in vocabulary, reading comprehension, and math compared to their non-Aboriginal peers. In most public school systems, this level of performance would qualify them to be classified as special needs students. Sadly, even though Aboriginal students attending non-Aboriginal public schools achieve higher average educational outcomes, their achievement still tends to be lower than that of non-Aboriginal students in the same school.

For some three hundred years, Aboriginal peoples living on the land now known as Canada suffered at the hands of settler peoples, and the education system has been a significant contributor to that suffering. The residential schools methodically undermined Aboriginal culture and harmed families for generations, disrupting the ties through which culture is taught and sustained. Because their explicit intent was to eradicate Aboriginal culture, the residential school system has been described as a form of cultural genocide.

For many Aboriginal students, this history has resulted in a tension between abandoning school or abandoning their cultural heritage. Aboriginal students may choose to stay away from school, or their family members may choose to keep them away. It is no surprise that opinions within the Aboriginal community on the role of education are mixed. Some encourage students to finish high school and to attend post-secondary education on the grounds that doing so will strengthen Aboriginal peoples' place in Canadian society. They argue that participating in public education can provide Aboriginal people with knowledge of how to defend themselves against oppression and discrimination. Others argue that while there can be gains from participating in the public education system, Aboriginal history and methods of teaching should be included in order for cultural wisdom, traditions, and pride to be passed on to future generations.

There is a consensus that Aboriginal peoples should be able to benefit from their rich cultural traditions while also participating in the advantages afforded non-Aboriginal Canadian people. Most would agree that making this a reality will require engaging educators, teachers, and schools in developing awareness, appreciation, and understanding of the social context of Aboriginal education. The ultimate goal is to ensure that every Aboriginal child, youth, and adult who enters the public educational system feels no more or less included, recognized, and valued in the classroom than anyone else.

REFLECTIVE TASK

Awareness of Colonialism

How would you rate your level of colonial awareness—that Canadian society is the product of taking land and liberty from people who were living on the North American continent before Europeans arrived? Is it something you ever think about? Are you aware of children in your classroom of Aboriginal heritage, or aware of their being under- or over-represented in your classroom? Perhaps you yourself are of Aboriginal heritage. If so, what is most salient about your experience with respect to being a teacher? Take some time to write down your responses to these and any other questions that occur to you about colonialism.

PROVINCIAL MINISTRIES OF EDUCATION

In every Canadian province and territory, the highest educational authority is the Ministry (or Department) of Education. The minister appointed to the education portfolio by the premier is also an elected member of the legislature and a member of Cabinet. In some jurisdictions the portfolio is combined with post-secondary education; in others the two are kept separate. Under the Canadian parliamentary system, the Cabinet determines what legislation is brought forward by the government; it also formulates policy on matters in which it has jurisdictional authority, including education. Since most provinces and territories have only a few basic laws governing education, and these are not often significantly revised, government influence on education tends be felt through the administration of the ministry.

The education minister has authority over the jurisdiction's education system, in terms of policy, funding, curriculum, and teacher licensing (except in Ontario, where that responsibility resides with the College of Teachers). However, the minister's role is affected by the government's overall priorities and by his or her ability to influence them. Some ministers play a powerful role in Cabinet, others not so much. Regardless, the minister is expected to publicly support and defend the government's policies, even if personally opposed. However, because ultimate legal authority over schooling rests with the provincial or territorial government, the minister always plays a central role in educational policy and funding.

Education ministers also participate in the general work of the government, including election campaigns. They are very unlikely to have time to learn all the details and activities of their portfolio, even if they happen to have a background in education. The ministry is administered by civil servants, whose work reflects ministerial policies and procedures as well as the broad guidelines set by the minister. A great deal of this activity is either routine or handled by committees, with the minister only approving the final result. Ministers are usually directly involved only in politically sensitive issues, in public crises, or in matters relevant to the ruling party's policy directions.

The minister is the *political* head of the ministry; the deputy minister is the *functional* head. The deputy minister is a civil servant appointed by the Cabinet. At one time, deputy ministers of education were almost always career educators—teachers, principals, or school superintendents. In recent years, however, provincial and territorial governments have tended to appoint deputy ministers who have backgrounds in finance, reflecting the fact that education spending has become a pressing political concern.

As the most senior civil servant in any government ministry, the deputy minister is responsible for day-to-day operations, budgeting, and program development. A typical ministry of education will have functional units to deal with, such as finance and legal, as well as those typically thought of as educational, such as curriculum and school regulations. All of these areas require expert staff, including professional educators. Clearly, education ministries tend to be complex organizations employing hundreds of people.

Guided by professional values but serving the minister and government, the deputy minister can be caught in the middle. Party politics are subject to short timelines, and sometimes decisions on difficult issues must be made without sufficient time to fully consider the best course of action. Yet, whereas the government is expected to be responsive to public opinion and the minister to follow the government's political agenda, civil servants are generally guided by their professional training and background. Their views on education are often similar to those of teachers in schools. It is not uncommon for a minister to try to push the ministry in a particular direction while civil servants are less than enthusiastic. They may even resist certain educational reforms that they view as too heavily motivated by partisan politics.

Effective relationships between politicians and bureaucrats can be strained by an adversarial party structure. Politicians often enter office from opposition, fresh from having spent years criticizing the previous government, and they usually perceive civil servants as aligned with their ousted opponents. Because deputy ministers serve at the pleasure of the government, they can lose their positions as a result of a change in the party in power, specially if they are seen as too closely identified with the policies of the previous government.

Education ministries reflect a mix of professional and political authority, and education governance is strongly affected by an intersection of two world views, which often clash. The resulting tensions are part of the governance process. When they are successfully navigated, they can contribute to the development of policies that are sensitive to both professional standards and public wants. When they are not, governance can become inefficient or ineffective, sometimes both.

Education has become a higher priority in Canadian politics, and government attention to school issues has intensified considerably over the past decade. Education ministers often spend a great deal of time conferring with various groups across their jurisdiction. Sometimes this is done in earnest; other times, governments use consultation to make it *appear* that they are listening to the public before implementing predetermined plans. The increased prominence of education on political agendas has brought more attention to schooling and teaching. While this is good news when it comes to making decisions about education more democratic at the provincial or territorial level, it has taken many decisions away from the community level. It has also made efforts to protect teachers' professional autonomy increasingly difficult as more and more groups demand a say.

WHAT THE CODES SAY

Adhere to Agreements

The teacher adheres to agreements negotiated on the teacher's behalf by the Association.

—From the Alberta Teachers' Association Code of Professional Conduct

SCHOOL BOARDS AND PARENT COUNCILS

School boards are situated between acting as the agents of provincial authority and as representatives of local municipal interests. Typically, the education minister has the right to create or eliminate school divisions or districts and will delegate routine operations to school boards. School boards are thus subject to ministerial control, including dissolution. Yet they are responsible for most of the daily administration of the public and separate schools in a geographical district.

At the time of Confederation, most provinces had a patchwork system of sometimes thousands of school boards. Due to the rural nature of much of Canada in the early 1900s, most of these boards administered a single school. Alberta alone had some six hundred school boards when it entered Confederation in 1905, and that number continued to rise quickly with the province's population. Consistent with the Canadian value of accommodating diverse local concerns, these small local boards were highly responsive to the communities their schools served.

These small school boards were in many ways well suited to the educational, economic, and political realities of the time, but they also had their limitations. The multitude of small districts resulted in large discrepancies in financial resources and quality of education. Provincial governments and many local boards felt that larger school districts would mean fewer redundancies and the pooling of financial and pedagogical assets.

Thus the provinces and territories have gradually consolidated small school boards into larger ones. Again using Alberta as an example, where there were once 5,000 local boards, there are now a mere 65, a trend mirrored in all other provinces. Current rural school boards are usually responsible for thousands of students in school systems spread out over thousands of square kilometres. The Toronto District School Board is the largest urban school board in Canada, with almost 300,000 students attending some 600 schools.

School boards generally hire and pay school personnel, develop transportation systems, build schools (although funds to do so are a provincial responsibility), close schools, and set budgets. Within limits, they can also modify the provincial curriculum. While the basic teaching materials are determined by the minister, supplementary learning resources are usually selected by the school board—an important role that can be a source of conflict regarding the authority of school boards. School boards also hire teachers, subject to the provincial acts and the collective agreements reached between the teaching associations and the boards. (The role of teachers' associations is discussed in Chapter 5.)

A school board is composed of members elected from the local community. It is meant to represent the diverse views of all subcommunities within that larger group rather than the views of the individual elected members. In particular, a school board cannot be ruled by a particular religious or moral point of view, even if that view is accepted by the majority of the school board.

Most school boards are subject to a local election every few years. This obliges them to reflect local educational interests. When school boards were responsible for very small jurisdictions, the most common number of board members (called trustees) was three or five. Today, school boards generally consist of seven to fifteen trustees, with some provinces having even larger numbers. It is normal in most provinces for trustees to be elected, either by the electorate of the school division as a whole or by smaller wards, each of which elects one or more trustees.

In recent years, an important modification to this process has been legal provisions to ensure the representation of specific minority populations on school boards. This has generally involved francophone and Aboriginal populations, and

African Canadian representation in Nova Scotia. In Ontario, school boards that operate secondary schools have been required since 1998 to appoint at least one "student trustee" to advise the board, but that person does not vote on board decisions or attend *in camera* meetings.

There are few restrictions on who can run for election to a school board. The *Manitoba Public Schools Act*, for example, states that anyone who is (1) a resident elector of the division, (2) at least eighteen years old, and (3) a Canadian citizen can run for election to the school board. Once elected, it is the trustees collectively who constitute the board as a corporate body with a legally defined range of duties. This collective constitution is important because it means that the board exercises its authority only as a single corporate entity and not through the actions of individual members.

As with their counterparts at the provincial level, trustees are usually assisted by a professional administration headed by a superintendent or director of education. The size of the board office administration is usually a function of the size of the division. The school board hires and can fire the superintendent, although firings are infrequent and it is much more common for superintendents to leave voluntarily, either retiring or moving to another position.

The social circumstances in which school boards function can fluctuate quite rapidly, from general disinterest characterized by acclamations in elections and dreary board meetings, to passionate involvement characterized by the electoral defeat of standing trustees and well-attended board meetings. Public interest can arise out of competing agendas either at the local level or between local and provincial levels. Issues likely to arouse interest include the setting of budgets, the negotiating of collective agreements for professional and administrative staff, the closing or opening of schools, the offering of programs other than those mandated by the province, and the selection of schools for specialized programs. When parties to a local dispute at the school board or district level cannot come to an agreement, they often call on the minister to intervene and settle the matter.

The shifting of authority away from school communities to large boards has been balanced by attempts in most provinces to extend legal status to some form of parent advisory councils at the school level. Many provincial school acts recognize the right of parents to be involved in the management of their children's education and allow for the establishment of parent advisory councils for individual schools or districts. These councils, as the name suggests, advise schools on such matters as improving scholastic achievement, suspending students, the conditions of the school premises, and extracurricular activities. In most provinces and territories, members of the council must be parents of children attending that school and are elected to one-year terms. Such councils vary widely in terms of structure: some have extensive by-laws and place restrictions on their members in order to avoid bias such as political partisanship.

Although parent advisory councils typically can only make recommendations, they play an important role in giving voice to the local community. Yukon, for example, encourages the development of school councils with substantial authority, subject to ministerial approval, over matters such as the selection of the school principal, the development of local curriculum, and the evaluation and dismissal of teachers. Similarly, Quebec allows the creation of elected school governing bodies comprising parents, teachers, support staff, and, at the secondary level, students, in order to ensure greater community input.

■ REFLECTING ON THE CHAPTER

As you look back on this chapter, what was the most surprising thing you learned? What new perspective does it give you about how Canadian society sees you as a teacher? How might you incorporate this new perspective into your evolving ethical self? What challenges does it present for you? What steps might you take to overcome these challenges? Take some time to write down your responses to these and any other questions that occur to you.

SUMMARY

France developed the first European system of education in Canada during the early 1600s under the control and sponsorship of the Roman Catholic Church. When the British conquered the French settlers they brought their secular system of education. The British passed a variety of acts intended to appease French Canadians by allowing them religious freedom, which included education. With the passing of the *Constitution Act, 1867*, a provincial system of public and separate schools was established to accommodate those professing a religious faith different from the majority in a community. Aboriginal education was and remains a federal responsibility, and has by all accounts failed in its mandate. Provincial ministries of education oversee policy, funding, teacher licencing (except in Ontario), and curriculum. School boards manage the administration of schools in a geographical district, subject to ministerial control. In response to increasingly large school boards, most provinces have legislated parent advisory councils to represent the local community in the running of a school.

QUESTIONS FOR DISCUSSION

1. Do you think the "Great Compromise" was good for education? How might you have resolved the problem of disparate educational systems? Why?
2. Should there be national standards for education? What are the advantages and disadvantages of your position?
3. Some commentators have criticized private schooling for taking away resources from public schooling, or for creating a multitiered approach to education. Do you agree with this? Why or why not?

CASE STUDY

WHO SITS NEXT TO DAUGHTER?

You are the seventh-grade homeroom teacher in a small school. In your school the parents are very involved, often to the point of what you consider to be interfering. One parent in particular, who is on your school's Parent Advisory Council, is displeased with the seating assignments in your class. She wants you to have her son sit beside a more popular child. You do not agree that this would be good for her son, who in fact struggles when socializing with higher-status classmates. Even if you could offer a tactful explanation for the move, it certainly would not benefit the child you originally assigned to sit beside him. Attempts to convince her otherwise have no effect, yet you feel it would be a mistake to bend under pressure. She is insistent, however, and accuses you of not doing enough to attend to the students' social needs.

1. What possible courses of action occur to you in response to this situation? What are the ethical pros and cons of each course?
2. What do you think the average person would expect a teacher to do in this situation? Do you agree with these expectations? If so, how would you present them in a persuasive manner to a fellow teacher struggling with what to do in this situation? If not, how would you persuasively correct an average person's expectations?
3. What difference would it make to your decision if your principal has been relatively more supportive of your professional autonomy over parental input? If your principal has been more supportive of parental input?

CHAPTER 5

THE PROFESSIONAL CONTEXT

CASE STUDY

ANYONE CAN TEACH

At a party, a fellow guest asks what you do for a living and you answer, "By profession, I'm a teacher." To which he replies, "Teaching isn't really a profession, is it." When you ask him what he means, he says, "Teaching is easy, isn't it? You start at 9 in the morning, teach lessons that have already been prepared for you, leave at 3:30 in the afternoon, and get twelve weeks' holiday." Warming to the topic, he adds, "Besides, anyone can teach." Struggling to maintain your composure, you manage to sputter, "But teachers are respected and trusted role models. Being a teacher takes education, training, qualifications, commitment, and dedication." Apparently taking some pleasure in your distress, he responds, "Maybe, but so do electricians, hairdressers, and mechanics." You gulp down the rest of your drink and look around the room for someone else to talk to.

1. What does it mean to be a member of a profession as opposed to an occupation such as electrician, hairdresser, or mechanic?
2. Are education, training, and qualifications sufficient to establish you as a professional? Are commitment and dedication also required, or merely desirable?
3. Do you think teaching is a profession? Why or why not?

The question is often raised, "Is teaching a true profession?" The reason it seems to keep being asked is that we all went to school, and we all have opinions about our teachers. They are considered fair game to praise or condemn. Some inspired us—perhaps even to pursue teaching as a career—and some were truly awful. Before becoming a teacher we assumed that we knew what it would be like to be one and how easy it is to teach. Bad teachers made teaching look easy because we thought it wouldn't take much to do a better job than they did. Good teachers made teaching look easy because we experienced only the ease of learning and were unaware of the talent and effort that went into making it so. Even if we accept that teaching is a demanding occupation requiring knowledge and skill to do well, is it really so different from being an electrician, hairdresser, or mechanic?

To be considered a profession, an occupation must be (1) an intellectual activity based on a specialized knowledge base rather than a routine, (2) practical rather than theoretical, and (3) oriented toward service to society. Many occupations might be said to meet the first two criteria, but few meet the third. The three most established professions, sometimes referred to as the *learned professions*, are the clergy, the law, and medicine. Each requires years of education and training to acquire necessary expertise and performs a vital service to society. The clergy tend to the spiritual needs of the faithful. Lawyers enact our legal system to maintain civil order. Physicians treat the sick and injured. Members of each of these professions are expected to serve the needs of all of society's citizens. Thus a profession is expected to adhere not only to practical responsibilities, but also to ethical responsibilities in serving the community.

When the learned professions emerged, there were no clear categories of who belonged and who did not, nor were there any clear criteria of what constituted admission to the profession. Members were typically self-taught, or they apprenticed under someone considered to already be a member. Nevertheless, societies afforded them privileged status because of the valuable role they played. Modern-day usage of the term *professional* can also refer to being engaged in an occupation as a paid job rather than unpaid, such as a "professional athlete." Here the word "professional" serves only as a distinction from the "amateur," who is not paid, and does not denote membership in a profession or, crucially, service to society. This is a secondary meaning, therefore, and serves only to confuse the issue. Professionals are those who belong to a profession and uphold their professional responsibilities. That is, anyone who does not *act* professionally by fulfilling their ethical obligations to society is not truly a professional. From a pragmatic point of view, this responsibility is enacted in a profession's collective ability to ensure that its members behave in an ethical manner.

So is teaching a profession? Some argue that teachers are "semi-professionals" because the practice of teaching is not based on a unique body of knowledge or theory. This has been a difficult claim to counter. Most teachers hold a rather low opinion of their professional training and say that they learned most of what they needed by actually teaching in the classroom. On the other hand, many scholars assert that there is a formal knowledge base to guide educational practice, although they can't seem to agree on specifics. To be fair, this situation is not all that different from that of established professions and so probably doesn't represent an essential claim.

Some have argued that teaching is not a profession because teachers' ability to self-regulate is limited by legislation, so they probably won't ever achieve the professional status enjoyed by doctors and lawyers. This is more of a "chicken-and-egg" argument, given that professional autonomy is granted when an occupation is generally perceived by a society as being worthy of it. If teaching was viewed as a profession, then teachers would be granted self-regulation. In fact, as will be discussed in the next section, some jurisdictions have vacillated back and forth on granting teachers autonomy on par with other professions.

Others have argued that teachers have such a relatively low status within society that they don't deserve to be classified as professionals. This speaks to the societal appraisal of the value of teaching and is influenced by perceptions of authority and power. Teachers are required to impart their knowledge to students and their parents in a public venue; in marked contrast, other professions tend to keep even their most basic specialized knowledge to themselves. Thus the mystique engendered by the practice of other professionals is unavailable to teachers. Similarly, students cannot be engaged in the process of learning in the impersonal manner that is characteristic of traditional professional practice. Instead, students and teachers must share responsibility for expending effort in order for learning to occur, and this minimizes the status imbalance that is characteristic of the more established professions.

However, proprietary knowledge, self-regulation, and social status are ultimately superficial characteristics of a profession. There is no question that teachers have a time-honoured role in society. Preparing children to be contributing members of a community is an essential occupation. In the classroom and in the school, students exercise their understanding of the concepts of fully functioning participation in the community and in society. And the teacher contributes greatly to this.

The road to professional status for teachers began in the late 1800s with efforts to form local associations. In the earliest days, these were populated by Department of Education officials, inspectors, clergy, and various influential members of the community. As a result, they tended not to address teachers' concerns, especially about working conditions. Teacher restiveness reached a peak around the time of the First World War as pay remained static while the cost of living nearly doubled. Across Canada, teachers' associations lobbied for pensions and better salaries, as well as for professional status. They argued for compulsory membership in their association, control over entrance standards to the profession, adoption of a code of ethics, and authority to discipline members who did not abide by the code. In 1935 the Saskatchewan legislature was the first in Canada, and the world, to pass a teaching profession act; it made membership in a teachers' professional organization mandatory for all teachers employed in publicly funded schools. Alberta followed soon after in 1936, and by 1960, membership in a provincial association was automatic or compulsory for all teachers in Canada. And most of those associations had acquired some disciplinary powers.

■ REFLECTIVE TASK

Experience with Professionals

What is your experience with professionals? Is there a member of your family who is a professional? Perhaps even a teacher? How has your familiarity—or lack of familiarity—influenced your conception of what a professional is? When you reflect on what it means to be a professional, what thoughts come to mind—money, social status, respect, something else? Do you have a negative reaction when you think of professionals, such as greedy "ambulance-chasing lawyers," self-serving physicians who practise "defensive medicine," or inept, "baby-sitting" teachers? Perhaps you want to distance yourself from any considerations of professionalism and focus simply on teaching? Or have you had a positive experience or even many positive experiences such that you have very favourable associations with the concept of professional? Perhaps you even have an idealized conception of being a professional. How have these experiences influenced your sense of yourself as a professional in relation to being a teacher?

PROFESSIONAL STANDARDS

The degree to which the public can trust a profession ultimately rests on that profession's ability to regulate its members. Professions set standards of admission to the profession, address those at risk of harming recipients of their services, and sanction those who do harm. Today, except in Quebec, all of Canada's teachers' federations/associations have adopted codes of ethics or codes of conduct that set standards of responsible teacher conduct. However, few have been granted complete responsibility for certifying and decertifying their members.

In the early 1980s, the governments of Ontario and Alberta proposed that their teachers' associations adopt a full self-governing role on the condition that they agree to split their organizations in two. One part would be a compulsory-membership college responsible for professional regulation, the other a voluntary-membership association responsible for collective bargaining. Teachers in both jurisdictions rejected the proposals, choosing to remain single associations. In 1987, the government of British Columbia, over opposition from the Teachers' Federation, passed the *Teacher Profession Act*, which created a College of Teachers with the power to certify, discipline, and otherwise regulate teachers. Similar legislation, called the *College of Teachers Act*, was passed in Ontario in 1996. The Ontario College of Teachers sets standards for teacher education and practice, as well as professional self-regulation and public accountability. As with the earlier Ontario and Alberta models, professional regulatory functions were intended to be separated from the collective bargaining of teachers' associations.

These gains in professional recognition did not last. In 2012 the British Columbia government dissolved the BC College of Teachers and took away teachers' self-regulation. Governance of teachers was assumed by the Teacher Regulation Branch of the BC Ministry of Education. Reflecting a similar public/political sentiment, the Ontario College of Teachers' disciplinary system has recently been reviewed in response to concerns that misconduct cases weren't being adequately investigated. Curiously, these pressures for greater scrutiny by moving from professional to political oversight are not based on the reality of how diligently teachers are disciplined under each system. Within a four-year period prior to being disbanded, for example, the BC College of Teachers cancelled or suspended the licences of nearly one hundred teachers, while in Alberta, with a similar number of teachers and under government oversight, fewer than twenty were disciplined.

Entrance Standards

One of the more obvious tasks of a profession is to set entrance standards deemed necessary to offer services to the public in a beneficial and nonharmful manner. As discussed in Chapter 4, one consequence of the great compromise that enabled Confederation has been that each province and territory has established unique standards for the professions, including teaching. By 1939 all teachers were required to have completed high school before entering normal school (later called teachers' colleges). In the early 1950s it was agreed nationally that all teachers should hold a post-secondary degree and that teacher preparation should take place under university auspices, but this ideal was slow to be realized. Indeed, the transfer of teacher training to the universities was not completed until the late 1970s.

In part to address the issue of idiosyncratic standards across jurisdictions, the federal, provincial, and territorial governments signed the *Agreement on Internal Trade* in 1994 with the goal of facilitating the mobility of Canada's people, investments, and services across the country. As a result of this agreement, teachers who hold valid Canadian certification in one jurisdiction can obtain certification in another without additional training and examination, although in some jurisdictions restrictions are placed on teachers who hold a certificate with a limited scope of practice.

Currently, most jurisdictions only allow persons who have obtained a bachelor degree in Education, or a bachelor degree in some other field plus an after-degree in Education, to call themselves teachers. Beyond this, there are varying requirements for specific coursework and supervised practice before and after the degree has been earned. Around 95 percent of Canada's approximately 400,000 elementary and secondary school teachers now have a university certificate, diploma, or degree, and close to 90 percent have obtained a bachelor's degree or higher.

Codes of Ethics and Conduct

Regulators of teachers must also ensure that properly qualified teachers practise competently. Nine jurisdictions employ a code of ethics for these regulatory functions, although the aspirational nature of true ethics codes (see Chapter 1) makes them poorly suited for the task. The other jurisdictions have a *code of professional conduct* or *code of ethics and standards*. A code of professional conduct defines minimally acceptable behaviour and is intended to function as enforceable rules of practice rather than as aspirational principles (as found in codes of ethics). Some jurisdictions address both functions by combining them into one document; in other jurisdictions, what is called a code of ethics is actually a code of conduct.

Whatever it is called, an enforceable code of conduct serves a number of functions. From a societal standpoint, it assures students, their families, and the community that they can expect teachers to behave in accordance with established standards of practice and conduct. This generates confidence that the profession is serving a public interest and is worthy of trust and support. From the teachers' standpoint, it offers a set of uniform rules and standards that define acceptable professional behaviour and provide a basis for properly regulating their conduct.

Codes of conduct are meant to be definitive, explicit, compulsory, and attainable such that any violation of them is a basis for formal disciplinary action. They are intended to be the standard against which to judge a teacher's conduct in such matters as disciplinary hearings. Even our courts of law usually assume that professional codes of conduct are adequate and will usually seek to make rulings that are consistent with them. Ideal codes of conduct have the following characteristics:

1. They are compulsory, attainable, and crucial in that any violation is a basis for formal disciplinary action.
2. They primarily protect the public interest and only secondarily protect professional interests through maintaining public confidence and trust in the profession.
3. They are as clear as possible concerning what behaviour is required and what is prohibited.
4. They deal with the teacher's behaviours, not the content or outcome of professional judgment.
5. They are sufficient unto themselves, without dependence for interpretation on additional explanatory materials.

As with entrance standards, each provincial and territorial regulator has the authority to establish or adopt a code of conduct. An important practical concern that arises from this situation is that teachers who move from one province or territory to another must practise in accordance with the code of conduct of the new jurisdiction. Fortunately, the various codes are mostly quite similar in content.

WHAT THE CODES SAY

Acknowledge Authority of Teachers' Union

The teacher acknowledges the authority and responsibilities of the BCTF and its locals and fulfills obligations arising from membership in her or his professional union.

—From the British Columbia Teachers' Federation Code of Ethics

PROFESSIONAL ACCOUNTABILITY

Various formal mechanisms have been established within teaching associations and by law to protect the public from harm by teachers. Currently, Ontario is the only jurisdiction in which teaching is recognized as a self-regulating profession, with a code of conduct implemented and administered by a teaching council that has the authority to dispense sanctions, including deregistration. Whether administered by the profession or by government, internal mechanisms for accountability are sufficient to deal with the vast majority of situations. When a code is difficult to enforce, the fault often lies not with the code but rather with difficulties around clearly articulating the consequences for unethical conduct. In those rare instances when professional standards and mechanisms are insufficient, external processes can be invoked.

In most jurisdictions, the regulator (be it a college or a government department), a member of the public, a school administrator, or another teacher can launch a complaint. Initially, the complaint may be made orally or in writing, although a written complaint must be made if it proceeds beyond preliminary considerations. In many jurisdictions the code of ethics or conduct requires that, if the complainant is a teacher, the named teacher (the *respondent*) be informed of the intent to make a complaint.

Typically, an appointed representative of the regulator will discuss with the person making the complaint (the *complainant*) the standards the teacher will be held to and the nature of the discipline process. If the regulator determines that the complaint is frivolous, intended only to cause trouble, or an abuse of process, no further action is taken. If it is none of those things, the complainant is given a choice: do nothing further, make a formal written complaint, or elect for an informal complaint resolution process (if the jurisdictional legislation allows for it). If the complaint is serious in nature, the regulator may proceed with an investigation regardless of the complainant's wishes.

If the complainant or regulator elects to proceed, the regulator's representative will normally send a letter to the respondent teacher requesting a written response and, if needed, a request to the complainant for further documentation. Typically, the respondent teacher's employer will also be notified of the complaint. The regulator may then appoint an investigator, who reviews all materials, contacts any relevant parties, collects any necessary further documentation, and prepares a report summarizing the evidence. The method of investigation usually varies based on the nature of information necessary to clarify the complaint; it may include interviews, a review of school files, and other correspondence. The regulator may also seek legal advice or an expert opinion as to whether any relevant codes or standards have been violated.

Once all necessary information has been gathered, the regulator typically has the option to dismiss the complaint, initiate a mediated or negotiated settlement, or proceed to a discipline hearing. If the complaint is dismissed, the complainant usually has the right to appeal. If a negotiated settlement is pursued, the teacher undertakes whatever actions are agreed to be necessary to remedy the wrongdoing. In some cases this may involve the teacher undertaking sensitivity training or upgrading, for example. If the teacher breaches the terms of the settlement, in most cases the regulator will forward the matter to a disciplinary committee. If the terms are completed successfully, the case can be closed.

If the case proceeds to a discipline hearing, the committee will hear evidence from the regulator and the teacher. At this point in some jurisdictions, the complainant becomes a witness and the regulator becomes the complainant. In other jurisdictions, the complainant maintains "status" and has the right to legal representation, to question witnesses, and so forth. Typically, legal counsel represents both the regulator and teacher. If an expert witness was involved, the witness testifies on behalf of the college and can be cross-examined by the teacher's legal counsel. In most jurisdictions the teacher is permitted to call his or her own expert to testify.

Disciplinary committees are better equipped to deal with a teacher who has a multitude of relatively minor offences over a period of time with different students, and can impose a greater range of penalties, including placing restrictions on a teacher's certificate such as the age of students that can be taught, or requiring that teachers take courses in topics such as boundary issues or anger management. In some instances, disciplinary hearings will be undertaken in addition to criminal proceedings. In *Ontario College of Teachers v. Newton* (1999), for example, a teacher who was criminally charged on a number of counts of assault and as a result agreed to a peace bond, was subsequently the subject of a discipline inquiry that exonerated her. The penalties available to discipline committees are diverse, from a written reprimand to revocation of the teacher's registration. Other possibilities include imposing terms, limits, or conditions on the teacher's practice involving, for example, supervision, fines, personal therapy, or successful completion of additional training.

Since the discipline committee acts in a quasi-judicial manner, and may impose rather severe penalties, there is a right of further appeal by the teacher to the lower courts in each of the provinces and territories. The legislation governing this right of appeal varies across jurisdictions, but most allow the courts to uphold, quash, or alter the committee's decision. In hearing an appeal, the courts will usually defer to the expertise of the regulator, and by extension the discipline committee, to govern its own affairs.

Due to the absence of a uniform system of classifying cases as well as to inconsistent reporting practices, it is almost impossible to form a precise idea of how many complaints are handled by provincial or territorial regulatory bodies. However, British Columbia and Ontario do publish discipline outcomes on their website. Some smaller jurisdictions, such as Prince Edward Island, receive only one or two complaints per year. The largest jurisdiction, Ontario, which has 180,000 teachers, receives more than two hundred complaints per year. In some jurisdictions, as many as fifty cases per year are handled through negotiated or alternate dispute resolution procedures, with many more than that handled informally. The numbers of complaints that go to a formal discipline hearing occur at a very low rate, from none to half of 1 percent (of the total number of teachers) per year in any given jurisdiction.

REFLECTIVE TASK

Reflective Teachers Wanted

Imagine a job advertisement that read as follows:

Teachers wanted who are inherently curious, who don't have all the answers, and aren't afraid to admit it. Someone who is confident enough in his or her ability to accept challenges in a non-defensive manner. Someone who is secure enough to make his or her thinking public and therefore subject to discussion. Someone who is a good listener and trusts other people to contribute to making good decisions if given the opportunity. Someone who is able to see things from another's perspective and is sensitive to the needs and feelings of others. Someone who is able to relax, step back and let others assume responsibility for their own actions. Some experience desirable but not as important as the ability to learn from mistakes.

Take some time to think about which of those qualifications you value. Which do you reject? Which do you possess? Which will take some work to develop or acquire? Why?

ESTABLISHING AND MAINTAINING COMPETENCE

Competence is the cornerstone of professional practice. Society expects professionals to be able to perform the critical tasks that define their profession. Incompetent actions on the part of teachers are unethical and unprofessional because they are unlikely to be of benefit, and under certain circumstances, they can be grounds for discipline if they fall below expected standards or cause harm. A teacher who is not competent to practise should not teach. Competence is generally considered to have four essential components: *knowledge, skill, judgment,* and *diligence.*

Knowledge

Knowledge involves having absorbed and understood a body of information sufficiently to be able to comprehend and conceptualize the range of professional issues that teachers can reasonably be expected to encounter. Knowledge is a necessary but not sufficient foundation for competence. In Canada, knowledge is initially demonstrated by completing a degree program in education, usually including a certain set of required courses. Knowledge can be understood as covering a continuum from basic information that all teachers should know, such as ethics, to specific knowledge necessary for specialized areas of practice, such as learning disabilities. Obviously, the knowledge base for teaching is not static, and continued study is considered necessary to maintain an adequate knowledge base. To be considered knowledgeable, teachers are expected stay current to those matters relevant to their practice.

Skill

Skill is the ability to apply knowledge effectively in practice. As with knowledge, skills cover a continuum from basic teaching skills of lesson planning and classroom management, to technical proficiency for specific teaching procedures. Much more difficult to assess and even more difficult to instil, but also considered to be necessary, are personal skills such as self-awareness, tolerance, and interpersonal sensitivity. It is generally accepted that supervised field experiences are necessary to acquire the fundamental skills for the practice of teaching. As with the knowledge base of teaching, the skills base is also not static, and teachers are expected to upgrade their skills as necessary to stay current with the field.

Judgment

Judgment involves knowing when to apply what knowledge and which skills under what circumstances. This requires the ability to reflect on how our values, attitudes, and experiences, as well as the shifting social context, influence our actions, choices, and recommendations. Good judgment incorporates increasing the probability that activities will benefit and not harm the students, parents, and communities to which teachers are responsible. It is acquired through reflective practice as described in Chapter 2. Judgment is much more difficult to assess than knowledge and skills and is usually indirectly addressed during supervised experience—a teacher-in-training who doesn't get into any serious trouble is assumed to have good judgment.

Diligence

Diligence involves consistently attending to our knowledge, skills, and judgment as they are applied in our professional activities while giving priority to students' needs over any other concerns. Diligence involves working hard to teach as best we can with each and every student, honestly evaluating our performance, and seeking additional training when appropriate. A diligent teacher seeks out professional guidance to identify the knowledge, skills, and judgment essential for good teaching. Being diligent also incorporates self-awareness of any personal or situational circumstances that might compromise our competence.

One consequence of individual teachers constantly striving to be better is that the average competence of the entire profession continues to rise over time. Teachers are expected to keep abreast of new developments in the field in order to maintain their competence. Thus, in order to remain competent, we must diligently strive to be better. Resting on our laurels only results in becoming less competent relative to the standards of the profession. The types of activities that may be necessary to maintain competence include continuing education, supervision, consultation, and retraining.

For various reasons, teachers may wish to enhance or change their scope of expertise. In that case, we are expected to obtain whatever additional knowledge and skills are necessary to practise competently in the new area. Teachers must become familiar with the standards of knowledge, skills, and judgment considered necessary for competent practice in the area they are considering expanding into, compare them with their own, and develop a plan to acquire what is lacking. The means for achieving this goal are identical for those used to maintain competence, although of course teachers will typically have to undergo more extensive training.

Another consideration in enhancing competence is whether doing so involves acquiring established and proven knowledge and skills, or more recent ones. With regard to the former, training or retraining is more straightforward and mainly has to do with learning about the area of practice. With more recently developed knowledge and skills, the issues are somewhat more complex. Teachers are expected to ensure that any new approaches and procedures they adopt will benefit and not harm their students. This requires critical evaluation of the new procedures and their incorporation into existing areas of expertise. Evaluation of the relevance and soundness of new procedures can be accomplished through several routes, such as examining the professional literature on the topic, consulting other teachers with expertise and experience in the area, and the generous exercise of critical judgment.

Equally important is that teachers themselves are always changing. The profession is widely regarded as being stressful. Teachers also age, experience joy and suffering, form new relationships and end others, and generally change as people. Thus our manifest competence also changes—often for the better, but sometimes for the worse. Teachers are also expected, therefore, to be diligent about paying attention to their own personal changes and reflecting on how these changes impact their competence.

Teachers are also expected to be diligent with respect to becoming impaired. Because competence is based on performance, not ability, circumstances may arise whereby our ability to apply our knowledge, skills, and good judgment becomes impaired. Reasons can range from burnout or distress, to substance abuse, to dementia. Whatever the reason, we are expected to do whatever is necessary to avoid becoming impaired and take appropriate steps to limit harm to others if we do become impaired, such as by withdrawing from classroom teaching for a period of time or seeking out personal counselling.

WHAT THE CODES SAY

Maintain Efficiency

The teacher should maintain his/her efficiency by study, by travel or by other means which will keep him/her abreast of the trends in education and the world in which we live.

—From the Nova Scotia Teachers Union Code of Ethics

RELATIONSHIPS WITH COLLEAGUES

The essence of being a professional is that each teacher is both regulated and a regulator. That is, it is not enough to be concerned only with your own behaviour. We are expected to be concerned about whether every teacher is providing benefit to society and not causing harm. All teachers will therefore find themselves at some point having to respond to unprofessional or incompetent conduct on the part of another teacher.

The circumstances of teaching are such that relationships with colleagues are a more sensitive matter than they are, for example, with lawyers and doctors. Teachers are expected to respect the expertise of their colleagues, to refrain from acting in ways that undermine professional authority, and to deal with disputes with other teachers in a respectful manner. Most codes of conduct prohibit teachers from publicly criticizing other teachers. Some, such as the Saskatchewan Teachers' Federation *Code of Ethics*, go even further: they set out when critical comments are to be made, and to whom they can be made, and they require that the teacher being criticized be given the opportunity to respond. In most jurisdictions, the Teachers' Act also prohibits malicious, careless, or irresponsible criticism of a fellow teacher that undermines the public's confidence.

This undermining of confidence in the profession is especially pertinent to teaching. To facilitate effective learning, teachers must have the confidence of students and parents. We are all familiar with the fate of the unfortunate substitute teacher who does not have the students' respect and fails to gain sufficient control over the classroom to properly undertake a lesson. If this occurred for all the teachers in a school, no real learning by any student would take place.

Just how important this provision is was brought to national attention by the case of James Keegstra, a teacher in Alberta. In this instance, teachers' actions implied that maintaining students' respect for teachers took precedence over denouncing him for teaching anti-Semitism to his students. Many have been critical of how the Keegstra situation was handled, but subsequent legal decisions have upheld that refraining from publically criticizing a fellow teacher is a foundational expectation of teachers.

As might be expected, this prohibition against openly disparaging other teachers has been challenged on the grounds that it restricts teachers' freedom of expression as guaranteed by the *Charter of Rights and Freedoms*. In *Cromer v. British Columbia Teachers' Federation* (1986), Ms. Cromer, a teacher who was also the parent of a student, made a number of derogatory remarks about her child's teacher during a parent advisory committee meeting. The court ruled that Ms. Cromer's interests in saying what she said were not sufficient to override the interests of maintaining trust in the profession of teaching.

In *Eggertson v. Alberta Teachers' Association* (2003), Ms. Eggertson, a teacher and the parent of two students, made critical comments to her children's current teacher as to the quality of a previous teacher. A complaint was made by the children's current teacher, and Ms. Eggertson was found by the Alberta Teachers' Association to have violated the *Code of Conduct* requirement that teachers' criticisms of one another be made in confidence to the proper official and only after the other teacher had been advised. On appeal, the court disagreed, noting that those present were not mere disinterested members of the public but were concerned about the children's progress such that open criticism would not undermine public trust. The court also noted that discourse between parents and teachers when the parents also happened to be teachers should not be stifled when the child's educative interests are at stake.

The following steps may be of some help when attempting to deal with these situations in an ethical and responsible manner.

Confirm the Issue

First, as best as you are able, try to assess the situation dispassionately. Are you certain you are able to determine the appropriateness of your colleague's actions? Are your motives personal, as opposed to upholding the standards of the profession? Do you have direct knowledge of your colleague's actions? You should be very reluctant to do anything based on rumours you have heard. Similarly, if you are approached by someone who claims to have first-hand knowledge of the unprofessional behaviour of a colleague, you should encourage that person to take appropriate action while being very careful about taking an active role yourself.

Consult

Before taking any action, teachers are expected to consult with trusted peers or with their teachers' association/federation. It is not a violation of most codes of professional conduct to do so. The role of the association in these situations is to help clarify issues and procedures. For example, do they agree that action should be taken? Are there any professional guidelines or standards relevant to the issue? Does the situation truly fall below acceptable professional standards? When you do discuss your concerns, make sure to protect the identity of your colleague and anyone else involved.

Speak with the Colleague

Questions or concerns about a teacher's professional conduct or competence should next be raised with the individual, unless it is a matter of harassment or abuse or it is a criminal offence. If the latter, there is a statutory duty to report the issue to the proper authorities. Taking this step may even successfully resolve the issue. Your goal at this point should be to correct the problem, not to punish. Try to be calm, respectful, and constructive—imagine how you would like to be treated if you had made a professional mistake and were being confronted. Try to be open-minded and to understand your colleague's side of the story. A face-to-face meeting in professional surroundings is usually best.

Involve Others

If your colleague is unwilling to address the issue, or if the action is of a seriously harmful nature, such as the sexual exploitation of a student, you are expected to take your concerns to the regulatory body in your jurisdiction that is best suited to investigating the situation and to stopping or offsetting the harm. You will likely be asked to make a written, signed complaint and possibly to testify in a disciplinary hearing. It is probably in your best interests, and in the interests of a fair process, that you record details of your actions and include time, date, and the basic content of any conversations.

REFLECTING ON THE CHAPTER

Take some time to think about what is most important in this chapter for you. Perhaps you might go back and reread the parts that resonated most for you. As you are doing so, you might want to think about other parts of the chapter that you think parents and students and community members might think are most important. If these are different, take some time to reflect on how the different emphases might be important in your development and career as an ethical teacher.

SUMMARY

While some controversy remains over whether teaching is a profession, Canadian society for the most part treats it as one. The degree to which the public can trust the profession of teaching rests on teachers' ability to protect the public from harm caused by their members. Teachers are therefore accountable for regulating themselves by setting entrance standards to the profession, developing codes of conduct to set minimum standards of competent practice, and sanctioning members who fail to meet those standards. Competence has four major components: *knowledge, skills, judgment*, and *diligence.* Teachers are expected to take steps to maintain competence and avoid becoming impaired. One of the more difficult situations they have to deal with is the possible incompetent behaviour of another teacher. A teacher who suspects a colleague of unprofessional or incompetent behaviour should first be sure to have adequate knowledge of the issue, then consult with others, attempt to resolve the issue with the colleague, and involve others if necessary or if the issue is a serious one.

QUESTIONS FOR DISCUSSION

1. What has been your experience with people who do not view teaching as a profession? Do you think teaching is a true profession? Why or why not?
2. Do you think the entrance standards for teachers are high enough? Or are they too high? Explain your answer.
3. To what extent do you think that burnout is inevitable in the profession of teaching? What self-care practices do you have in place to facilitate your continued personal and professional well-being?

CASE STUDY

LOYALTY QUESTIONED

You teach students who are performing below their grade level by taking them out of class for private lessons. One day, while you are with a student, the rest of the class had a music lesson during which they destroyed school property. The music teacher relayed the names of the guilty parties to the principal, including the student who was with you, and they were suspended. The mother of the innocent student called the principal the next day and argued that her son should not be suspended because you corroborated her son's claim that during the time of the incident, he had been in your lesson. The principal reassured the mother that you had probably forgotten that you let him out before the end of the lesson. Later the principal calls you into her office for a talk and accuses you of not being loyal by speaking with the mother and contradicting the music teacher.

1. Do you think that what you did was wrong in this situation? Does an alternative course of action seem more correct? What

do you honestly think you would do if you were confronted with this situation in real life? What does this tell you about your ethical self?

2. How compelling do you find the argument that teachers must be loyal to one another in order to maintain trust in the profession? Can you formulate a counter-argument?
3. What do you think the average person would expect a teacher to do in this situation? Do you agree with these expectations? If so, how would you present them in a persuasive manner to a fellow teacher struggling with what to do in this situation? If not, how would you persuasively correct an average person's expectations?

CHAPTER 6

STUDENT RIGHTS, PARENT RIGHTS

CASE STUDY

RATE MY TEACHER

You are the teacher responsible for overseeing the students' after-school computer design club. One especially talented student has designed a website that allows users to post comments from their smartphone, tablet, or personal computer. What makes her Web design unique is that it has protections built in such that users cannot be identified or linked to the comments they post. The site will enable students to rank the teachers in the school in terms of how well they teach and how much fun their classes are. It also enables selected comments from student surveys about the teachers. She tells you she intends to have the website up and running in the next few days. When you tell her that would be a terrible thing to do, she says it's within her rights and you can't stop her.

1. How much control should you exercise over the website? Does it make a difference if the website forms part of a school assignment?
2. To what extent do you think you have an obligation to protect your fellow teachers' reputations (and your own, for that matter) from these reviews?
3. Would it make a difference if the school was not directly involved in the website—for example, if it was posted on the server of the student's personal account?

The term "people's rights" encompasses a number of different concepts. In its broadest interpretation, one speaks of rights that would exist even if they were not codified by law. For example, almost everyone recognizes that infants have the right to be nurtured and cared for by their parents (or guardians) and teachers and that this right exists even in countries that have no laws that specifically require it. These are sometimes called "natural rights" or "fundamental rights." A natural right is something we possess by virtue of being human. We don't have to do anything to earn this right; it is ours automatically. Natural rights include the right to a fair trial, the right to free speech, and the right to be free from arbitrary discrimination.

In its narrowest interpretation, one speaks only of rights set out by statute and protected by law. These are sometimes called "legal rights," and they typically flow out of natural rights. When there is sufficient social and political will to have a natural right established in law, legal recognition of it may follow. The most obvious legal rights are those set out in the *Charter of Rights and Freedoms* that are granted to everyone, including children, in Canada. *Charter*-protected rights are to a large degree inalienable. As set out in Section 1 of the *Charter*, they are "subject only to such reasonable limits prescribed by law as can be demonstrably justified in a free and democratic society" and to the opting out clause, Section 33. Still important, but more prone to legislative change, are rights contained within other provincial and federal statutes, such as human rights codes and the right to an education as contained within school acts.

A somewhat broader interpretation of legal rights includes international agreements that Canada has ratified. In the case of students, the most important agreement is the *UN Convention on the Rights of the Child*, which came into force on 2 September 1990 and was ratified by Canada in 1991. Article 28 of that document provides:

> 1. State Parties recognize the right of the child to education and with a view of achieving this right progressively and on the basis of equal opportunity,* they shall, in particular:
>
> (a) Make primary education compulsory and available free to all;
>
> (b) Encourage the development of different forms of secondary education, including general and vocational education, make them available and accessible to every child, and to take such appropriate measures such as the introduction of free education and offering financial assistance in case of need;
>
> (c) Make higher education accessible to all on the basis of capacity by every available means;
>
> (d) Make educational and vocational information and guidance available and accessible to all children;
>
> (e) Take measures to encourage regular attendance in schools and the reduction of dropout rates;

*United Nations' Convention on the Rights of the Child, Article 28. <http://www.ohchr.org/en/professionalinterest/pages/crc.aspx>

2. State Parties shall take all appropriate measures to ensure that school discipline is administered in a manner consistent with the child's human dignity and conformity with the present Convention.

The *Convention* is enforceable under international law but is not part of Canadian law. It is still important, though, because when the courts interpret *Charter* provisions, they are guided by that convention, because it is an international commitment that Canada has made, and also because it sets a benchmark against which to measure the protections provided by the *Charter*.

An even broader definition of students' rights includes statements of principle enshrined in the codes of ethics of the teaching profession. For example, the Manitoba Teachers' Society *Code of Professional Practice* (2014)" provides that

"The Member speaks and acts with respect and dignity, and deals judiciously with others, always mindful of their rights."

There is, of course, no *Charter* right or any other law that requires a student to be spoken to with respect and dignity. Yet this expression of how teachers are expected to conduct themselves is important, not only because a teacher who fails to abide by it could be subject to discipline, but also because it creates an expectation of a certain environment in which the student and teacher operate.

This expectation placed on people to treat one another as autonomous individuals, and as thinking, feeling persons, underpins the broadest sense of students' and parents' rights. It is a way of thinking that has moved from educational philosophy to the administration of education.

■ REFLECTIVE TASK

Relationship with Parents

This might be a good time to reflect on the role your parents (or whoever raised you) played in your life. Was it your parents who most influenced your values and beliefs about right and wrong? Or was it someone else? What was the nature of their influence? For many people, parents and early family environment have been very important, although often in ways we are not completely aware of. For others, the ethical values of our families were quite explicit—for example, if a parent was a judge or religious leader. Even in these instances, the expressed views of these individuals were often not always completely congruent with their actions. If that is the case for you, how has it influenced your ethical beliefs? Take some time to reflect on and record your answers to these and any other questions that arise for you.

RIGHTS OF STUDENTS AND THEIR PARENTS

Whether one is speaking of natural rights or legal rights, it is typically accepted that the rights of an individual are to some degree prescribed by their age. Even John Stuart Mill, in *On Liberty* (1869), argued that the doctrine of only interfering with the rights of any person when self-protection is at stake does not apply to "young persons below the age which the law may fix as that of manhood or womanhood." In much the same way, while the *Charter* guarantees certain rights to all, including children, the law does not treat children as if they were adults; rather, it acknowledges that they are developmentally lacking in the ability to take proper care of themselves. The duality of viewing children as having rights but also as requiring the protection of adults creates a tension for teachers who are responsible for the care of their students.

Every jurisdiction in Canada has set a legal age of majority. Above this age, people are assumed to be competent to make decisions for themselves. Below it, competence is not assumed and the child's parent or guardian has a legal duty to provide care and supervision. In most jurisdictions the age of majority is eighteen, although in some it is nineteen. Note that the acceptance of the late teens as an appropriate age to be viewed as an adult is a relatively recent construct. In Western Europe in the late eighteenth century, children were essentially viewed as adults at the age of eight and were often expected to "make it on their own" from that age onward.

Thus parents (or guardians) are legally obligated to provide care and support for their minor children, and this translates into the legal right to direct and supervise them. Proxy consent from parents or guardians is thus sought for many activities involving persons under the age of majority. This age criterion is based as much on convenience as on ethical and legal considerations, however. The ethical expectation of respecting autonomy obligates us to not interfere with the self-determination of anyone capable of taking proper care of themselves. However, the day-to-day functioning of many social institutions would grind to a halt if we had to determine the capacity to consent of every individual for every decision he or she has to make.

This is why, besides the age of majority, the law also recognizes the principle of a *mature minor*. Minors can be considered "mature" if they are capable of being self-sufficient, productive members of society and are able to navigate and participate in the social and economic institutions of society. Although chronological age is only one of several relevant factors, the case of *C. (J.S.) v. Wren* (1987) suggests that a minor would likely not be considered mature before the age of fifteen. In fact, most minors aged fifteen and older of average intelligence are able to understand society's institutionalized expectations as well as adults do. Therefore, the law expects that minor students whose capacity for and understanding of an activity is equal to that of someone of the age of majority should not have their rights restricted based solely on their age.

In some instances, of course, there may be a conflict between what a mature minor views as the proper course of action, and that of his or her parents. Although the courts in Canada have not decided the issue in the context of education, there is some case law (e.g., *Gillick v. W. Norfolk and Wisbech Area Health Auth.*, 1985) that in some circumstances the minor's view is paramount.

Other legal exceptions may apply to the normal requirement for parental consent, and teachers should be aware of the legislation in their jurisdiction. In Alberta, for example, students under eighteen may be considered "independent" as defined in the *School Act* and thus be responsible for making their own educational decisions.

Even when they have obtained parental consent for a minor child to participate in educational activities, teachers are expected to provide the student with as much information as he or she is able to understand and to obtain the child's agreement to proceed. Immature minor students who do not want to participate in activities that their parents have consented to on their behalf should be provided with as much choice as possible regarding aspects of the activity that are negotiable, and every effort should be made to secure the students' agreement. Ultimately, if the minor student steadfastly refuses to participate in the activity, it may be that there will be little, if any, benefit to the student, and the parents should be so informed. Teachers are expected to refrain from forcing a student to participate in an activity that is of no benefit.

Decisions regarding education are not made solely by students and educators, of course. The common law has long recognized that parents are in the best position to make the decisions necessary to ensure the well-being of their children, including as they relate to education. The role of parents is rooted in the presumption that they should make important decisions affecting their children both because they are more likely to appreciate the best interests of their children and because they have a deep personal concern for fostering the development of their own children. The parental right to exercise control over their child's education is also protected by Sections 2(a) and 7 of the *Charter*.

Respecting the right of parents to control their children's education requires sensitivity to their wish to instill certain beliefs, which may not be shared by the majority of the school community. But, as Chief Justice Beverley McLachlin stated in *Chamberlain v. Surrey School District No. 36* (1998), although parental involvement is important, it cannot override the imperative placed on public schools to mirror the diversity of the community and to teach tolerance of difference. This expectation also holds true for those parents who remove their children from public secular schools in order to furnish them with a religious education, as established in *Canadian Civil Liberties Association v. Ontario* (1990), *R. v. Jones* (1986), and *Zylberberg v. Sudbury Board of Education* (1988). Even in the case of private schools that exist primarily to promote religious beliefs, parental interests may have to be tempered when the curriculum is not consistent with what is provincially mandated. Deciding what exceptions to make to the standard curriculum in response to parental interests is not a task reducible to a formula, and educators are expected to review the particular facts of each situation.

WHAT THE CODES SAY

Mindful of Students' Rights

The teacher speaks and acts toward students with respect and dignity, and deals judiciously with them, always mindful of their individual rights and sensibilities.

—From the British Columbia Teachers' Federation Code of Ethics

RIGHT TO AN EDUCATION

Under Section 7 of the *Charter*, "everyone has the right to life, liberty, and security of the person and the right not to be deprived thereof except in accordance with the principles of fundamental justice." The scope of this clause goes far beyond mere freedom from physical restraint. It has been interpreted by the Supreme Court as encompassing the right to make fundamental personal decisions that are rooted in the basic concepts of human dignity, autonomy, and privacy. Of particular interest is that the section has also been held to be a guarantee of the right to an education. In *R. v. Kind* (1984) the judge observed:

> I am of opinion that a child's right to education is included in the liberty guaranteed to it in section 7 of the Charter. However, in its role of protector and guardian of these rights on behalf of all parents, the government of this province has assumed the obligation of educating all children of school age in this province out of public funds. It is indeed a legitimate goal of the state to insist upon minimum education standards for all children within reasonable limits.*

If a child has a *Charter* right to an education, then a school administrator's decision to suspend a student may become the subject of scrutiny by the courts. The courts have long shown considerable reluctance to involve themselves in schools' internal discipline decisions unless the parties specifically invoke the *Charter*. In *Haines v. Neudorf* (1995), for example, the court dismissed an application for judicial review on the basis that the school board was entitled to prolong the suspension of a student who provided sexual favours for a number of students in the back of a bus. The court ruled that the suspension was within the board's powers. However, the court did suggest that the school had probably failed to give the student the opportunity to be heard and present a defence in the face of a ten-day suspension. While this issue has not yet come before the Supreme Court of Canada, in the lower court case of *Edward Gianfrancesco and Jessica Gianfrancesco v. The Junior Academy Inc.* (2003), damages were awarded for breach of natural justice when a school expelled a student without hearing under the school's "zero tolerance" policy.

As part of their mandate to protect some students, school administrators often have to consider limiting the rights of other students to an education. *Hawreluik v. Shamrock School Division No. 38* (1987) provides a troubling example of a case where these conflicting rights came into play. A number of children were charged under the *Young Offenders Act* with multiple counts of sexual assault on other students at the school. The board wrote to the parents of the accused advising them that their children were being put on "short bounds," which severely restricted their movements during school hours. The board justified the restrictions on the basis that they prevented intimidation and/or retaliation against the alleged victims and would prevent the laying of baseless allegations against the suspected offenders, while still allowing the students to attend school.

Judicial review of these restrictions was sought *prior* to the criminal trial, and thus prior to any decision as to whether the students were guilty or innocent. The court held that the board had acted within its duties to "administer and manage the educational affairs of the school division" and to "exercise general supervision and control over the schools of the division," and on that basis the restrictions

*R. v. Kind (1984)

were within the board's authority. No claim was made that the board had failed to adhere to the requirements of natural justice in limiting the students' rights without offering them the opportunity of a hearing. The court very pointedly stated:

> On this application the board does not have to justify the necessity of the "short bounds" placed on the applicants. It is not for me to decide the rightness or wrongness of the decision of the board. I do not sit on appeal from the board. I am only asked to determine whether the board possessed the authority under the Act to impose the restrictions.*

The difficulty in determining whether the board was, in fact, justified in its decision can easily be seen. On the one hand, the board had a responsibility to protect the other students in the school and to administer the school in a way that made it, as much as possible, a safe place in which to learn. However, there was also a significant curtailment of the rights of the alleged offenders, who had not been found guilty of any offence, and who had not had the opportunity to present their side of the case in any formal way.

Given the seriousness of the allegations, it seems likely that if the court had had to decide the issue, it would have found that the board acted in a reasonable manner, given that the accused students, while subject to constraints on their activities, were still being allowed to attend the school. It is very doubtful, however, that it would have been reasonable for the same board to suspend the students pending the outcome of their criminal trial.

This balancing of rights was similarly reflected in *R.B. v. Keewatin-Patricia District School Board* (2013), where the Ontario Human Rights Tribunal dealt with the issue of a nine-year-old student in grade three who was suspended from school for inappropriate behaviour, including swearing, spitting, yelling, stomping on a child's leg, and being noncompliant with his teacher. The tribunal determined that the student had been denied meaningful access to an education because of the school board's very negative relationship with his mother and not because the board was unable to meet his needs. The tribunal found that this was not an appropriate basis on which to justify his dismissal, given that there would be significant harm to the student if he were excluded from his school, and far less harm to the board if he were returned.

■ REFLECTIVE TASK

Experience as a Student

Thinking back on your own experience as a student, what conversations do you remember having that you felt your teacher should not share with others? What do you think were the most influential factors that shaped how important this was for you?

---

*Hawreluik v. Shamrock School Division No. 38 (1987)

PRIVACY AND CONFIDENTIALITY

Privacy is the right of an individual to choose the time, circumstances, and extent of his or her personal information being shared with others. It is a basic human right guaranteed in the *Charter of Rights and Freedoms*. Confidentiality relates to the expectation that information about a student will not be disclosed to anyone except under agreed-upon conditions.

Section 8 of the *Charter*, which deals with the right to be secure against unreasonable search and seizure, has received considerable judicial commentary in the context of students' privacy rights. The leading case is the Supreme Court of Canada's decision of *R. v. M.R.M.* (1998). A vice-principal had been advised by a number of students that another student had been selling drugs on school property and would be doing so at a school dance that evening. The vice-principal arranged for an RCMP officer to be present when he asked the student to empty his pockets and roll up his pant leg. A bag of marijuana was found hidden in the student's sock, and the student was charged with possession of a controlled substance.

The key issue in the resulting criminal trial was whether the vice-principal's search was reasonable, given that no warrant had been obtained beforehand. At trial level, the court found that the search was contrary to the *Charter* and the evidence was disallowed, resulting in the case against the student being dismissed. This decision was reversed on appeal, largely on the basis that the school administrator had a duty under the *School Act* to control the activities in the school and that the student, knowing this, had a diminished expectation of privacy.

The first issue the Supreme Court addressed was whether the student had a reasonable expectation of privacy, and if so, to what degree. The Court had little trouble finding that the student had a reasonable expectation for privacy of his body and the contents he carried and that this expectation was not displaced merely because he was in a school. However, a student would be aware that a school is supposed to be a safe environment in which discipline is enforced, and thus students may at times be required to submit to searches and have items seized. Because of this, the Court held that school authorities need only establish that there are reasonable grounds to believe there has been a breach of school regulations and that a search would disclose evidence of this. Reasonable grounds may be established through information provided by a student who is considered to be credible, from information received from more than one student, or from the educator's own observations.

Also, that search must also be reasonable in the circumstances. So when a student is suspected of carrying a weapon, a search that is immediate, thorough, and extensive would be considered reasonable. On the other hand, the belief that a student is carrying chewing gum contrary to a school policy would not justify such a search. The gender of the parties is also relevant. For example, a male teacher should not perform a search of the person of a female student unless the circumstances are extraordinary. Finally, the search should be as minimally intrusive as possible—thus, performing a strip search before asking the student to reveal the contents of a backpack would be unjustified.

One important factor in *R. v. M.R.M.* was that the police officer stood by silently while the search was being conducted. The argument that the search was to enforce school policies, and not part of a criminal investigation, could not have been made if the officer had conducted the search. Thus, in *R. v. S.B.* (1996), where a high school resource officer, dressed in his police uniform and acting on information obtained through a *Crime Stoppers* program, requested that the occupants of a car parked on school property exit the car and place any narcotics they had on the vehicle, the evidence was excluded on the basis that there was a *Charter* violation.

In cases involving searches of lockers, there is an even lower expectation of privacy, particularly where, as is common today, students are told that the lockers are school property and can be searched by the school. *R. v. W. (J.J.)* (1990) established that even in the absence of such a policy, locker searches are considered acceptable so long as the school administrator has reasonable cause for the search. However, a blanket search of all lockers for the vague purpose of finding evidence of some misdoings would likely not constitute a reasonable search.

With respect to confidentiality, teachers are expected to only share information about a student with the student's parents (or legal guardians) and with other teachers as necessary to provide a proper education for the student. When it comes to anyone else, personal information should only be disclosed with appropriate consent. This applies even to seemingly trivial information such as hobbies or interests—it is difficult to know what disclosures will be experienced by the student as a betrayal. The rationale for this position is respect for the student's privacy, given that children as young as six are sensitive to such issues and become increasingly concerned about control over their personal information as they grow older.

Thus, a student's school record is considered confidential information. Teachers are expected to ensure that grades, class assignments, and any other materials collected as part of the students' education are not disclosed to anyone who does not have a legitimate interest in accessing them. Many of the education acts set out the limited conditions in which the information can be divulged to a third party, subject to the waiver of this right by the student or, in appropriate circumstances, by the guardian or parent. As well, confidentiality issues may be addressed by teachers' codes of ethics. For example, the *Code of Professional Practice* (1995) of the Manitoba Teachers' Society states that "a Member respects the confidential nature of information concerning students and may give the information only to authorized personnel or agencies directly concerned with the individual student's welfare."

Robinson v. Northmount School for Boys (2014) recently upheld the principle that information that properly forms part of the school record of a student cannot be disclosed without the appropriate consent. However, information about other students, including another student's name and address information, may not receive such privacy protection if it originated in other documents where it was used for other purposes. The information may still receive privacy protection pursuant to municipal privacy legislation, notwithstanding that it is not protected under the *Education Act*.

An important exception to confidentiality relates to suspicions of child abuse. All Canadian jurisdictions except Yukon have legislation making it mandatory to report such suspicions regardless of any implied or contracted confidentiality agreements. And in all jurisdictions except Saskatchewan, failing to do so is a criminal offence.

The issue of confidentiality is made complicated by the fact that minor students are not fully autonomous individuals in the eyes of society or their parents. Where a minor student's parents have given consent for their child to participate in educational activities, what will and will not be disclosed should be clarified with them and the student. Legally, the parent or guardian who consents to activities on the minor student's behalf has the right to know the nature of those activities. Thus, a minor should not be promised that information will be kept from a parent who has legal custody.

If a minor student requests certain confidences, the degree to which confidentiality can be honoured is directly related to whether the student is sufficiently competent to be treated as a mature minor. If so, the parent or guardian no longer has the right of access to the student's confidential information. If not, the teacher must still deal with the matter of limits to confidentiality. That is, the student must be informed that his or her parents or guardians do have the right of access to all information contained in school records. Whether or not the student agrees to have information disclosed to a parent, teachers are expected to inform the student about what information will be shared and to whom.

The issue of confidentiality is troubling to many school officials when protecting the privacy of a student conflicts with ensuring that the school environment is safe for all. The *Youth Criminal Justice Act* attempts to address this by restricting access to records and by preventing the media from publishing the names of youth offenders. However, Section 125(6) of the *Act* allows the disclosure of information without prior court approval by a Crown prosecutor, a police officer, a provincial director, or a youth worker to, among others, representatives of a school board for the purposes of ensuring compliance with the terms of a youth court order, to ensure the safety of staff, students, or other persons. Under Section 127(7), when such information is released to the school it must be revealed only to those employees who need to know for the purposes for which it was released, and it must be destroyed once that purpose is passed. The information is also not to be kept with other information that forms the student's school record.

WHAT THE CODES SAY

Regard Student Information as Confidential

A teacher regards as confidential, and does not divulge, other than to appropriate persons, any information of a personal or domestic nature concerning either pupils or their homes.

—From the Newfoundland and Labrador Teachers' Association Code of Ethics

FREEDOM OF EXPRESSION

A hallmark of a democratic society is the promotion of freedom of expression, which is recognized as a fundamental freedom in Section 2 of the *Charter*. The classic rationale for freedom of expression lies in its importance for the search for truth, self-fulfillment, and self-governance. Without the protection of free expression, citizens in a democratic society are unable to adequately govern themselves. Free speech on the part of students—and teachers (see Chapter 12)—is considered necessary to prevent education from degenerating into a propagation of official dogmas and ideologies. But, as with all rights, freedom of expression has limits.

The seminal case on freedom of speech post-*Charter* is *R. v. Keegstra* (1990), in which high school teacher James Keegstra was charged with the criminal promotion of hatred through his teaching that Jewish people were "treacherous," "subversive," "sadistic," "money-loving," "power hungry," and "child killers" who sought to destroy Christianity. Students who espoused different views were academically penalized in his classroom. In that case the Supreme Court of Canada, following a long line of precedent, adopted an expansive definition of "expression": "if the activity conveys or attempts to convey a meaning, it has expressive content and prima facie falls within the scope of the guarantee." Assuming this requirement is met, the second part of the test for a breach of this *Charter* right involves determining whether the impugned action restricts such speech regardless of its content. If both these requirements are met, the issue then turns on whether such a restriction is demonstrably justified in a free and democratic society as per Section 1 of the *Charter*. In *Keegstra*, the *Criminal Code* provisions were found to be a justified restriction.

What is and is not justified was also addressed in *Lutes v. Prairie View School Division No. 74* (1992), where a grade nine student was given a month-long noon-hour suspension for singing a popular rap song titled "Let's Talk about Sex" that had been banned by the district. In apparent defiance of the ban, the student sang the song during the lunch break, off school premises, in the presence of a school district official who was allegedly involved in the banning of the song. The school determined that the student's act had been rude and disrespectful, and warned that if the noon-hour suspension were not adhered to he would be suspended from school altogether. The student sought judicial review of the decision on the grounds that it violated his right to free speech.

The Court rejected the school's argument that the student had been appropriately disciplined for being rude, ruling that the student's freedom of expression rights had been violated and that the suspension was not demonstrably justified in a free and democratic society. In the court's words, "the problem arose as a result of overreaction to an inoffensive song that carried a powerful message." The court ruled that the student could seek damages from the school.

It is an interesting question whether freedom of speech could be applied to dress codes. In an effort to control gang actions within schools, for example, some boards have banned certain jewellery and colours of shoelaces. There is little doubt that pre-*Charter*, this would have been within the right of the school authorities, as demonstrated by the oft-cited case of *Ward v. Blaine Lake School Board* (1971), in which an eleven-year-old, in conjunction with twenty others, was suspended because his hair was longer than allowed by the school appearance code. The court held:

> I am of the opinion that the power of prescribing within reasonable limits the extent of cleanliness required of pupils attending school, the extent of clothing they should wear, their general appearance,

> including hair grooming, was within the powers of the Board under the heading "administering and managing the educational affairs of the school district" and "exercising a general supervision and control over the schools of the unit." In these days of the so-called "permissive society" one does not need to indulge in much in the way of flights of imagination to envisage how difficult it would be to conduct a class of boys and girls where they could wear as little or as unusual clothing as some children or some parents might see fit. This would include not only care and cleanliness and covering of various parts of the body but preventing of unusual types of dress and hair styling which might be calculated to distract the pupils from their work in the classroom or adversely affect a proper and reasonable air of discipline in the school.*

Were the case to be decided today, likely the matter of hair length would be viewed as trivial to the safe administration of a school and a different result would be reached. However, the fact that what was once a matter of serious dispute became trivial over time warns us not to be overzealous in justifying free speech infringements in the name of proper school management.

The individual teacher is in the "front line" position to determine how custodial and bureaucratic rules are enacted in the classroom. The extent and nature of institutional control varies considerably from school to school and, to a lesser extent, from classroom to classroom within a school. Teachers, and students, typically feel considerable pressure to maintain appropriate decorum in the classroom. Decisions about what is appropriate are rarely made by the students themselves, or by the teacher, for that matter. Often they are made by administrators and, in many cases, previous administrators.

Ultimately, the question of freedom of speech and expression for students addresses what we want our students to learn. If students are denied the opportunity to freely express their thoughts and ideas in the classroom, what kind of citizens will they be? Will they internalize the skills and dispositions necessary for exercising political and civil rights? And will they think beyond pursuing questions of their own welfare and consider the welfare of others? It is to these questions that teachers are expected to address their attention.

REFLECTING ON THE CHAPTER

Go back and review the notes you made for the chapter as you were reading it. Did any aspect stand out for you as diverging from what you expected about student and parent rights? If so, what was your belief or understanding before reading the chapter? Are you convinced you were misinformed? Or do you still harbour some doubts? If you do, you may want to do some of your own research into the topic. You may even want to look up the legal decisions cited and read them for yourself. Whatever you need to do to be sure of your knowledge, take some time now to satisfy yourself that your understanding is sound.

*Ward v. Blaine Lake School Board (1972).

■ SUMMARY

Students' rights can arise from a number of different sources, including laws and statutes, codes of ethics, and our beliefs in the basic entitlement of all humans. However, the rights of a student may be limited by a number of different factors, including their age and developmental abilities, the need to safely administer schools, and the rights of others. Important rights for students are contained in the *Charter* and, to a lesser extent, in the *UN Convention on the Rights of the Child*. These include the right to an education (and not to be unreasonably deprived thereof), the right to security of the person, and the right of free speech. When circumstances require that a student's rights be restricted, teachers are expected to endeavour to do so in the least intrusive manner possible.

■ QUESTIONS FOR DISCUSSION

1. When does the school's role of socialization give way to respect for the individual preferences and rights of the student? What ethical and legal principles are relevant to your point of view?
2. To what extent should the rights of the individual child take precedence over the rights of parents to decide how their children should be raised? Don't forget to provide ethical and legal justification for your position.
3. If a student turned in a class paper in which the assignment was to produce a work of fiction, but the content contained a graphic, detailed description of a plan to bomb the school, would you alert law-enforcement authorities? Why or why not?

CASE STUDY

■ MUSIC AVOIDANCE

You have been concerned that your students tend to group together based on cultural background. You have noticed in particular that the only two students of a fundamentalist religious faith seem to be trying hard to make friends, with no success. As the holiday season approaches, you decide to involve the class in a multifaith musical production and proudly observe that it is having a positive impact on morale and cultural acceptance. Just as you are starting to feel pretty good about yourself, the parents of the two quiet students complain that, according to their faith, music is to be avoided at this time of year. They insist that you cancel the musical or excuse their children from it. All your good work will be ruined if the holiday production is called off, and no matter which of the parents' edicts you follow, the rest of the class will dislike their children.

1. How do you go about weighing the rights of the students and the rights of the parents in this situation?

2. How compelling do you find the argument that schools should accommodate the religious beliefs of all of the families in a school? Can you formulate a counter-argument?
3. If another parent argued that the school musical is an expression of free speech, how would you respond?

CHAPTER 7

AUTHORITY AND DISCIPLINE

CASE STUDY

UNRULY CLASS

Your class is being particularly unruly today. In fact, from the first day of the school year this group of students has been a challenge. For the most part you feel they are great kids, and you genuinely like them. It's just that some are rather excitable, and tend to get the others worked up, and the next thing you know, the classroom is out of control. On many days there is no time for teaching as you rush about trying to restore order. You find yourself feeling nostalgic for the district's former "zero tolerance" policy whereby any infraction of a rule was punished, regardless of accidental mistakes, ignorance, or extenuating circumstances. You believe that everyone deserves a second chance and so have never consistently implemented the policy, but today you are tempted to dust it off and use it to negate the influence of the disruptive students.

1. What role should your belief in the correctness of the school's abandoning its "zero tolerance" policy play in your decision of how to act?
2. Would isolating the excitable students from the others be an acceptable form of discipline? If so, how would you justify it? If not, what makes it unacceptable?
3. How would you propose to balance the rights of the unruly students against those of the students who are having their learning disrupted?

The complexity of the ethical and legal dimensions of classroom life is nowhere more evident than when a teacher exercises discipline in the classroom. In the above example there are at least two possible ways of thinking about the situation. One is in terms of legitimate power: children are supposed to do as you say as a representative of societal authority, and it is your job to instill respect through the administration of punishments for disrespect. When authority is given precedence, your job is to teach the civic virtues of self-restraint and respect for lawful authority.

Another way to think about classroom discipline is in terms of social order: the children are out of control, and it is your job to restore harmony so that learning can occur. When you give precedence to social order, you set aside your authority and prioritize classroom management—for example, by organizing where students sit, requiring them to raise a hand before asking a question, and so on. You see your students as confused and undirected rather than rowdy and disobedient.

Each way of thinking about discipline prompts different actions on your part. And each has its own ethical and legal issues.

Teachers—especially new or trainee teachers—often feel reluctant to impose control in the classroom for fear of interfering with the students' autonomy. But as any teacher with any experience can attest, a classroom of students left to their own devices will soon become so chaotic that the only autonomy any student can exercise is to contribute to the chaos or withdraw. The teacher's responsibility is to decide how to establish a framework of limits so that every student is able to learn, but to do so in a way that does not completely disregard their individual rights. Teachers must decide how to responsibly exercise *authority*.

Schools are unlike other organizations in that they create "offences" that would not be considered wrong or would not be subject to punishment in other social settings. For example, going to the bathroom at the wrong time can be an offence in a school but would rarely be considered so in other places. The same is true of being discovered in the hallway during classes, talking out of turn, or copying someone else's work. In a setting where large numbers of young people are required to attend, and are supervised by a relatively small number of adults, some rules will be necessary to keep order. The challenge that faces educators is how to strike the appropriate balance between the requirements of order necessary for effective education and the degree of autonomy that everyone is entitled to.

Moreover, the educational mandate of schools imposes expectations on educators that are not found in other situations. In an educational setting, everyone is expected to be concerned about the development of students as persons—with their intellectual and moral growth, not simply their behaviour. We don't want students merely to comply with our instructions. We want them to understand why those instructions are necessary and why it may be in their best interests to do as they are asked. This means that teachers are expected to try to *teach* students, not simply keep them out of trouble.

Every event in the school, even a transgression by a student, can thus be seen as an opportunity to educate. For example, if a student is suspected of plagiarizing, the teacher might take this as an opportunity to discuss with the class what plagiarism means, why it is frowned upon, and what the conventions are for crediting other people's work. There are times when it may well be more important to have all students learn from a situation than to punish one student for doing something inappropriate.

Also, what is required for educational purposes may not be the same as what a strict view of the law might demand. Because schools are expected to care about students, teachers will want to think very carefully about the best course of action when a student is suspected of a crime. Do teachers simply call the police, or do they try to work with the student to help him or her cope with the problem? Teachers are expected to help students achieve their potential, yet doing so may sometimes conflict with narrower legal expectations that pull teachers toward acting as agents of the state.

As well, for teachers to prepare students to be good citizens, they must educate them about their rights and responsibilities. How can students become responsible adults if, while in school, they are not informed about rights, or if their opportunities to learn to exercise rights and responsibilities are highly restricted?

Power is a constant in classrooms. It resides neither completely within an individual nor completely within a group, but rather in the complex interplay between them. Power is thus both personal and social. That is why, while it is misleading to say that the teacher "has" power, it is also misleading to say that power arises completely out of social structures. Rather, the individual characteristics of the teacher are expressed within the social expectations of the teacher's role. Students give a certain amount of power to a particular teacher in part because they recognize the legitimate power that teachers have in our society, and in part as a function of how much the teacher expects (or demands) it. It follows that each particular teacher differs in his or her willingness and ability to take some or all of the power offered (or surrendered) by a particular group of students. It is in this give and take of power in teacher-student relationships that particular ethical and legal issues can arise.

So what do we mean when we speak of power in the classroom? Power is one person's ability to get another to do something he or she would not otherwise do. Getting students to do things they might prefer not to do is a pretty good description of what teachers do every day. This is an ethical issue for two reasons. First, teachers must get students to do things that are in the students' best interests and thereby provide care; and second, there are limits on how much power anyone—including teachers—ought to use in order to achieve even legitimate ends and thereby respect autonomy.

A teacher's authority ultimately flows from being good at promoting student autonomy (i.e., from being a good teacher) and from having a broad and rich understanding of societal standards. A teacher, it follows, is justified in passing judgment on how students ought to behave in order to be good citizens. Thus a teacher is expected (a) to use her or his authority to *educate*, and (b) to be able to explain and justify the enforcement of rules. While the busy ebb and flow of the classroom does not always allow time for explanation, justification is expected to exist in the mind of the teacher and to be based on more than mere whim or personal preference. That is why the example the teacher sets is so central to his or her role (see Chapter 9). Society and students alike benefit when they learn to obey rules through an appreciation of good and sensible reasons for doing so, instead of simply doing as they are told.

■ REFLECTIVE TASK

Good and Evil

If only there were evil people somewhere insidiously committing evil deeds, and it were necessary only to separate them from the rest of us and destroy them. But the line dividing good and evil cuts through the heart of every human being. And who is willing to destroy a piece of his own heart?

—From the Solzhenitsyn, Aleksandr. The Gulag Archipelago, 1918–1956: An Experiment in Literary Investigation. Translated from the Russian by Thomas P. Whitney (Parts I-IV) and Harry Willetts (Parts V-VII); abridged by Edward E. Erickson, Jr.; foreword by Anne Applebaum. New York: HarperPerennial, 2007.

Think about the good and evil in your own heart. What occurs to you? Do you struggle to remember evil deeds you committed as a child, or perhaps more recently? Or do they come immediately to mind? Can you even acknowledge that you have an evil side? Or do you think that Solzhenitsyn (who spent eight years as a prisoner in a Soviet labour camp) is mistaken and that there really are good people and evil people? Take as much time as you need to reflect on these and any other questions that occur to you.

IN LOCO PARENTIS

The doctrine of *in loco parentis*—literally, "in place of the parent"—refers to the legal authority given to public or private institutions to act as a temporary guardian or caretaker of a child and to assume some or all of the responsibilities of a parent. In the context of education, it concerns itself with the limits of discipline in the teacher–student relationship. The Saskatchewan *Education Act* (1995), for example, allows that teachers may discipline students in a manner "that would be exercised by a kind, firm and judicious parent." William Blackstone's *Commentaries on the Laws of England* (1765–1769) is typically credited with providing the earliest common law source of the doctrine:

> [The father] may also delegate part of his parental authority, during his life, to the tutor or schoolmaster of his child; who is then *in loco parentis*, and has such a portion of the power of the parent committed to his charge, viz. that of restraint and correction, as may be necessary to answer the purposes for which he is employed. (Book 1, Chapter 16, p. 361)*

Throughout the eighteenth and nineteenth centuries, the courts usually declined to hear challenges to the doctrine, and when they did, they rejected those challenges. In fact, prior to the *Charter of Rights and Freedoms*, teachers were not generally expected to adhere to any particular standards of natural justice when dealing with students because they were considered to stand *in loco parentis*. Prior to the *Charter*, judicial reasoning in Canada was generally grounded in deference to the good faith behaviour of teachers. Public expectations were

*Blackstone, William. (1765–1769). Commentaries on the Laws of England, Book 1, Chapter 16, p. 361.

represented by local school board policy and the discretion of the teachers. Thus, school law was mostly found in the actions of school boards, ministry officials, and professional teacher organizations rather than in the written decisions of judges.

Canadian courts granted broad discretionary powers to teachers as representatives of school authorities based on an interpretation of the relevant school act and long-standing principles such as *in loco parentis*, and judicial reasoning reflected the belief that teachers rarely behave in a capricious, arbitrary, or unreasonable manner. The courts were—and to a lesser extent still are—reluctant to interfere with the reasonable exercise of this discretion. A teacher's authority to discipline students under common law is therefore based on society's willingness to delegate considerable latitude to teachers as state agents carrying out the important function of "peace, order and good government" through the doctrine of *in loco parentis*, as articulated in *Murdock v. Richards* (1954):

> It is sometimes said that the parent, by sending the child to school, has delegated his discipline to the teacher; but since many children go to public schools under compulsion of the law, and the child may well be punished over the objection of the parent, a sounder reason is the necessity for maintaining order in and about the school. (p. 769).*

Before the *Charter*, the approach of the courts was deference to teachers' discretion and a preference for the virtues of discipline and obedience over the individual rights of students. More recently, the doctrine has received important challenges as the courts seek to balance the parental role of teachers against the reality that teachers derive much of their power from being agents of state institutions and, as such, ought to be subject to limits on their authority to infringe on people's rights. The courts are therefore increasingly favouring the protection of students' rights instead of deferring to teachers' judgment. Post-*Charter*, the doctrine of *in loco parentis* continues have an important, though increasingly lesser, influence in legal cases involving a range of students' rights as they relate to, for example, freedom of speech, acceptable punishments, and privacy protections. In particular, the broad discretion afforded teachers as surrogate parents is inconsistent with the protection of students' *Charter* rights.

Many teachers tend to understand the doctrine of *in loco parentis* to mean that they ought to deal with students in a caring and compassionate manner by, for example, making disciplinary decisions based on how they would treat their own children. The problem with this thinking is that a given teacher's child may be quite unlike the student for whom he or she is responsible. Also, given that the doctrine has been eroded considerably over the past several decades, it is no longer the primary source of a teacher's authority. Indeed, in *R. v. Ogg-Moss* (1984), the Supreme Court of Canada ruled that it "has little, if any, relevance in institutional settings" such as schools. The Court ruled that the combination of "authority of the *in loco parentis* doctrine and the power conferred on teachers by statute" has resulted in an "almost omnipotent, legal status" for teachers. Instead,

*Murdock v. Richards (1954)

the *in loco parentis* role has diminished, and teachers are now more commonly understood to be acting as agents of the state and are to be treated accordingly in law.

The courts do continue to defer to teachers' exercise of discretion to the extent that they seek to balance students' rights with the interests of order and discipline. Judges remain cautious when addressing questions about methods of discipline and the limits of a teacher's disciplinary role. However, the broad discretion arising out of the *in loco parentis* doctrine is increasingly considered inconsistent with current understandings of students' rights post-*Charter*. Given that the authority delegated to teachers under most education acts can easily be misunderstood as legitimizing the principle of *in loco parentis*, teachers would do well to be mindful of mistakenly believing they have the authority to exercise discipline in ways that are contrary to students' *Charter* rights and freedoms.

WHAT THE CODES SAY

Show Justice to Students

The member will strive to show consistent justice and consideration in all his or her relationships with pupils.

—From the Nunavut Teachers Association Code of Ethics

PUNISHMENT

Punishment is the deliberate infliction of a disadvantage for a wrong that has been voluntarily committed. It is meant to decrease the likelihood that the wrong will be committed again; it does so by enhancing the offender's autonomy by presenting a choice of reoffending and paying the price, or obeying the rule and reaping the benefit. Properly implemented, punishment helps to maintain social order and to morally educate the punished—not merely to suppress behaviour. Teachers, parents, police, and courts of law are socially sanctioned arbitrators of punishment; all of them routinely and legitimately exercise a right to punish children under certain conditions.

Given that teachers are expected to influence the morality of children in the direction of what is desired by the community at large, there will be times when punishment is an appropriate response to behaviour that is legitimately prohibited. It is expected to contribute to and protect the educational development of students toward being good citizens. This means that punishment ought not to coerce students to the will of the more powerful teacher. Nor—it must be said even if obvious—should it be the deliberate infliction of harm.

Traditionally in our society, parents have been viewed as having the right to discipline children, short of what would constitute abuse. Abuse of children by *any* person—be it parent, teacher, or family member—is a serious problem in Canada that has received widespread attention in recent years. But except in the most blatant instances, there is little consensus as to where to draw the line between a teacher disciplining a student and abusing a child.

To differentiate punishment from what in law would normally constitute assault, Section 43 of the *Criminal Code* was enacted in 1892. Predicated on the (even at that time) historical value that parents have the right to discipline their children, and that teachers also have this right by way of *in loco parentis*, it states:

> 43. Every schoolteacher, parent or person standing in the place of a parent is justified in using force by way of correction toward a pupil or child, as the case may be, who is under his care, if the force does not exceed what is reasonable under the circumstances.

Although enacted in the late 1800s, the reasoning behind Section 43 dates back to Roman law and then English common law, which also allowed corporal punishment by husbands against wives, employers against servants, and masters against apprentices. Today, only in the case of children does the law condone such behaviour. A cross-sampling of recent cases involving acquittals under the section shows that there are divergent views as to what is reasonable. A teacher using a karate demonstration on four grade ten students (*R. v. Wetmore*, 1996), pushing one student against a blackboard and slapping another on the head (*R. v. Plourde*, 1993), and attempting to kick a twelve-year-old and then holding him against a wall while slapping him in the stomach (*R. c. Caouette*, 2002), have all been deemed acceptable by the courts.

It was inevitable that Section 43 of the *Criminal Code* would be subjected to *Charter* challenges. One such challenge was commenced in 1998 (*Canadian Foundation for Children, Youth and the Law v. Canada [Attorney General]*, 2004), based on the argument that the section was unconstitutional by virtue of the "life, liberty and security," "cruel and unusual punishment," and "equality before the law" provisions of the *Charter* (ss. 7, 12, and 15, respectively). The position of the Canadian Foundation for Children, Youth and the Law was that hitting children breached their fundamental rights of respect for human dignity and equal protection under the law. It argued that Section 43 justified physical assault in order to protect parents and teachers who mistakenly believed that assaulting children is necessary for their own good.

The foundation asked the court to repeal the section and thereby open the way for new legislation that would follow the view prevailing throughout Europe and in most of the American states—that is, that physical punishment is not acceptable in schools. The example of England was provided: there, physical punishment in the school system was banned and restraint only allowed in proscribed circumstances.

A number of other interested parties were allowed to make submissions to the court, including the Canadian Teachers' Federation (CTF), which opposed the repeal of the section because it allowed a defence in situations when a teacher needed to physically intervene to prevent violence or establish control. The CTF stated that it did not condone physical punishment by teachers, and it took no position on whether Section 43 was unconstitutional, arguing instead that there were common and appropriate physical interventions in the classroom that had rightly been decriminalized as a result of the section. These included removing a student from a classroom, taking a noncooperative student to the principal's office, gaining a student's attention during the course of a verbal reprimand, and restraining a cognitively impaired student. Given that even trivial physical interventions by teachers often formed the basis of a parental complaint or police investigation, the removal of Section 43 would make teachers more vulnerable to unjustified allegations and severely limit their ability to maintain order in the classroom.

The foundation's submission to repeal Section 43 was ultimately rejected by the Supreme Court. The Court stressed that the section required that the force used be "reasonable," which precluded conduct that would constitute "cruel and unusual punishment." Also, the Court noted that the need to address the best interests of the child was not fundamental to our societal notion of justice and therefore was not contrary to Section 7 of the *Charter*. Finally, the argument that Section 43 was unconstitutional because it treated children in an unequal way from adults was rejected on the basis that the equality provision does not require identical treatment under the law, only equal treatment. Teachers who exercise authority in the classroom by use of physical force, therefore, continue to be protected by Section 43, subject to the requirement that the force be reasonable in the circumstances.

Determining what constitutes "force which is reasonable in the circumstances" is done on a case-by-case basis. However, in *R. v. Robinson* (1899), the court did establish that any pain inflicted must be temporary in nature, result in no serious injury, not threaten to cause injury to life or limb or disfigurement, and not be prolonged past the endurance of the child.

R. v. Imbeault (1977) refined this standard by establishing that the courts will assume that any punishment inflicted is reasonable and for sufficient cause until the contrary is shown, with the onus on the complainant to prove the contrary. However, if it can be shown that the punishment was motivated by anger or was intended simply to cause physical harm, the teacher's actions will not be protected by Section 43. Also, the punishment meted out must be proportional to the behaviour. Thus, in *R. v. Godin* (1996), where two students had already been involved in three separate fights with each other on the same day, a teacher stepping in and physically separating them during the course of which he slapped them on their faces with an open palm was held to be acting reasonably in the circumstances. The court in this case noted that the fighting was not an isolated incident and that the teacher had little time to consider alternatives.

Deciding whether punishment is warranted does not entail purely an objective test, however. In *R. v. Haberstock* (1970), a teacher slapped a student for name-calling that had occurred three days earlier. The teacher had been supervising the playground on a Friday afternoon when a group of students leaving on a school bus shouted names at him. The teacher's reprimand occurred at the earliest opportunity the following Monday. When it was determined that the child was in fact innocent, criminal charges were brought against the teacher. The court found that the teacher's action was reasonable and justified by an honest belief that the student was guilty.

By contrast, in *R. v. Kanhai* (1981), the defendant teacher was administering a twelve-minute running test. Students were required to either run or jog for its duration. At the end of the test the teacher told a student who had repeatedly walked despite being instructed otherwise that he would have "an appointment";

he then grabbed him by the hair and ushered him into his office. There was no evidence that the student talked back or resisted in any way. During the course of this, the teacher gave the student a "firm head rubbing against the door." The court was troubled by the degree of force used and the more fundamental question of whether it was used "by way of correction." The court held that the punishment was not justified because the student was complying with the teacher's reprimand.

For some students, force can never be justified. In *R. v. Ogg-Moss* (1984), a twenty-one-year-old student with an IQ of less than 20 and incapable of speech was struck for spilling milk. The Court ruled that the punishment was not protected by Section 43 because the person administering the punishment knew that the recipient was incapable of remembering the punishment within minutes of it taking place. The punishment could therefore not have been intended as a form of correction. While some have suggested that punishing a mentally handicapped child is never justified, the Court was reluctant to state that all such persons cannot be punished.

■ REFLECTIVE TASK

Being Punished and Rewarded

What has been your experience with punishments and rewards? Have you generally been treated fairly by teachers and other authority figures in your life? Or were you mistreated? Or perhaps favoured by a teacher such that you felt you didn't deserve the praise or favours you received? How has your experience with discipline shaped your practice of it? Have there been times when you meted out rewards and punishments impulsively rather than reasonably? Take as much time as you need to reflect on these and any other questions that occur to you.

NATURAL JUSTICE

The provisions regarding natural justice in Sections 7 and 11 of the *Charter* have important implications for schools. While the authority of teachers to discipline students comes from their *in loco parentis* status as well as legislation that allows schools to make and enforce rules, neither of these sources provide particulars, and few higher-court cases have applied *Charter* guarantees to students. On the whole, the courts have accepted that schools can make and enforce rules that can reasonably be considered necessary for maintaining order. That said, there has been a gradual shift in societal expectations toward schools having rules consistent with the *Charter's* emphasis on natural justice.

The basic elements of natural justice are as follows: (1) the person deciding the matter is free from bias, (2) the accused has the opportunity to mount a defence, (3) the accused is entitled to legal representation, (4) the accused can appeal the decision, and (5) the matter is conducted fairly. School discipline practices often appear to violate these principles. For example, teachers often accuse students of wrongdoings and dispense punishments without explaining precisely what they did wrong or providing them with an opportunity to be heard. Students are usually compelled to give self-incriminating evidence, are rarely presumed innocent until proven guilty, and are almost never given the opportunity to appeal, let alone have legal representation.

To maintain order, schools establish various rules and place restrictions on students that are not ordinarily found in other social settings. Examples include rules governing movement (where students can be), privacy (lockers, personal possessions), appearance and dress, and conduct (smoking, fighting, taking turns). Canadian courts have consistently upheld the right of schools to restrict students' freedom for the purpose of maintaining an orderly atmosphere in the school. These restrictions can extend to such obvious matters as studies, attendance, and homework, as well as who students are permitted to associate with and where in the school they can choose to be.

The courts have begun to insist that such rules be clearly justified and that their application respect students as persons. School authorities are expected to be able to demonstrate that any limitations placed on students' rights and freedoms are actually necessary for the orderly conduct of schools. Society's willingness to tolerate rules that are set and enforced in an arbitrary fashion is diminishing, and the courts are paying greater attention to principles of natural justice. This attention is gradually influencing ministries of education and school boards, and even some parent councils.

For example, *J. O. v. Strathcona-Tweedsmuir School* (2010) involved the expulsion of a student accused of having sex in a public washroom at a school dance held at a golf club in response to member of the club complaining to the school. The student claimed that she was not feeling well and that she had asked her boyfriend to accompany her to the washroom to take care of her. Other students corroborated the student's account, but the principal refused to hear it or investigate further, stating that the school had been deeply embarrassed by the incident. The student and her parents sued the school for breach of contract and mental distress. The court held that "expulsion decisions must not be arbitrary, discriminatory, or made in bad faith" and that the school had an obligation to ensure that whatever procedure it chose was fair. The school was found to have fallen considerably short of meeting its duty of fairness because the student's side of the story was not considered.

Issues of order such as this illustrate the dilemma posed by the schools' educational mission. It is hard to understand how a school can teach its students to respect the law, the rights of others, and democratic processes when these are not manifest in its own operations. If students are treated arbitrarily, subjected to rules they neither support nor understand, or denied the opportunity to express their opinions, how can it be said that a school is doing what it should? Teachers are expected to keep order in the school, but they are also expected to tolerate diverse behaviour and points of view in order to fulfill their educational mandate.

Some teachers may worry that their authority will be undermined if the pendulum swings too far toward natural justice and away from professional judgment. However, societal expectations do appear to be gradually changing; schools are becoming more democratic and just. The foundation of a teacher's authority is shifting away from the *in loco parentis* doctrine, as grounded in provincial legislation, toward respecting students as persons, as grounded in the *Charter*. Thus teachers find themselves having to reconcile traditional expressions of authority with respect for the rights and freedoms of their students as citizens.

So in the school setting, respect for natural justice requires that any student accused of misbehaving be given a fair hearing. Ideally, students are given notice of what they are accused of as well as the opportunity to respond to the allegations on their own behalf. Rules need to be clear and specific, not vague and general, and students need to be informed of them in advance, including any procedures for appeal of decisions. In this way it is possible to both maintain school order and respect student rights.

WHAT THE CODES SAY

Treat Students with Respect

Members are dedicated in their care and commitment to students. They treat students equitably and with respect and are sensitive to factors that influence individual student learning.

—From the Ontario College of Teachers Standards of Practice

CLASSROOM MANAGEMENT

Although typically thought of as a technical problem of establishing and maintaining order, classroom management is very much an issue of authority and therefore of ethics and law. Teachers establish rules, correct infractions, give feedback and rewards, resolve conflicts, and recommend suspensions from school. The task of creating an educative classroom climate involves working through complex value issues related to authority, autonomy, and responsibility. However, the teacher's responsibility for managing and organizing cannot be separated from that for teaching and learning—students learn as much from how they are taught as from what they are taught.

One of the more challenging aspects of classroom management has to do with the impact of discipline on all of the students involved, whether as actors or as audience. Teachers are expected to know how to discipline individual students without embarrassing them, and to do so in a way that reminds the entire class of what is inappropriate behaviour.

Teachers and schools are expected to have enforceable rules that contribute to the decorum necessary for learning. Systems of punishment that are so severe that they diminish the educational function of the school violate the school's primary function and are therefore unacceptable to the community at large. Punishment that makes it impossible for the student to continue in the educative process, such as suspension or expulsion, runs contrary to the core ethical value of providing care. Because teachers are expected to educate as many students as possible, suspension from school should be considered only after all other forms of punishment have been tried and have failed, or there is good reason to believe that they would fail if employed. Thus every effort should be made to keep students in class, where they have some access to educational opportunities. However, this obligation to be just and considerate in dealing with each student does not undermine the teacher's authority—for example, under Section 231 of *The Education Act, 1995*—to exclude a student from the classroom in the interests of the other students.

Perhaps one of the more difficult questions to answer is this one: When does classroom management become manipulation? Manipulation involves applying nonrational, covert processes to bring about behaviour change. It is inconsistent with our understanding of the teacher's legitimate role, which is to provide education through rational, overt means. Many teachers have fallen into the habit of assigning "busywork" that has no legitimate educative end, simply to maintain order in the classroom. When the means of learning are separate from the ends, the students are being manipulated. When students are given rational reasons (within their ability to understand), and the pedagogical means are inseparable from the educative ends, true education is taking place. For example, students might be assigned the task of learning about life in the trenches of the First World War. This could involve acting in a play that takes place during trench warfare, reciting *In Flanders Fields*, and writing their own poem. Each of these learning tasks would complement and indeed enable the others. Ultimately, for every aspect of teaching, a teacher is expected to be able to answer the question that most dread: "Why are we doing this?"

A teacher who keeps in mind that students are actively learning as much from how they are treated as they are from the curriculum will also realize that the values of respect for student autonomy and providing care are as important, if not more so, than the goals of classroom management. Teachers are expected to help students learn much more than reading, writing, and arithmetic. They are expected to help them learn how schools are administered and, by extension, how authority, power, respect, and responsibility are manifested in our society.

■ REFLECTING ON THE CHAPTER

Many people, teachers and nonteachers alike, struggle with authority. Some are reluctant to acknowledge their own power and risk wielding it mindlessly—the proverbial "baby with a handgun." Some bristle when anyone exercises authority over them and risk overreacting to legitimate restrictions on their autonomy. Some too quickly surrender their autonomy to anyone willing to seize authority. Do any of these descriptions resonate with you? Did any of the topics covered in this chapter prompt you to reflect on your relationship with authority or trigger a strong reaction? What has been your experience with authority—both receiving and expressing? How might your experience shape how you will deal with the authority that comes with being a teacher? Take as much time as you need to reflect on these and any questions that occur to you in response to reviewing this chapter.

SUMMARY

Power is inherent in teaching, and teachers are expected to responsibly exercise the authority that comes with it. A primary source of a teacher's authority comes from acting *in loco parentis*—in the place of the parent. Traditionally in our society, parents have been viewed as having the right to discipline children, short of what would constitute child abuse. Section 43 of the *Criminal Code* is intended to allow a teacher to act in a manner that in law would normally constitute an assault if the student's conduct merits punishment and if that punishment is reasonable in the circumstances. Teachers are increasingly being expected to maintain order in the classroom in a manner consistent with the *Charter's* provisions for natural justice. This means that, at a minimum, any student accused of misbehaving is given a fair and impartial hearing. When disciplining, teachers are expected to contribute to and protect students' educational development.

QUESTIONS FOR DISCUSSION

1. To what extent should students be held responsible for their actions? How ought a teacher to handle a student who significantly disrupts classroom decorum through no fault of his or her own, for example?
2. A student approaches you and says he broke a window. Do you praise him for being honest, punish him for playing with a baseball inside the school, or respond in some other way? Explain.
3. Do you believe in "an eye for an eye"? If so, how closely must "the punishment fit the crime"? What ethical principle or system is consistent with your belief? How well does your belief mesh with what is expected of teachers?

CASE STUDY

BOYS WILL BE BOYS

You are a new grade three teacher, and Martin has been assigned as your mentor. You are team teaching with Martin, as well as taking over his class entirely while he completes other duties. Martin describes your teaching style as engaging, if perhaps a bit too liberal. By way of example, he makes reference to how you allow the female students to take leadership roles in the classroom. In fact, you find that Martin treats the students differently based on gender stereotypes. You notice, for example, that he is more likely to correct a female student who is rude or impolite than he is a male student. In one particular instance, a boy has been verbally aggressive in the class and showing the other students what you consider to be age-inappropriate sexually explicit pictures on his phone. When you bring this up with Martin, his response is, "Boys will be boys."

1. To what extent do agree with Martin's differential treatment of students based on their gender? How is your answer affected by the fact that Martin's actions closely reflect those of Canadian society?
2. Do you think that Martin is exercising an appropriate degree of authority in the classroom? If too much, in what way might he tone it down? If too little, how might he exert more?
3. How much difference would it make if the community of which the school is a part was strongly in favour of differential gender roles in accordance with Martin's actions? If the community's standards were quite different? Explain.

CHAPTER 8

PROTECTING STUDENTS FROM HARM

CASE STUDY

SUBSTITUTE RUGBY TEACHER

You are a substitute teacher covering for a junior high school gym class. You are eager to show how valuable you can be to the school and thereby increase your chances of being hired into a permanent position. To your dismay, the class has been learning to play rugby—a sport you have never played or taught. You've seen it from time to time on big-screen TVs in restaurants, and it looks to be a brutal sport. The students are eager to begin, however, and are asking to take to the field. You have some serious concerns about your lack of knowledge in light of the risks of physical injury that may be presented if you allow the students to play. Despite a nagging dread, you tell them to be sure to remember what they've learned in previous classes, be careful, and (with fingers crossed) proceed with the scrimmage.

1. What do you think are your responsibilities in this situation regarding the students' physical safety?
2. What do you think the students' parents, and your fellow teachers, expect you to do in this situation?
3. If a student was hurt playing rugby in this class, who do you think would be liable for the injury: (a) You for letting them play? (b) The school for making you responsible for a class for which you were not properly prepared? Or (c) partly you and partly the school? Explain.

Undoubtedly, the vast majority of teachers would never harm a student on purpose. But the unique nature of education imposes a duty upon teachers beyond that of merely refraining from intentionally causing harm. Because parents are obligated to send their children to school (unless they provide home schooling), they are entitled to expect that teachers will take precautions to prevent harm to students in the school environment. Thus, teachers are expected not only to educate students but also, like parents, to take responsibility for their safety and well-being.

Obviously a teacher, or a school district, cannot guarantee the safety of students any more than parents can of their children. That said, teachers are expected to meet a reasonable (i.e., not perfect) standard of care. The classic description of the standard to be met was established in the British case of *Williams v. Eady* (1893), in which it was ruled that a schoolmaster must take care of his students, with consideration of the usual nature of children, and their tendency for mischief and propensity for meddling, "as a careful father would take of his boys, and there could not be a better definition of the duty of a school master" (42). The court found that the schoolmaster had failed to satisfy this standard when he left a bottle of phosphorus in a locked cupboard in the classroom; the students found it, set it on fire, and burned themselves. The standard was affirmed a century later in *Myers v. Peel County Board of Education* (1981) when the Supreme Court of Canada ruled that "the standard of care to be exercised by school authorities in providing for the supervision and protection of students for whom they are responsible is that of the careful or prudent parent, described in *Williams v. Eady*" (31).

When a student is injured while in the school's care, the parents or guardians are entitled to seek damages. An attempt is then made to apportion responsibility for the mishap. If the school or one of its employees is found to be negligent (see Chapter 3), then the parents may be able to claim financial compensation, which can be quite substantial. For example, if a student is paralyzed, he or she will need lifelong care and support, which is expensive. If the school is at fault, it may be required by the courts to provide these funds. The law governing these matters is found not in statutes but in the common law of court decisions and precedents created over many years.

That school authorities have a special duty of care toward the students in their charge is now firmly established in Canadian common law. The standard of the fictional "careful or prudent parent" includes the duty to protect students from any reasonably foreseeable risk of physical or mental harm. Given the large numbers of students who go to school each day across the country, the variety of temperaments, proclivities, and abilities they possess, and the array of activities they are involved in, it is rather amazing how little harm befalls them. But as we all know, accidents and even tragedies do occur. Over time, a body of law has grown that helps demarcate what the responsibilities of teachers and schools are for keeping students safe.

Over the years, teachers have been expected to intervene more and more when students are taking part in potentially dangerous activities. The standard of care has moved from solely parental to also include skilled practitioner, reflecting the changing nature of teaching. What the courts seem to disagree on is when the parental and when the skilled practitioner standard applies. However, trends in the case law with respect to revision of the teacher's duty to protect students from harm can be discerned.

REFLECTIVE TASK

Comfort with Responsibility

What has been your experience with being responsible for the well-being of others? Have you been in a responsible role for much of your life, such as having to take care of younger siblings from the time that you were a child? Or were you mostly taken care of by others? Are you a parent now yourself? How about taking on responsible roles in organizations such as student councils—did you take on leadership duties or were you a "free rider"? What is your relationship with responsibility? Do you feel it is an obligation or burden, or do you seek it and enjoy it? Take some time to think about how comfortable you feel with being responsible for the safety and well-being of the students in your care.

SUPERVISION OF STUDENTS

A teacher has little chance of keeping students safe if they are being improperly or inadequately supervised, and this is the area of education law that has seen the most attention. Aspects of the classroom situation, while clearly a factor in the degree of supervision a teacher can offer any one student, are not typically accepted by the courts as a defence against failing to properly supervise. Obviously, there are times when it is impossible to monitor all students simultaneously. Teachers are therefore expected to be aware not only of the risks posed by the activities but also how reliable the students are. Thus, with students who are known to be more prone to taking risks than others, it is only reasonable for the teacher to avoid placing them in a position where they are involved in hazardous activities without sufficient supervision. Teachers are expected to put responsibility for students' safety above all other considerations, including following a course curriculum or a lesson plan. A teacher who feels there is an unacceptable degree of risk—due to class make-up, or the equipment available, or any other reason—is expected to refrain from the activity.

In *Myers v. Peel County Board of Education* (1981), illness of the grade twelve gym teacher resulted in the grade eleven teacher having to teach a double-class of some forty students. The teacher had given two students permission to practise their gymnastic manoeuvres without his supervision. They had been informed in advance of the importance of having a "spotter" (someone positioned to catch the gymnast or at least break their fall). At one point, the spotter turned to leave just as one of the students attempted a difficult manoeuvre for the first time. The student fell; broke his neck, and was rendered quadriplegic. The Supreme Court of Canada held that the level of supervision was not sufficient in that a careful or prudent parent would not have allowed the child to undertake such a risky activity without supervision.

A large part of the Court's reasoning in *Myers* was based on the inherent and unusual dangers posed by the gymnastic rings—and, for that matter, most gymnastic activities. The question then arises as to whether "the prudent parent" test is appropriate for classroom activities that the average parent would have no experience in, such as supervising a chemistry laboratory or using parallel bars, as was the case in *McKay v. Govan School Unit* (1967). In *McKay* a jury had found liability on the part of the school board on the basis of the prudent parent test. This finding was appealed on the basis that the jury had been improperly advised as to the standard of care expected of a teacher. The Saskatchewan Court of Appeal, in allowing the appeal, ruled that while the prudent parent standard might apply to a teacher supervising a baseball or hockey game, a physical education teacher is expected to exercise the skill and competence of an ordinarily competent instructor in the field. The Court of Appeal thereby imposed a higher standard of care than that adopted by the jury and incongruously overturned the finding of fault! The Supreme Court of Canada ultimately overturned the Court of Appeal's ruling and restored the jury's finding of liability, while accepting that a higher-risk activity requires a higher standard of care on the instructor's part.

This is not to say that gymnastics are so inherently dangerous that they have no place in the curriculum. In *Thornton v. Prince George* (1976), it was established that it is not a breach of the duty of care on the part of the school authorities to permit a student to participate in a gymnastic manoeuvre if (a) it is suitable to the student's age and condition (mental and physical), (b) the student is progressively trained and coached to do it properly and avoid the danger, (c) the equipment is adequate and suitably arranged, and (d) the manoeuvre is properly supervised. Thus, the Alberta Court of Appeal held in *MacCabe v. Westlock Roman Catholic Separate School* (1998) that the teacher was liable for a grade eleven student being rendered quadriplegic after unsuccessfully attempting a complicated gymnastic move from a box horse. The court ruled that the teacher had failed to satisfy the criteria set out in *Thornton*. Applying the same reasoning, in the British Columbia Supreme Court case of *Hamilton v. Delta School District No. 371* (2010), the district was not found liable when a grade eleven student suffered a broken nose while playing floor hockey in a physical education class. The court determined that the student was properly trained to play, that safety equipment would not have prevented the injury, and that the game was properly supervised.

Note that under *Thornton*, a teacher is also expected to be cognizant of the student's individual attributes. Thus, a younger student will typically require greater supervision than an older one "who should have known better" (*Catherwood v. Heinrichs*, 1996), as would a student who lacks the requisite physical abilities to perform a task safely (*Boese v. St. Paul's Roman Catholic Separate School District No. 20*, 1980).

In the case of students with disabilities, the standard obviously becomes much higher. In the Supreme Court of Canada decision in *Dziwnka v. The Queen in Right of Alberta* (1971), a student who was deaf and mute was injured while using a table saw with the guard removed. The student was a competent woodworker, and the teacher had adequately instructed the student and warned of the dangers of the operation. The Court observed that if the student could hear and speak, then no liability would have been found. However, because the condition of the student prevented a rapid warning of danger, liability was imposed.

Even if a teacher was not at fault when a student was injured, liability may be found if, after the injury, his or her conduct was such that the injury was exacerbated. In *Freer v. Okanagon-Skaha School District No. 67* (2002), a student who was unable to play because his broken leg was still in a brace slipped while watching his class participate in a soccer game. He told the supervising teacher that he thought he had rebroken the leg. The teacher advised the student to walk back to school, put ice on his leg, and call his mother to take him to the hospital. The court held that neither the teacher nor the school was negligent for failing to adequately supervise the student; even so, they were found liable for causing him additional pain and suffering by requiring him to walk unassisted.

Nevertheless, there is no duty to supervise commonplace activities that the students can reasonably be expected to perform on their own. In *Robinson v. Calgary School District 19* (1977), for example, the fourteen-year-old student's claim that the school board was negligent in failing to prevent him from sliding down a banister, even though he had been warned on a number of previous occasions, was dismissed. It is interesting to note that the court in their judgment observed that the student, while a disciplinary problem, was of normal intelligence. The courts tend to take a robust view of teens bearing some responsibility for their actions.

In the case of younger students, the need to provide safe premises and adequate supervision is that much higher. In *George v. Port Alberni School District 70* (1986), the school was successfully sued for not having temporary teaching trailers hooked up to the school address system used to advise students when it was safe to load onto school buses. In that case, a five-year-old student was struck by a school bus when he was discharged from school in the erroneous belief that all the buses had arrived. In contrast, in a similar accident when a sixteen-year-old student was run over by a school bus that unexpectedly backed up, the Court in *Germschied v. Richardson* (1987) noted that the plaintiff was of an age that he should have known better and apportioned liability accordingly.

Often, an injury occurs that is unforeseeable, or it occurs in the course of an activity that is so low in risk that no prudent parent would have hesitated to allow their child's participation. Examples include a ball that bounces out of control during a game of catch, causing the loss of an eye (*Plumb v. Cowichan School District No. 65*, 1993), a teenager doing a baseball-like slide on fresh fallen snow and rendering himself quadriplegic (*Fraser v. Campbell River School District No. 72*, 1988), a student falling from a tree during a baseball game and fracturing a wrist (*Catherwood v. Heinrichs*, 1996), and one student pushing another in the playground, causing a fractured elbow (*Gu v. Friesen*, 2013). All of these were accepted by the courts as unforeseeable accidents and not as the fault of the teacher or school.

WHAT THE CODES SAY

Assume Responsibility for Safety of Students

The teacher should assume responsibility for the safety and welfare of his/her pupils, especially under conditions of emergency.

—From the Nova Scotia Teachers' Union Code of Ethics

BULLYING

Bullying is an old problem well known to educators, students, and parents. Historically it has tended to be seen as mere "schoolyard fighting" rather than assault, and children have long been admonished to "learn how to stand up to bullies" (usually of their own accord). This sentiment is still voiced from time to time, even in the courts, but societal attitudes are changing.

It is generally accepted that bullying involves a student being repeatedly exposed over time to negative actions such as physical contact, words, threatening gestures, or intentional social exclusion by one or more other students. It can occur directly or indirectly, such as by spreading malicious gossip. Bullying is not friendly teasing or horseplay, although younger students may not always be able to tell the difference between playful and abusive conduct. Often it is the element of repetition that distinguishes bullying from friendly joking. Bullying usually occurs in the context of relationships in which there is a real or imagined physical, psychological, or social imbalance of power between the victim and the bully (or bullies). It is often directed at victims because of perceived or real differences relating to physical appearance, intelligence, ethnicity, gender, sexual orientation, or economic status.

Consistent with the recognition that society has an interest in maintaining a proper educational environment, parents have turned to the courts to sanction a teacher who bullies their child. In *Gould v. Regina (East) School Division No. 77* (1996), the court did not accept that a teacher had bullied a student by speaking loudly and permitting other students to bully her, although it did note that the teacher's actions bordered on educational malpractice (see Chapter 3). Similarly, in *A.S. v. Toronto District School Board* (2001), the court found that, while the school board had done nothing wrong by suspending an eleven-year-old student who had put nails in his teacher's coffee cup, the case could proceed against the teacher for yelling at and intimidating the student.

When one student bullies another (or a group of them bullies one or more), schools are expected to take appropriate steps to restore a positive educational environment. Indeed, a school that fails to respond strongly enough to bullying may be considered to have condoned and supported the conduct. In *Hopkins v. Mission School District No. 75* (1998), the court upheld the five-day suspension of a student for providing encouragement while watching a gang assault at school because doing so contributed to an intimidating school environment and the administration was right to have acted as it did.

Schools have a societal and legal duty to ensure that all students are able to benefit from a positive school environment. In the landmark case *North Vancouver School District No. 44 v. Jubran* (2005), a student was taunted and harassed during his high school years for being "gay," even though the bullies did not believe he was homosexual. The school board made a number of attempts to address the bullying, including meeting with the students involved and warning them of escalating consequences should the bullying continue, and imposing one detention and two suspensions. These steps seemed to succeed in stopping the behaviour of the particular students disciplined, but other students continued with the bullying. Other steps eventually taken included putting into place a formal Code of Conduct for the school, a copy of which was sent home with the students and discussed with them during assemblies. The principal contacted a consultant, as a result of which workshops were held with the teaching staff on the issue and the school set up a peer counsellor program.

The British Columbia Human Rights Tribunal held the school board liable for the discriminatory behaviour of the bullies because its disciplinary response to their actions was not up to the standard of a "kind, firm and judicious parent" as set out in the provincial *School Act*. On judicial review, however, the British Columbia Supreme Court determined that the student had not been discriminated against. He appealed, and the British Columbia Court of Appeal upheld the tribunal's ruling in his favour. An application for leave to appeal to the Supreme Court of Canada was denied, thereby affirming that the school board was liable for not doing enough to address the bullying.

In *E.B.J. v. Upper Canada District School Board* (2001), two teenaged boys were suspended from their school, one for pulling out a knife he carried in order to protect himself from further bullying, and the other, who had also been repeatedly bullied and intimidated, because he wrote a story for class about a boy who was bullied and who brought a bomb to school. The authorities assumed that the boy was actually planning to set off a bomb at school and had him arrested and placed in custody for thirty-four days, after which the charges were withdrawn and he was released. Their father argued that they could not receive adequate instruction in one of the school board's schools because the school environment was not safe for them. The court agreed, and ordered the school board either to arrange placement for the students with a neighbouring school jurisdiction or to pay their tuition at a private school.

"Cyberbullying" is currently of particular concern in Canadian schools. It is different from other forms of bullying in that it is perpetuated through electronic or digital media such as cellphones, blogs, chat rooms, and social networks such as Facebook and Twitter. Sending harassing or threatening e-mails or text messages, posting derogatory comments about someone on a website, spreading online rumours, or stalking someone online are all examples of cyberbullying. Responding to cyberbullying is a challenge because it often—though not always—occurs away from schools, yet its effect on students and the school environment can be severe.

The impact of cyberbullying was central to *R. T. v. Durham Catholic District School Board* (2008). Here, a grade eight student corresponded with another student in the same grade at the school via Facebook. When setting up her profile on Facebook, the student used a name and identifying information similar to the victim's so that she was able to contact the victim's friends. Among other things, the student wrote to the victim: U DON'T WANT ME TO GET MAD BECAUSE THEN ILL KILL YOU RIGHT IN UR SLEEP OR AT SCHOOL ON MONDAY. The victim's father informed the school of his concerns about his daughter's safety. The school suspended the student pending an investigation, after which she was expelled. The student's mother filed an appeal of the expulsion.

In reviewing the evidence, the Child and Family Services Review Board noted that the student was bright, that she understood what she was doing, and that her actions were premeditated. The board held that her behaviour was of such a nature that it would be very detrimental to the school climate if she were permitted to return to the school. It upheld the decision to expel her.

Efforts have been made to address cyberbullying through legislation. Ontario amended its *Education Act* in 2007 (and again in 2009 and 2011) in order to gain jurisdiction over cyberbullying and authority over students' activities out of school that are likely to have an impact on the school climate. Bullying was specifically named in the amendments as grounds for suspension, and reporting by school staff to principals and by principals to parents was made mandatory. The current Ontario *Education Act* mandates school boards to develop bullying prevention and intervention plans and to take a tougher stance against bullying.

In 2013, Nova Scotia's *Cyber-safety Act* became the first in Canada to deal specifically with cyberbullying. It enables a victim of cyberbullying to obtain a protection order, in violation of which the bully can be fined up to $5,000 or imprisoned up to six months, or both. Under the same act, parents who fail to properly supervise their minor child's online activities can be found liable for cyberbullying.

While these legislative changes involve only two jurisdictions, it is clear that educators and school boards have a statutory and common law duty to provide a safe and positive learning environment for students. That includes addressing incidents of cyberbullying. Teachers are expected to respond to bullying whether it is initiated on or off school premises if it substantially and materially disrupts the learning environment at the school.

REFLECTIVE TASK

Experience with Bullying

None of us gets through school, or indeed life, without experiencing bullying as a target, perpetrator, or witness. Take some time to think about your experience with bullying. Were you a victim of a bully or bullies? How serious was it for you? Do you still feel the effects? Did you ever bully another person? If you did, you most likely were a victim of bullying as well. How did your experience as a victim impact your bullying of another, if at all? And if you were lucky enough to never be bullied, what was your experience of witnessing others being bullied? Did you stand up for them or intervene in some way? If not, why not, and how did being a bystander affect you, if at all? Take some time to think about and record your answers to these and any other questions that occur to you around bullying.

EXTRACURRICULAR AND OUT-OF-CLASS ACTIVITIES

A number of court cases have brought to the forefront a teacher's responsibility for students during extracurricular activities. When a school outing is mandatory, the courts view these activities as an extension of schooling, even when outside regular hours and/or not on the school premises. That means the teacher has both the right and the responsibility to control the student's activities. In fact, as noted in *Bain v. Calgary Board of Education* (1993), because the risks posed by such activities may be less familiar than those encountered during normal school hours, there is a stronger onus on the teacher to supervise. Thus, in *Madsen v. Mission School*

District No. 75 (1999), the British Columbia Supreme Court found the school board liable for a grade twelve student's dislocated shoulder when a classmate pulled him to the ground during a physical education class involving a game of "capture the flag." The game was played off school grounds at a local park with a broad expanse of hills and trees. The court held that a prudent parent would not have accepted a low level of supervision in that setting, particularly given the rough nature of the game.

Typically, parents are asked to sign a consent form for extracurricular activities. It usually specifies that their children will be under the control of the teachers and adult supervisors. No consent form can cover in minute detail all possible activities and all possible associated risks, but it is expected that reasonable specifics will be included so that parents can make an informed decision as to their child's participation. When an activity deviates significantly from that described in the consent form, the school board is liable; so is the teacher if he or she is acting outside the scope of his or her employment. Examples include an unscheduled side trip to a swimming hole during which two students drown (*Moddejonge v. Huron County Board of Education*, 1972), and permitting students to attempt to climb a mountain (instead of going to a movie, as was planned), as a result of which one falls and suffers brain damage (*Bain v. Calgary Board of Education*, 1993).

Many parents expect the school to be responsible for the safety of their children throughout the school day, even when the student has permission to leave the school property. *Lutes v. Prairie View School Division No. 74* (1992) found that students can be disciplined for their conduct occurring off the school premises during a lunch hour break. The courts in Canada generally draw a distinction between students who are bussed to the school and those who are not. For bussed students, the duty of supervision continues from when they board the bus in the morning until they leave it at the end of the day. For students who do not take buses, liability is imposed from the point that the students enter school property (*Hoyt v. Hay*, 1978) and usually ends when they leave the property.

Schools can also be found liable for the condition of the premises under occupier's liability—a legal principle that applies to many situations, including schools. If an injury is sustained as a result of the condition of the premises, then a lawsuit may be brought against the school even if the person injured was trespassing. As with most legal principles, the standard is that of "reasonable care" and not perfection. Thus, as in *Thiessen v. Winnipeg School Division 1* (1967), if a person slips on a tiny piece of apple in a classroom used as a student lunchroom, the school division will not be found liable if it can show that a reasonable maintenance system was in place. The standard is somewhat higher with students because they are compelled to attend school, which means that schools also have a duty to supervise students (*Cropp v. Potashville School Unit 25*, 1977). So if students are directed to enter the school by a certain entrance that is unsafe, the school can be found negligent not only for their failure to provide safe premises but also for their failure to supervise. Teachers would likely not be considered the occupiers of the school grounds in law, but they still have a professional responsibility to students to be attentive to the conditions of the premises. In some instances this may consist of nothing more than being aware that there is a regular maintenance program in place. In other situations a more proactive response may be required, such as asking a janitor to shovel snow from a path commonly used by students, or picking up broken glass on a playing field.

The matter of a student's out-of-school behaviour negatively impacting the educational environment was addressed in *Kawartha Pine Ridge District School Board v. Grant* (2010). The Child and Family Services Review Board addressed whether the school had the authority to expel a student for using and selling drugs away from school property. The board noted that the student's buying, smoking, and selling drugs over a six-week period at friends' houses and parties was insignificant compared to the pervasive, pre-existing drug culture at the school as testified to by the principal. The board ruled that there was insufficient evidence to conclude that the student's activities had any impact on the already negative school climate, and ordered the student to be reinstated.

Although not directly the responsibility of the individual teacher, one area of law that has seen a significant degree of change over time is the imposing of vicarious liability on school boards for activities conducted without their knowledge by teachers or by individuals over whom they have some measure of control. As noted in *M.B. v. BC* (2001), an organization can be found vicariously liable for the activities of an employee even in the absence of negligence on the organization's part in hiring or supervising that employee when the ultimate responsibility for the performance of a duty cannot be delegated. It is, in effect, a "no fault" imposition of liability and thus much different than negligence (see Chapter 3).

Where negligence normally involves an individual's action or lack of action, with respect to education the school district usually assumes the legal liability. Therefore, even though a student may have been injured while under a teacher's care, it is the school board's insurance coverage that will pay for any damages. However, if a teacher's conduct were such that no employer would authorize it or bring it within the scope of its employment terms, the victim would be left with no legal recourse. Instead, as found in *Bazley v. Curry* (1999), it is fairer to place the loss on the employer who introduced the risk and had the better opportunity to control it, rather than on the victim. The most notable examples are the tragic sexual abuse of First Nations children in residential schools (*W.R.B. v. Plint*, 2001; see also Chapter 4) and the sexually predatory adults who assaulted children under the auspices of Boys and Girls Clubs (*T. (G.) v. Griffiths*, 1999).

In the leading decision of the Supreme Court of Canada in *E.D.G. v. Hammer* (2003) a night janitor at a public school repeatedly assaulted a grade three student when she was sent down to the boiler room by her teacher to clean blackboard brushes. Neither the teacher nor the school's administration had any reason to suspect that at least twenty sexual assaults were taking place over a two-year period. Having reviewed the statutory responsibilities of the school board under the *School Act*, the Court ruled that they were not so broad that the school could be held to be liable for sexual abuse by the janitor whose activities they had no cause to have knowledge of. Although the Court was considering only the wording of the British Columbia *Act*, its reasoning would almost certainly apply across Canada.

WHAT THE CODES SAY

Physical Welfare Is a Chief Aim of Education

A teacher accepts that the intellectual, moral, physical and social welfare of his/her pupils is the chief aim and end of education.

—*From the Newfoundland and Labrador Teachers' Association Code of Ethics*

RESPONDING TO HARMS

When an accident occurs the immediate concern is, of course, the well-being of the injured student, but teachers are also expected be vigilant about protecting themselves and the school board from unreasonable findings of liability. Because an injured party may not seek a legal remedy for a number of years, memories may fade and the names of potential witnesses may be forgotten. It is prudent for a teacher to interview the injured student and any witnesses as soon as reasonably practicable to determine what has happened and why. This is important to prevent further incidents of the same sort; also, when kept as a written record, it can be an important source of evidence in court as well as an aid in remembering at that time what took place. Most schools have an incident reporting form that, as a minimum, should be filled out. Depending on the severity of the injuries, additional records should be kept, including signed and dated witness statements from the students if the severity of the harm warrants doing so. Whatever actions a teacher takes, in all cases he or she is expected to advise the school administrators of any significant events. Teachers are expected to consider first the safety of the students and the urgency of the situation in reporting any incident. Typically, they are required by statute to report it to the principal by the end of the school day.

It should be obvious that it is best to be careful not to make incriminating statements in the heat of the moment against yourself, the school board, or the students. Rather, teachers are expected to deal with the accident first by providing whatever first aid is appropriate and within their ability. Requests from students for assistance and medical aid should be taken very seriously, given that teachers have been found liable for failing to do so on many occasions. Only after every reasonable effort has been made to ensure that the student is properly attended to should any attempt to determine fault be made. Teachers are also expected to inform the parents of the student of all but the most minor of injuries on the school grounds because of the possibility that it might make the student more susceptible to further injury later. Informing the parent is also advised because it could be that the student, particularly if young, may complain of symptoms only after a number of hours and may not attribute them to the accident. While bumps and scrapes are a normal part of growing up for everyone, hindsight is sometimes critical of the best efforts of those involved at the time, and prudence is usually the wisest course.

In the very rare cases where a lawsuit is commenced, the school board either will have insurance or will be self-insured to provide coverage in case of liability being found. Assuming your activities fall within the scope of your employment, this insurance will protect you as well. However, you will be expected to cooperate with the insurance company and its lawyers, which will likely be time-consuming and is often unavoidably stressful for all involved. In the ideal world, no accidents would occur. In the real world, the best we can do as teachers is take what care we can, be conscious of minimizing risks, and respond in a professional manner when accidents inevitably occur.

REFLECTING ON THE CHAPTER

One approach that many people find helpful for understanding a topic is to shrink it down to a few essential ideas. You may find some benefit in doing so with this chapter. Go back through the chapter, and through any notes you may have taken, and extract the essential points regarding your responsibility for protecting students from harm. See if you can distill each section into one or two key ideas. Record your ideas and any reflections prompted by the exercise of doing so. For example, did you find the task difficult, easy, tedious, interesting, or helpful? What does this tell you about your level of understanding of the material?

SUMMARY

Although the standard of care for supervision expected of a teacher is expressed as "that of a reasonable and prudent parent," this may be modified by the degree of risk an activity poses, the particular attributes of the student in question, the condition of the equipment used, and a host of other considerations. A young or disabled student, a more dangerous activity; all may require greater vigilance on the part of the teacher. In some instances, such as gymnastics, where the reasonable person would expect specialist training on the part of the teacher, a higher standard is imposed on the teacher to have the knowledge and level of care of the ordinary, competent instructor in that field. This may require a teacher to have special training or to refuse to take part in such activities. Not all injuries, however, are the result of negligence; in some cases the accidents are unforeseeable or the likelihood of their occurrence is too remote to allow recovery. The guiding principle, restated, could be, "If this was my child, what would I expect of the teacher?"

QUESTIONS FOR DISCUSSION

1. In the summary we restate the principle as being, "If this was my child, what would I expect?" Why is this possibly misleading?
2. Is the standard of care of the reasonable, careful, or prudent parent even appropriate in this day and age? Would a more appropriate test be that of a reasonable or prudent teacher? What changes in the expectations of teachers would occur if the latter standard were adopted?
3. To what extent do you think the courts should be involved in resolving disputes initiated by parents who contend that their child has suffered due to incompetent teaching? Why not have the parent and teacher sort things out between themselves in a civil trial? Explain.

CASE STUDY

FACEBOOK SUICIDE

A student in your school committed suicide a short while ago. Some other students decided to create a Facebook page to memorialize her. They ask you if you think this is a good idea. They seem sincere in wanting to do something positive by way of paying their respects, and they tell you they will moderate the page. You and the other teachers in the school talk it over, and you give your approval. One condition of approval is to "follow" the students' memorial page in order to monitor it. At first, all goes well. The page is done in a sensitive manner, with tasteful pictures of and quotes attributed to the deceased student. As other students begin posting comments to the page, however, some refer to considering suicide themselves.

The posts are not anonymous, and with minimal effort you could follow up to determine whether these students are indeed at risk of suicide.

1. Do you think you should contact the students making the suicidal posts? Why or why not?
2. What do you think the parents of the students making the suicidal posts would expect you to do in these circumstances? What do you think the students themselves would expect you to do?
3. How would your responsibility be affected if the students had created the Facebook page on their own, with no involvement of the school and without your approval?

CHAPTER 9

PERSONAL LIFE, PUBLIC ROLE

CASE STUDY

GAY PRIDE TEACHER

You are a teacher in a Catholic school. A variety of news outlets have been covering the story of a teacher acting as a spokesperson for the local Gay Pride Parade. While being interviewed he clearly identifies himself as a teacher in the Catholic school system. Besides being supportive of gay rights, he criticizes the Catholic Church for its position on the issue. The incident has become a talking point for many teachers, administrators, parents, and students in your school. During a Parent Council meeting a parent puts forward a motion to have your school release a public statement opposing the views expressed by the Gay Pride teacher and supporting heterosexuality as the only socially acceptable interpersonal union. Feeling vaguely uncomfortable with the motion, you—almost imperceptibly—hesitate. However, the parent notices and asks you if you are a homosexual and if you promote the privileges of perverts.

1. What do you think are the expectations on a teacher in a Catholic school around expressing discomfort with opposing equal rights for those who are homosexual, regardless of how you actually feel about the issue?
2. What difference would it make if you were gay? If you were not?
3. What difference would it make if the teacher were a spokesperson at a rally for a political party critical of the current government?

A central concept of teaching is that teachers are role models. Many of our own teachers from our schooldays have faded from memory, yet some have not. For most of us, exemplary teachers inspired us to strive to realize our potential, and many of us to become educators ourselves. Likewise, we remember other teachers less favourably and seek to avoid being like them. Who among us does not want to be remembered as one of the good teachers in the lives of our students? Without going too deeply into the philosophy of teaching, most will agree that what made those teachers "good" was not how much of the subject material they helped us master. Rather, it was how their unique character—their personality, interests, passions, opinions—inspired us in just the right way at a crucial point in our education. No matter how meticulously curriculum is circumscribed, it is the teacher who interprets and applies it, and the teacher who inspires, or discourages.

While most will agree that this is how it should be, a dilemma arises when *who* the teacher is as a person—as opposed to simply the choices he or she makes—is perceived as being at odds with the role model a teacher is expected to provide. As discussed in Chapter 5, teachers share many attributes with people in other professions. They are required to belong to a professional body such as the provincial teacher association, they have a code of ethics or conduct they are expected to uphold, and they are extended a high degree of autonomy in how they fulfill their professional duties.

Teaching is a profession. But unlike other professionals, a teacher can be competent (i.e., teach knowledgeably, skillfully, with good judgment, and with respect for students' autonomy) yet still cause harm by failing to be an *example* of a good citizen. And remember that the ethical principle of providing care is central to all professions, including teaching. Thus the question can be asked by the members of the community: Is this teacher the kind of *person* who should be teaching our children?

Teachers' associations generally recognize the importance of role modelling. Only the British Columbia Teachers' Federation's *Code of Ethics* and the Manitoba Teachers' Society's *Code of Professional Practice*—which are essentially identical documents—remain silent on this issue. The others expect that teachers will act "in a manner which maintains the honour and dignity of the profession"* (see the Alberta, Newfoundland and Labrador, Prince Edward Island, and Saskatchewan teachers' codes) and not engage in "conduct unbecoming of a member of the profession" (see the New Brunswick code) in order to avoid bringing "dishonour to the teacher or the profession"** (see the Nunavut, Nova Scotia, and Yukon codes). The Ontario College of Teachers' *Ethical Standards for the Teaching Profession* also addresses the importance of role modelling by stating that teachers are expected to "model respect for spiritual and cultural values, social justice, confidentiality, freedom, democracy and the environment."

Clearly, the role teachers play in society, and especially in the community in which they teach, is very important. Parents who are seeking the best surgeon to operate on their child probably will not care if the surgeon is a cruel spouse, a neglectful parent, and opposed to charitable organizations, as long as he or she has the required surgical expertise. For parents who are seeking the best teacher

---

*Alberta Teachers' Association
**Yukon Teachers' Association

to educate their child, however, these same characteristics are relevant. They are understandably concerned about the values and personal qualities revealed by a teacher's behaviour both in the classroom and in the community.

This can place teachers in a bind. In particular, while parents rightly expect teachers to model exemplary citizenship, there is no unanimity as to what that means. Even for teachers in private or separate schools, where school and community values tend to be more clearly articulated, disagreements still arise.

Then there is the question of the degree to which a community can impose its expectations on the teacher as an individual, especially outside the classroom, without violating the teacher's personal rights. Given that what is considered acceptable behaviour varies across jurisdictions and over time, it is inevitable that teachers' personal and professional values will sometimes conflict with the expectations of a given school community.

As discussed in Chapter 4, the development of educational institutions in Canada was intricately tied to religious affiliation. That is why, when questions about community expectations versus the personal rights of teachers have reached our courts of law, religious freedoms are often involved. Related issues arise when it comes to the teaching of controversial subjects (see Chapter 12). Teachers are well advised to be knowledgeable of the difficult question in ethics and law of how to balance the individual rights of teachers relating to their private life, with the rights of the community they are responsible to as role models for their children.

■ REFLECTIVE TASK

Someone Highly Ethical

Think about someone you consider highly ethical. It can be someone you know well, such as a parent or fellow teacher, or someone you know only by reputation. Ideally, it would be a colleague whom you would want to consult when faced with an ethical dilemma. What qualities or behaviours do they exhibit that prompt you to believe them to be ethical? How might you strengthen your relationship with that person? If it's a public figure, you might read or reread their autobiography or biographies written about them, for example. If it's someone in your life, you might invite him or her for coffee or lunch. Spend some time reflecting on what makes someone an ethical exemplar and developing a plan for creating a stronger connection with someone who is one.

PUBLIC BEHAVIOUR

The *Charter of Rights and Freedoms* contains a guarantee of freedom of speech. Even so, teachers are not unfettered, even outside the classroom. The leading case on this question is *Ross v. New Brunswick School District No. 15* (1996). A teacher, Mr. Ross, made numerous anti-Semitic claims through books, articles, and television appearances. The school board knew about his comments, but it took no disciplinary action until a parent of the Jewish faith complained that the board's failure to act amounted to condoning his views and promoting discrimination in the school system. The board then placed Ross in a nonteaching position and ordered him to refrain from publicly expressing any anti-Semitic views.

Ross appealed the board's decision to the New Brunswick Court of Queen's Bench, which ruled that the board had infringed on his freedom of speech outside the classroom. The matter was then taken to the Court of Appeal, which upheld the lower court's decision, saying that while "the author of the discrimination is a teacher, who might be considered a role model to students," there were no "pressing and substantial reasons" for censoring him in this particular case, given that the conduct took place entirely outside of the classroom. The same court noted that it was only in the clearest circumstances that an individual's rights of free expression could be restricted. In its view, those circumstances had not been established in this particular case.

The Supreme Court of Canada accepted that Ross's freedom of expression and religion had been infringed by the disciplinary order, but that this could be justified under the *Oakes* test (see Chapter 3) if it could be demonstrated that doing so addressed a pressing and substantial concern in a free and democratic society, and that it was done in a manner that was proportional to that goal. The Court determined that the test had been met, given the unique role of teachers as role models in promoting an inclusive educational environment:

> It is on the basis of the position of trust and influence that we hold the teacher to high standards both on and off duty, and it is an erosion of these standards that may lead to a loss in the community of confidence in the public school system. I do not wish to be understood as advocating an approach that subjects the entire lives of teachers to inordinate scrutiny on the basis of more onerous moral standards of behaviour. This could lead to a substantial invasion of the privacy rights and fundamental freedoms of teachers. However, where a "poisoned" environment within the school system is traceable to the off-duty conduct of a teacher that is likely to produce a corresponding loss of confidence in the teacher and the system as a whole, then the off-duty conduct of the teacher is relevant.*

The Court also addressed how off-duty and classroom behaviour is connected:

> In the case of the teacher who has proclaimed the discriminatory views publicly the effect may adversely impact on the school community. It may raise fears and concerns of potential misconduct by the teacher in the classroom and, more importantly, it may be seen as a signal that others view these prejudicial views as acceptable. It may lead to a loss of dignity and self-esteem by those in the school community belonging to the minority group against whom the teacher is prejudiced.*

---

*Ross v. New Brunswick School District No. 15 (1996).

The content and nature of Mr. Ross's actions was so reprehensible that his removal from the classroom setting would be seen as justified by most observers. But at other times, it can be difficult to separate unacceptable conduct from legitimate political discourse. Consider *Metropolitan Separate School Board v. Ontario Catholic Teachers' Association* (1994), where an eminently qualified religious studies teacher was barred from teaching in that program on the basis of her public criticism of the Catholic Church's attitudes toward the role of women in the church. Many Catholics, especially in North America, are troubled by the non-ordination of women in the Catholic faith. The teacher had been quoted in a number of newspaper articles as a spokesperson for a group critical of the Church's position. In some of those articles, she was identified as being employed by the board, and the school board felt that she was using the board as a "soap box" to express her own views. From their perspective, while she was entitled to express those views, her identifying herself as a teacher in a particular separate school board could not be condoned. In addition, the board had received a number of letters complaining of the teacher's deviation from traditional Church orthodoxy.

The board argued before a Labour Board of Arbitration that Section 93 of the *Constitution Act, 1867*, allowed it to refuse to appoint her on the basis of her public criticism. In this, they relied on a number of earlier decisions—in particular, *Essex County Roman Catholic Separate School Board v. Porter* (1978) and *Essex County Roman Catholic Separate School Board v. Tremblay-Webster* (1984)—that supported the right of Catholic schools to dismiss for denominational cause.

The arbitration board conceded that the school board had the right to decide who could teach a particular subject. But it also held that in this case the board's decision had been made not for denominational reasons but for political ones. It found that her identification as a teacher of religion in articles critical of the Church was uncomfortable for the school board, which had chosen to deal with her by removing her from her post. This, the arbitration board held, was not a denominational decision but merely taking the easy way out. It ordered the board to reinstate her as a teacher of religion at the school.

The British Columbia Court of Appeal decision in *Kempling v. British Columbia College of Teachers* (2005) deals directly with the off-duty public behaviour of teachers. Here, the British Columbia College of Teachers found Kempling guilty of professional misconduct because he wrote and published an article and some letters to the editor in the local newspaper expressing condemnation of homosexuality and explicitly linking his views to his standing as a teacher. The College of Teachers found that his writings demonstrated that he was not prepared to accommodate the core values of the education system, which include the recognition of homosexuals' rights to equality, dignity, and respect. The college also found that, despite the lack of direct evidence that his actions caused a poisoned school environment as required in *Ross*, it was reasonable to infer that they would.

Mr. Kempling appealed the decision of the college to the British Columbia Court of Appeal and eventually to the British Columbia Supreme Court. At both levels, the college's decision was upheld by applying the *Oakes* test. The Court ruled that Kempling's right to free speech could be infringed based on his published statements causing direct harm to the integrity of the school system by virtue of his being a teacher.

It has yet to be settled whether words and images posted to social media sites by teachers can be grounds for legal sanctions or dismissal, but it seems very likely that they would be considered public behaviour. To the extent that anything posted by a teacher would poison the school environment or bring the profession or the teacher's competence into disrepute, legal and/or professional repercussions would not be inconsistent with existing case law.

WHAT THE CODES SAY

Do Not Bring Dishonour to the Profession

Members at all times conduct themselves in order that no dishonor may befall the profession.

—*From the Yukon Teachers' Association Code of Ethics*

PRIVATE BEHAVIOUR

A teacher's general behaviour as a member of the community beyond the classroom is often relevant to her or his fitness as a role model. In *Stolen v. British Columbia College of Teachers* (1995), for example, the courts found that it is was within the jurisdiction of a teacher's professional body to investigate allegations of spousal assault. Obviously the circumstances surrounding the allegations would be germane to the reasonableness of any finding that body made. It is, however, a strong reminder of the unique nature of a teacher's role in society.

Caldwell v. Stuart (1984) provides insight into how personal conduct can sometimes lead to professional concerns. Ms. Caldwell, a practising Catholic, was hired by a private Catholic high school as a teacher of mathematics and commercial subjects. Although the school would have preferred to have an all-Catholic staff, shortages of applicants meant that 30 percent of the teachers were nonadherents. In the case of Catholic applicants, a certificate was required from their parish priest that the teacher was a practising Catholic. Non-Catholics were expected to adhere to the tenets of their own faith.

After teaching at the school for five years, Caldwell married a divorced man in a civil ceremony. On learning of this, the school advised her that it would not be renewing her contract in the subsequent year on the basis that her conduct violated its teaching contract, which required Catholic teachers to exhibit the highest model of Christian behaviour. Her complaint to the Board of Inquiry under the *British Columbia Human Rights Code* was dismissed on the basis that the *Code* allowed for discrimination based on "bona fide qualifications in respect of his occupation or employment." This adverse decision was upheld by the Supreme Court of Canada, which observed that Caldwell would have been entitled to reinstatement had she been hired in a secular or public school, but in a Catholic school there is a religious element that forms part of the nature of a Catholic education. One qualification of teachers in such a setting is that they act as exemplars to the students through their adherence to the Catholic faith. The Court observed that the special role teachers play allows such discrimination, even though a Catholic school would not, for example, be allowed to impose similar requirements on a janitor. In reaching this decision, the Court concluded by noting that "freedom of religion remains and the right to separate schools continues" as guaranteed by Section 92 of the *Constitution Act*.

In *Shewan and Shewan v. Abbotsford School District No. 34* (1987), a husband and wife, both of whom were teachers, submitted a relatively modest semi-nude photograph of the wife to a so-called men's magazine, which published it. The local school board, on learning of the photograph, suspended both teachers for six weeks (which raises the issue of the hypocrisy of whoever perused the magazine, recognized the teacher in the photograph, and brought it to the board's attention). The teachers won an internal appeal on the basis that the board should have applied a more lenient nationwide standard of acceptable behaviour and not a local community standard. The matter went to the British Columbia Court of Appeal on the issue of what constituted "misconduct" and whether the standard to be applied should be one of a local or nationwide nature.

The Court of Appeal noted that the BC Teachers' Federation condemns the public display of all pornographic material and that it defines pornography as exploitation for a sexual purpose. Both teachers admitted that they regretted their actions and that the magazine was not the sort of publication they would recommend to their students. The court ruled that the teachers' actions violated local community standards and undermined respect for the education system and their own ability to carry out their roles as moral exemplars. In a passage subsequently adopted by the Supreme Court of Canada in *R. v. Audet* (1996), the Court of Appeal noted:

> The reason why off-the-job conduct may amount to misconduct is that a teacher holds a position of trust, confidence and responsibility. If he or she acts in an improper way, on or off the job, there may be a loss of public confidence in the teacher and in the public school system, a loss of respect by students for the teacher involved, and other teachers generally, and there may be controversy within the school and within the community which disrupts the proper carrying on of the educational system.*

In the Internet Age, interesting issues arise as to how a teacher's private "browsing" habits may affect his or her suitability as role model. In *Ontario College of Teachers v. King* (2003), Mr. King, while a member of the college, was teaching at a private kindergarten in Hong Kong. As part of his equipment, both a laptop and a desktop computer had been made available to him. All staff were provided with a policy on Internet use, which included a prohibition on visiting pornographic sites. A firewall program identified King as having visited a number of sites containing child pornography, though he had not downloaded content from them. All of this activity occurred outside school hours and was unknown to any of his students. Furthermore, such viewing did not constitute a crime in Hong Kong. King was dismissed from his position at the school; he then faced a hearing in front of the Ontario College of Teachers as to whether his conduct was unbecoming a member.

---

*R. v. Audet (1996).

The college found that the viewing of the material was reprehensible and appalling, and that it was immaterial where or when it occurred, and on that basis suspended King's certificate and ordered that he undergo psychiatric testing as well as sensitivity training.

REFLECTIVE TASK

Did the Right Thing

Think about a situation where you did the right thing and that you feel proud about. It might have been last week, last month, last year, or even many years ago. What, specifically, was it about what you did that made you feel proud? Was it that you had to overcome opposition to doing the right thing? Was it that it took courage on your part? Was it that other recognized what you did? Was it that the outcomes were satisfying for you or others? Or something else? After taking as much time as you need to fully articulate what was good about what you did, ask yourself how you can take what you learned from that experience and apply it to being more ethical in the future. You might want to make a specific written commitment to do things that you believe will make you more ethical.

CRIMINAL BEHAVIOUR

The requirement that a teacher's private life not bring the profession into disrepute can extend to criminal activity and result in a teacher being reprimanded for professional misconduct. In *Ontario College of Teachers v. GWD* (1999), a teacher was found guilty of professional misconduct when he became involved in an altercation with the police and was convicted of assaulting an officer in an attempt to resist arrest, even though the act took place outside school hours and no students were involved. Similarly, a conviction for trafficking in cocaine—and, incidentally, being known in the drug subculture as "Teacher"—was grounds for dismissal (*Ontario College of Teachers v. Hungerford*, 1999). Other conduct that has been found to be actionable includes engaging the services of a prostitute (*Ontario College of Teachers v. Knott*, 2000) and attempting to bribe a school official in order to protect employment during a period of downsizing (*Ontario College of Teachers v. Kuhn*, 1998).

Community standards are changing, and conduct that once was cause for dismissal, such as simple possession of marijuana, would likely no longer be accepted as such in the public school system. However, in a school established in part for religious reasons, an argument could be made that a higher standard of behaviour is required of teachers and that the conviction could be grounds for firing.

Wrongdoing that predates a person entering the teaching profession may also result in censure, as in *Ontario College of Teachers v. Haines* (1999), where an applicant lied about her qualifications in order to obtain a teaching certificate. This constituted professional misconduct even though she was not a teacher at the time. *Ontario College of Teachers v. Raciot* (2001) took this principle a step further (or back). Ms. Raciot applied to the University of Ottawa for entrance into their Bachelor of Education program for French studies. The program required a candidate to hold a Bachelor of Arts degree. In fact, Raciot had completed only one-third of the requirements for a BA, but through an administrative error, this was overlooked. She successfully completed her Bachelor of Education program and on that basis was issued a teaching certificate and employed by the City of London school board.

When the administrative error was discovered, Raciot admitted the deception and offered to make up the missing courses. The University of Ottawa elected not to revoke her degree in Education, but the Discipline Committee of the College of Teachers characterized her behaviour as "disgraceful, dishonourable and unprofessional. In addition, the Committee believes that this reprehensible behaviour must be dealt with severely as it undermines the integrity of the profession, which depends upon its members providing accurate information concerning their qualifications." Her teaching certificate was revoked, and a substantial fine imposed.

In *Toronto District School Board v. Ontario Secondary School Teachers' Federation* (2011), a special education teacher in grades one through three was found guilty of engaging in an unwanted kiss and sexual touching of a female acquaintance in a shopping mall parking lot while off duty. The trial judge declined to enter a conviction, in part because it would likely negatively impact his employment, and sentenced him to a conditional discharge with probation. On learning of the finding of guilt, the school board terminated his employment because he was "an appreciable threat" to people at the school, because his continued employment would damage the board's reputation, and because he was no longer capable of performing his duties due to his "impaired moral authority." The teacher appealed his termination and at arbitration provided an expert medical opinion from a psychiatrist that he was not a risk to offend against children, students, colleagues, or parents.

When the board challenged the arbitrator's decision, the court found that it was appropriate because the board had not established that the teacher posed a danger to students, staff, or parents. With respect to reputation and moral authority, the only evidence on this issue was a letter from the school principal, who described him as an asset to the school. As such, the court affirmed that there is no general presumption of just cause to terminate a teacher for an off-duty criminal offence, even though the threshold is lower by virtue of a teacher being entrusted with the care and safety of children.

In *R. v. Cole* (2012), a teacher responsible for his school's computer network, including students' e-mails and files, downloaded nude pictures that one sixteen-year-old student sent of herself to another. A school board technician accessed the teacher's computer to check for a virus and found the photos in a hidden folder. The technician alerted the principal, who provided the teacher's computer to the police. They copied the hard drive without obtaining a warrant, believing they had authority to do so because the school board owned the computer. The teacher was charged with possession of child pornography and unauthorized use of a computer contrary to the *Criminal Code*. The teacher argued that all teachers at the school had access to board-issued password-protected computers on weekends and vacations for their exclusive use, and that they stored personal data in addition to their work data. This had led him to believe he had a reasonable expectation of privacy. The Ontario Court of Justice agreed, ruling that the evidence was inadmissible because the computer had been seized without a warrant. However, the Court of Appeal found that the board's search of the computer had been within its responsibility and obligation to ensure a safe school environment for its students. The case was ultimately taken to the Supreme Court of Canada, which ruled that the images obtained from the teacher's computer were admissible into evidence because their exclusion would "have a marked negative impact on the truth-seeking function of the criminal trial process."

WHAT THE CODES SAY

Unethical to Discredit the Profession

It shall be unethical for a teacher, while acting in a professional capacity or otherwise, to engage in misconduct of a reprehensible and serious nature which, in the opinion of the Professional Conduct and Standards Committee, discredits the teaching profession or raises serious concerns as to the teacher's integrity.

—From the New Brunswick Teachers' Association Code of Professional Conduct

SEXUAL ORIENTATION

Most people would identify freedom from discrimination as central to a just society. Barring an individual from employment solely on the basis of gender or ethnic heritage, for example, is widely accepted as unfair. Applying such a universal statement to the individual circumstances of a teacher, however, may not be so easy, as illustrated by the Supreme Court of Canada in *Vriend v. Alberta* (1998).

Mr. Vriend was employed as a teacher at King's College, an institution in Alberta set up to promote learning in a Christian environment. During the three years of his employment he had received regular pay increases and positive work evaluations. On being asked by the president of the College whether he was homosexual, Vriend indicated that he was. Shortly afterwards, the college's Board of Governors passed a position statement condemning homosexuality and requested his resignation solely on that basis. Vriend refused to resign and filed a complaint with the Alberta Human Rights Commission.

The ethical and legal dilemmas posed by *Vriend* are profound. The school had been founded largely to foster an environment where Christian values could be promoted. According to the college, given that the Bible condemns homosexual relationships it was inappropriate for Vriend to continue on the staff. To require that the college continue to hire gays and lesbians was contrary to the freedom of conscience and religion guaranteed not only in the *Charter*, but also by a long series of legal decisions in Canada.

However, discrimination against gays and lesbians has been increasingly recognized as a social evil, especially in a school setting, where tolerance should be promoted. The Supreme Court of Canada had already clearly stated in *Egan v. Canada* (1995) that gays and lesbians "whether as individuals or couples, form an identifiable minority who have suffered and continue to suffer serious social, political and economic disadvantage" and that sexual orientation should be protected from discrimination under the *Charter*.

Vriend went to the Supreme Court of Canada on the narrow issue of whether Alberta's *Individual's Rights Protection Act* was unconstitutional by virtue of denying rights based on sexual orientation. The Court held that the failure to include sexual orientation was an indirect way of permitting discrimination against gays and lesbians. Furthermore, by refusing to protect sexual orientation in the same manner that other attributes such as age or gender were protected, the *Act* discriminated between homosexuals and heterosexuals in that the former class of people was unfairly impacted by the omission in the legislation. Finally, the Court was highly dismissive of the province's submission that the *Act* did not create discrimination against homosexuals (because the *Act* was silent on it) but rather that it existed in society. The Court described the argument as superficial because the *Act* was intended to protect against such discrimination as unfortunately existed in society. As the *Act's* stated purpose was to protect the rights and dignity of all persons in Alberta, the omission of sexual orientation could not be demonstrably justifiable and the legislation was unconstitutional.

Reaction to *Vriend* was mixed. Some commentators read it as a declaration by the Court that religious schools could not practise faith-based hiring practices; others stated that the case allowed religious schools to refuse employment to teachers based on their sexual orientation. In fact the decision did neither. It *did* reiterate the protection that gays and lesbians are afforded in Canadian society, and it found that legislatures, either through omission or commission, must recognize this protection when drafting their human rights codes. The right of separate schools to specify the personal characteristics of the teachers they employ, as role models of virtuous character, however, remains intact.

The Supreme Court of Canada had the opportunity to readdress the conflict between religious expectations and personal rights in *Trinity Western University v. British Columbia College of Teachers* (2001). Trinity Western was a private institution associated with the Evangelical Free Church of Canada. It had been established for the purpose of offering an "academically responsible education within a distinctive Christian context." In 1985, Trinity Western, in conjunction with the secular Simon Fraser University, started a teacher training program that offered baccalaureate degrees in education on completion of a five-year course, four years of which were to be spent at Trinity Western, the fifth at Simon Fraser University. In 1995, Trinity Western applied to the British Columbia College of Teachers for permission to assume full responsibility for the program.

Trinity Western University, consistent with its religious mandate, required students and staff to sign a community standards document that stated that they were, among other things, to:

> refrain from practices that are biblically condemned. These include but are not limited to drunkenness (Eph. 5:18), swearing or use of profane language (Eph. 4:29, 5:4; Jas. 3:1–12), harassment (Jn. 13:34–35; Rom. 12:9–21; Eph. 4:31), all forms of dishonesty including cheating and stealing (Prov. 12:22; Col. 3:9; Eph. 4:28), abortion (Ex. 20:13; Ps. 139:13–16), involvement in the occult (Acts 19:19; Gal. 5:19), and sexual sins including premarital sex, adultery, *homosexual behaviour*, and viewing of pornography (I Cor. 6:12–20; Eph. 4:17–24; I Thess. 4:3–8; Rom. 2:26–27; I Tim. 1:9–10). Furthermore married members of the community agree to maintain the sanctity of marriage and to take every positive step possible to avoid divorce. [Emphasis added.]*

The BC College of Teachers rejected Trinity's application on the basis that:

> Labelling homosexual behaviour as sinful has the effect of excluding persons whose sexual orientation is gay or lesbian. The Council believes and is supported by law in the belief that sexual orientation is no more separable from a person than colour. Persons of homosexual orientation, like persons of colour, are entitled to protection and freedom from discrimination under the law.**

The Supreme Court of Canada, in reviewing the decision of the College of Teachers, observed that it was correct to consider the protection of gays and lesbians in determining whether to accredit a private institution. However, it had failed in not also taking into account the right of religious freedom of Trinity Western University. The effect of the College of Teachers' decision was to limit the freedom of association of a particular religious group. Not only was Trinity Western University affected but so also were those students who, because of their religious affiliation, would be forced to attend a secular university for at least one year.

There was no evidence before the Court that teachers graduating from the Trinity Western program fostered discriminatory practices in the public school system, either through their teaching habits or by conduct in their personal lives. The freedom to hold beliefs, the Court observed, was wider than the freedom to act on those beliefs. Thus while a teacher might be censured for acting in a discriminatory manner, having such beliefs was within their rights. In the absence of such evidence, which could have been obtained by asking for reports on student teachers and opinions of school principals and superintendents, or by examining discipline files involving Trinity Western graduates and other teachers affiliated with a Christian school of that nature, there was no basis for denying the university's application.

---

*Trinity Western University, General University Policies, p. 296. <https://www.twu.ca/academics/calendar/ac0910-general-university-policies.pdf>

**Trinity Western University v. British Columbia College of Teachers

■ REFLECTING ON THE CHAPTER

Now might be a good time to reflect on your personal characteristics that are relevant to being a teacher. Do you have any habits or tendencies that you have tried unsuccessfully to discontinue or that you have lied to others about? These are just the kinds of activities that could land you in trouble with your school community. What is your relationship with these behaviours, given that you yourself at some level consider them undesirable? How could you go about changing or stopping them? Or do you perhaps not really want to stop?

What about characteristics that are not possible to change but that might not be approved of by the community at large or a vocal minority of the community? Have you had experience defending yourself or someone you know against discrimination? How successful were you? How might you do so more effectively in the future when your career as a teacher may depend on it?

Take some time to reflect on these and any other questions that might occur to you about the public and private roles of teachers.

SUMMARY

Teachers are expected to teach by example as well as by classroom instruction. They are seen as role models and, as such, are expected to display consistency between in-school and out-of-school behaviour. This means that a teacher's personal life and public role are not as separate as they are for other professionals or members of the general public. In addition to the burden this entails, difficulties certainly arise because just what behaviours are allowed and disallowed varies within and across communities. In general, teachers are expected to be reliable and trustworthy moral exemplars. They are expected to refrain from any public activities that might cause the school environment to be negatively affected, particularly by voicing opinions that are disrespectful of others or by undermining confidence in the teaching profession. Denominational schools present a particularly challenging circumstance, for teachers are expected to be upholders of religious tenets, including those relating to sexual orientation and behaviour.

QUESTIONS FOR DISCUSSION

1. What sort of role model do you think you represent? Which of your personal characteristics and qualities are central to this representation? Which of these characteristics and qualities could you change? Which would you like to change to make you a better role model? Why?
2. What harms are done to students by setting a bad example? What are the benefits of being a good role model? Consider, for example, teachers who smoke during breaks—is this contrary to setting a good example? Explain.
3. Should school boards warn prospective teachers about certain acts that, while not illegal, are considered by the local community to be unacceptable and therefore may be grounds for sanctions? What about circumstances where a community is in transition and standards are in flux?

CASE STUDY

SUBVERSIVE BLOGGING

You are teaching at an elementary school, working with students in grades three through five. You manage an anonymous blog on education policy that does not indicate your name, although you do make public that you are a practising teacher in an effort to establish the credibility of the content. When the district superintendent reveals changes to the yearly testing plans, you post an impassioned commentary that is critical of the district and the province for failing to incorporate the knowledge and views of educational experts. The parent of a student in your homeroom class sees your post and, after considerable effort using her knowledge of Internet code, determines your identity. She then circulates a letter to your principal, the district superintendent, and the local newspaper accusing you of spending too much time undermining the educational climate of the district and not enough time teaching.

1. Do you think the blog post violates any ethical standards of your teachers' association? If so, which ones? Do you think the expectation, or lack thereof, is just?
2. What difference does it make, if any, that you directed your criticism at the district and not toward a fellow teacher or the parent of a student in your school?
3. Would it have made any difference if you had not identified yourself on your blog as a teacher? Why or why not?

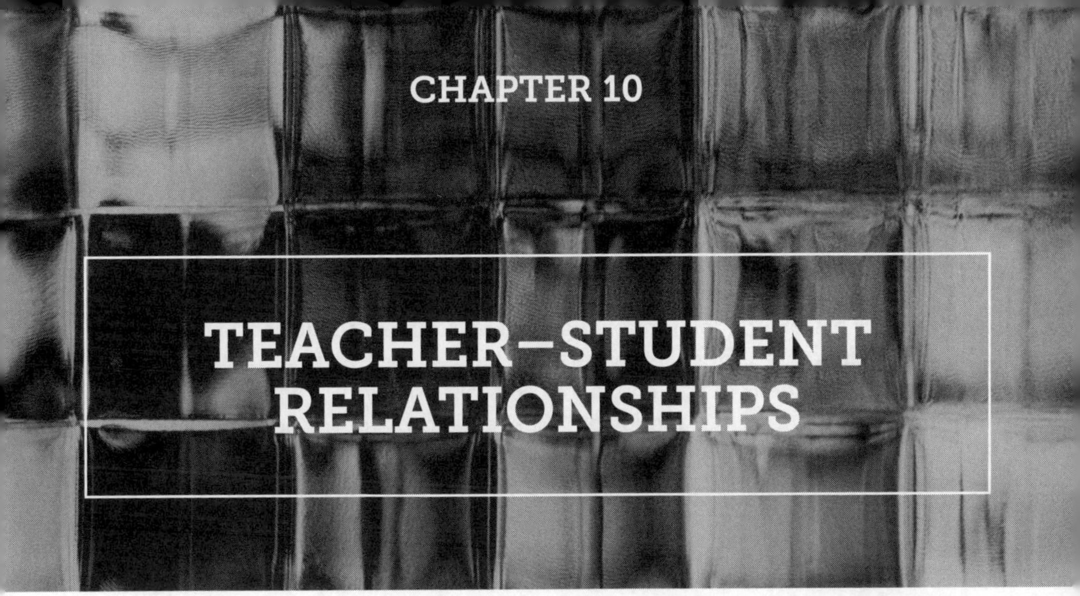

CHAPTER 10

TEACHER–STUDENT RELATIONSHIPS

CASE STUDY

COMMON INTEREST

You are in your first posting as a teacher and find yourself enjoying the company of a particular student. The student is a minor, though physically and emotionally very mature, and shares a common interest in jazz music. The two of you often strike up a conversation outside of class about music and your favourite musicians. Truth be told, if the student were a little older, and you were a little younger, and you weren't the student's teacher … well, you would probably find yourself romantically involved with each other. Fortunately, the school year comes to an end without incident. You have time to let your ardour cool and gather your wits before the next term starts. However, during the summer break you meet the student at a local jazz club. The student is celebrating having attained the legal drinking age and offers to buy you a drink.

1. Does it make a difference that you are not currently the student's teacher? What difference would it make if the student were attending another school next year?
2. What difference would it make if the student's parents were present at the jazz club and clearly approved of a relationship between the two of you?
3. Of what importance is the student's age? What difference, if any, would it make if the student were of the age of majority? What difference, if any, would it make if you were only a few years older than the student?

Good teachers do not treat pupils with the polite but disinterested formality that good doctors and lawyers, for example, show toward their patients and clients. While doctoring is aided by a calming bedside manner and lawyering by establishing trust with clients, effective teaching and learning depends on a good teacher–student relationship. The development of positive relationships with students is central to their motivation, intellectual development, and achievement, as well as to establishing a supportive and safe classroom environment that enables learning. It is the foundation for holding students' interest and fostering their imagination, and it is often by taking a personal interest in students that teachers find ways to engage them in the curriculum. Establishing and maintaining educative relationships requires time, sensitivity, respect, caring, and considerable emotional investment on the part of teachers.

Also part of teaching is the reality that teacher–student relationships are reciprocal. That is, teachers influence students, and students influence teachers. This shared influence can manifest itself in student success and teacher satisfaction, or their opposites. Students look to the teacher for guidance and approval, and teachers take pleasure in being liked and respected by students—and feel the sting of being detested by them. Reciprocity, then, involves a great deal of personal involvement as relationships are developed, negotiated, and maintained. And it naturally entails relational tensions around issues of caring, conflict, and betrayal.

Often, the very actions that teachers employ to promote student engagement, such as showing interest in a student or helping a student through a difficult time, can be those that are considered "unprofessional" by other teachers or that students may choose to exploit. Many veteran teachers remember being young and inexperienced and how being "too friendly" with students caused relational problems that affected the quality of their teaching. Especially in their first year of teaching and with older students who are closer in age to them, young teachers often have a greater need to be liked or to be friends with students. This places them at greater risk of putting their own needs ahead of their students' and of finding themselves in awkward relationships with students that they later regret.

The reciprocal nature of teacher–student interactions can manifest itself in strong emotions in the classroom, both pleasant and unpleasant. Keeping themselves and the classroom in a productive zone of emotion—on an "even keel"—can be a challenge as teachers negotiate their relationships with students. For example, teachers often find themselves having to regulate their negative emotions, such as anger, frustration, and anxiety, in order to maintain effective relationships. These constant emotional demands can give rise personal problems. Many teachers decrease their level of personal investment in teaching as a means of self-protection. Others experience overinvolvement that can lead to emotional exhaustion and in some cases prompt them to leave the teaching profession.

More so than in most other professions, teaching relationships present challenges. Issues such as the proper use of self-disclosure, the propriety of spending time with students in noncurricular activities, and how to allocate attention to individual students arise for all teachers at one time or another. Questions like "When does caring become cherishing?," "Where is the line between teacher and friend?," and "What do I do when I don't like a student?" often rear up. How teachers resolve them can make the difference between enthusiasm and fatigue, excitement and frustration. If a teacher emotionally disengages from students, student involvement in learning typically drops off accordingly, resulting in a vicious circle leading to dissatisfaction and cynicism for all involved. How a teacher negotiates relational involvement or withdrawal is therefore central to their effectiveness and professional identity. Indeed, it is often a recurring theme in their careers.

Society expects teachers to act conscientiously within the appropriate parameters of the teacher–student relationship. There are gradations in the degree of involvement with students, and the consequences of being too involved or not sufficiently involved range from trivial to harmful depending on the circumstances and the student. At times, greater involvement is in the best interests of the student, such as physically comforting an upset student when the normal expectation of refraining from doing so might harm the relationship. Determining where "the line" is between too much and not enough poses a difficult challenge for even well-intentioned and well-experienced teachers.

Teachers are expected to keep the best interests of the student as the primary concern when establishing and managing teacher–student relationships. As the professional in the relationship, it is the teacher's responsibility to ensure that he or she gains only a salary (or fee paid for a service) and, ideally, a sense of satisfaction for a "job well done." Beyond that, it must be only the student's development, education, and interests that are promoted via the relationship. This responsibility manifests itself in various ways—for example, in not meddling in the affairs of students that are outside the purview of their teaching responsibilities. But except for behaviours of a sexual nature or obvious conflict-of-interest activities such as accepting pay for tutoring one's own students, the parameters of acceptable relationships often are not clear-cut matters of right and wrong. Rather, the best course of action depends on many factors, and decisions require careful consideration of the issues, including how vital the teacher's personal emotional engagement is to effective teaching.

REFLECTIVE TASK

Exploitive Relationship

Take some time to think about the important relationships in your life. In particular, think about a relationship (or relationships) in which you felt exploited or betrayed. What made these relationships special or impactful (for good or ill)? You may also want to think about a relationship in which you were the one who let the other person down so that you would gain. What went wrong? To what extent are there residual feelings for you from past relationships that impact your current relationships? What might you do to come to some resolution of these feelings?

MULTIPLE ROLE RELATIONSHIPS

As teachers form relationships with students, they necessarily inhabit many different roles, including instructor, authority, evaluator, confidant, friend, and mentor. Each of these roles has different and sometimes conflicting expectations. Multiple role relationships are present when teachers function in their professional teaching role and in some other significant role in relation to the same person. That other significant role can be professional, authoritative, emotional, or some other. These multiple roles can be highly beneficial for students—because they create additional helpful relationships— but they can also become quite difficult to navigate when the expectations of one role are incompatible with or interfere with the other. So teachers are expected to avoid multiple relationships whenever there is a risk of causing harm to the student.

Because of the power imbalance between teacher and student roles and students' limitations due to their developmental age, students are rarely able to negotiate role expectations effectively or to defend themselves against harmful violations of role expectations. As well, students are typically unaware of the teacher's role expectations or their own; they may even at times initiate behaviour or make requests that are not in their best interests. The challenge for teachers is that, because these multiple relationships are inherent in the teaching role, they cannot be completely avoided.

Overlapping relationships in which a teacher has contact with a student, but not a significant role, can be problematic but obviously are not completely avoidable. Such overlapping relationships can arise in situations where, for example, the teacher is active in a religious or cultural community of which students and their parents are also a part, or is active in a local support association for parents (such as for learning disabilities). Overlapping relationships require the teacher to be alert to signs that the student or parent is treating the teacher as a teacher (e.g., discussing student academic progress) and not as an individual citizen, and to take steps to clarify that questionable role expectations will not be fulfilled.

"Boundaries" refers to the framework that defines the expectations for the people involved in different roles. They clarify the role expectations that make the teacher–student relationship safe and beneficial for the student; they constitute the field on which ethical and legal expectations are enacted. They constrain, constrict, and limit the power, control, and influence that teachers have over their students. Establishing and maintaining healthy boundaries is a large part of what makes the relationship one that ensures that students are cared for and protected from harm, and that teachers are not at risk for legal and ethical misconduct. Indeed, boundary violations are the grounds on which teachers are most frequently disciplined.

When harm is inflicted in the teacher–student relationship, it most often flows from the inherent power imbalance between the two, which flows in turn from the teacher's authority and influence, both of which have been sanctioned by the community. Because that imbalance favours teachers, it is they who are responsible for managing boundary issues and who are held accountable should problems related to boundaries occur. Almost all teacher codes of conduct and ethics in Canada admonish teachers to "recognize that a privileged relationship with students exists and refrain from exploiting that relationship for material, ideological or other advantage."

The idea of boundaries was first developed to describe the interpersonal rules governing family role relationships. Boundaries in this context define appropriate family roles (e.g., parents are responsible for children) in relation to developmental differences (e.g., younger children go to bed earlier than older children) to ensure that all family members, and children in particular, have their needs met (e.g., parents turn to each other for nurturance, not to their children). The maintenance of role boundaries within a family, especially between parents and their children, are considered crucial to healthy development. In an optimal family situation, boundaries are flexible, allowing family members to feel close to one another while still having a sense of separateness. In healthy interpersonal relationships, role boundaries are neither too diffuse nor too rigid; rather, they are flexible enough to meet individual needs without stifling individuality.

The concept of boundaries is used to distinguish between what is appropriate and inappropriate in a particular type of relationship. Like the membranes around the cells of living organisms, the boundaries that figuratively surround each party in a relationship are ideally firm enough to ensure the integrity of the individual but also permeable enough to allow communication. If role boundaries are so rigid that members are uninvolved with one another, then each individual's development is impeded through denial of their basic need for nurturing. Conversely, if boundaries are so diffuse that the members are overinvolved in one another's personal domains, each individual's autonomous functioning is impeded through denial of their need for self-determination.

Feminist scholars introduced role boundaries into professional ethics to explain why the (mostly sexual) exploitation of (mostly female) individuals by (mostly male) authority figures is so tragically common. The concept was found to be sufficiently useful such that all professionals, including teachers, are now expected to maintain appropriate boundaries in relation to those under their care. However, the way that boundaries are used in professional matters is somewhat problematic, particularly for teachers. Because the concept of boundaries originated in the recognition of harms caused by the lack of them, there is a tendency when prescribing professional role boundaries to favour those that are more rigid over those that are more flexible. Yet effective teaching requires more involved relationships—that is, more flexible boundaries—than most other professions, and this presents unique challenges for teachers. If teachers are to promote the development of students instead of merely protecting them from harm (see Chapter 8), they need be able to strike a balance between underinvolvement and overinvolvement without violating society's expectations of what appropriate boundaries are.

WHAT THE CODES SAY

Never Exploit Relationship with Students

A member recognizes that a privileged relationship exists between the member and his/her students and shall never exploit this relationship.

—From the Yukon Teachers' Association Code of Ethics

MANAGING RELATIONSHIP BOUNDARIES

Teachers are expected to accommodate all of the multiple role expectations within a circumscribed relationship. Relationships with students outside of the teaching relationship, where either the teacher or the student is in a position to give special favours, or where one holds any type of power over the other, present particular difficulties. Requesting favours from students or any other assistance that involves another relationship in addition to the primary teaching relationship, such as babysitting, risks changing the relationship for the worse. For example, a student who receives a gift from a teacher could feel pressured to reciprocate to avoid receiving a negative evaluation. Conversely, accepting a significant gift from a student risks altering the teaching relationship and could leave the teacher feeling pressured to reciprocate by offering "special" treatment. A frank but sensitive discussion of the student's motives can usually provide the necessary information to make an ethical decision. That decision should be based on a judgment of whether the teacher–student relationship would be changed in such a way that the student might be harmed or disadvantaged.

Socializing with students outside of school-sanctioned activities is a special case. In *Ontario College of Teachers v. Markson* (2001), a fourteen-year-old male student was asked to assist a female teacher in the computer lab. The student developed a "crush" on the teacher. The parents, observing this, brought the matter up with the teacher, who indicated that a teacher should never be alone with a student. Despite this, the student and teacher met that summer on five occasions, during which no sexual conduct took place, except for a hug and a kiss on the cheek by the student. However, a series of sexually explicit notes and e-mails ensued between the two in which the teacher confided that the thought of other females being involved with the student "drove her crazy" and that "the only experience I want to ever have is with you only from now on." The contents of these notes and e-mails came out after the boy's mother discovered a note while doing his laundry, and after the father subsequently searched his own laptop, which the student had been using.

The teacher was cited on a number of bases, including unprofessional conduct and abusing a student physically, sexually, verbally, psychologically, or emotionally. While the latter charge was dismissed, she was found by the college to have acted in an unprofessional manner.

Other examples of professional misconduct have included taking a student for drives in the teacher's car, purchasing small items for a student, and giving a student the teacher's home or cellphone number (*Ontario College of Teachers v. J.L.*, 2001). Teachers' colleges have noted that infatuation between teenage students and teachers is not uncommon and that the teacher is expected to discourage such feelings by physically and emotionally distancing himself or herself from the student.

Simple friendships can also present problems for both teachers and students in that the role expectations in a friendship are for a higher level of personal disclosure and reciprocity than in a teaching relationship. Expectations of reciprocity can lead to feelings of betrayal when the teacher later makes evaluative decisions in his or her role as teacher. Such relationships can become quite difficult for both teacher and student, for they increase the risk of misunderstandings and exploitation. Indeed, many teachers struggle with setting relationship role boundaries in the context of their emotional interactions with students.

Teachers must be very careful about self-disclosure, which can shift the focus from the needs of the student to those of the teacher or change the relationship into one that is more personal than professional. This blurring of role expectations can confuse students and degrade their educational experience. A certain level of self-disclosure can be an effective teaching tool—for example, the teacher can tie examples from her own life to topics being covered in the curriculum. That said, sharing too much personal information with students can leave teachers feeling vulnerable and make them less effective as a result. Student self-disclosure can also create problems—knowing too much can lead to, for example, increased subjectivity when grading the student. As always, the key question is, "Are my actions [in this case self-disclosure] for the student's benefit?" Self-disclosures such as telling stories or recollecting incidents can be a powerful teaching tool when used judiciously, so long as they do not involve irrelevant details about personal problems, fantasies, or sexual preferences.

Teachers in large urban centres have a much easier time avoiding multiple relationships because the students in their school represent a smaller proportion of the people in their community. Thus they can more easily separate their professional lives from their personal lives. Urban teachers also benefit from the relative anonymity of the large city so that overlapping relationships are less common. Rural teachers, by contrast, typically have dramatically different experiences as a result of less (often much less) anonymity and more contact with students and their families. Also, the pool of potential schools is usually much smaller so that not teaching one's own children, for example, can be next to impossible. Unless one is willing to live as a hermit, overlapping relationships are a fact of life in small communities. So the management of role boundaries and multiple relationships is far more complex in rural settings. Yet living in a small community does not absolve a teacher from meeting the same standards for professional conduct as their urban peers (*Ontario College of Teachers v. H.J.R.*, 2001). Teachers in rural communities who want to avoid the pitfalls of multiple relationships must be especially committed to the core ethical values of teaching and adept at upholding them in a flexible manner, while possessing a generous capacity for tolerating ambiguity in their relationships.

REFLECTIVE TASK

Healthy Relationships

So much of the focus with teacher–student relationships is on what teachers should *not* do. Yet we know from studies of expertise and goal setting that the best way to get better at something is to focus on what we *want* to do, and not on what we want to avoid doing. If we apply this logic to teaching, we would set a goal to have healthy relationships with our students that balance their need for connection with their need for individuation. You might want to take some time to think about relationships you have had that nurtured your development, and what made them that way. In particular, what were the boundaries—the role expectations—of the relationship and how were they negotiated and communicated? What steps might you take to emulate such relationships with your students?

SEXUAL BOUNDARIES

In Canadian law and in all codes of conduct and ethics for teachers, there are *no* circumstances in which sexual activity between a teacher and a student is acceptable. Sexual activity between a student and teacher is *always* considered detrimental to the student as well as to the school environment, whatever rationalization or belief system a teacher might use to excuse it. Sexual or romantic liaisons are a violation of the teacher–student relationship that undermines the trust that students and parents should be able to have in teachers.

It is obviously difficult to know exactly how often teacher–student sexual boundaries are violated because victims of sexual assault are usually very reluctant to come forward and many students don't know how to recognize sexual harassment. In the only study of Canadian students, Winters and colleagues (2007) found that 25 percent of university students reported that a grade-school teacher had touched them in ways that made them uncomfortable, 6 percent received hugs or kisses from a teacher that they did not want, and 3 percent received sexual attention from a teacher that they did not want. None reported that a teacher had tried to have sex with them forcefully, manipulatively, or otherwise without their consent. Tellingly, 37 percent reported having experienced sexual harassment, as legally defined, by a teacher. However, only 4 percent responded in the affirmative to the question "Were you sexually harassed?" and, even among those students who experienced sexual harassment, only 13 percent felt they had been.

In one of only three Canadian studies of offenders, Dolmage (1995) reviewed Ontario cases over a five-year period and found that 47 teachers (46 men and 1 woman) had been charged with sexual assaulting a student. Around half the cases, representing 0.06 percent of all male teachers in the province, resulted in a conviction. Moulden and colleagues (2010) reviewed RCMP files from 1995 to 2002 and identified 113 cases involving male teachers convicted of sexually assaulting a student (9 cases involved women but were not included in the study). The offenders were from nineteen to sixty-nine years old, and one-quarter of them victimized more than one student. Victims ranged in age from three to sixteen, with 56 percent being female. Jaffe and colleagues (2013) reviewed cases of teacher misconduct in Ontario from 2007 to 2012 and identified 110 cases of sexual misconduct, 100 of which involved male teachers. Most (57 percent) taught at the secondary level, and 62 percent of their victims were female. Half the cases involved one student; one-quarter of the offenders victimized three or more students. Seventy of the teachers had their licence revoked, 14 were suspended, 11 resigned or retired, and 15 were reprimanded.

As discussed in Chapter 7, a teacher's authority arises in part through delegation *in loco parentis*. From this, two consequences follow directly with respect to sexual misconduct. First, teachers are responsible to the parent independent of any responsibility owed to the student. The parent, having given to the teacher the right of control and direction over the child, is owed a duty that the teacher will not exercise that power in a manner directly contrary to what would be appropriate for the parent. Thus, a parent can sue a teacher regardless of the student's wishes, as in *Young v. B.C. College of Teachers* (2001) where the court found liability against the teacher for engaging in a relationship that the student was in favour of but the parents were not.

The second consequence is that a special relationship arises between teacher and student where the teacher is placed in a "position of authority" or a "position of trust." A position of authority includes the power that arises by virtue of the unequal status between the teacher and student. A position of trust arises out of the relationship between teacher and student in which all of the persuasive and influencing factors that adults hold over young persons come into play, and the young person is particularly vulnerable to the sway of these factors. Therefore, unlike for example cases of sexual assault, consent on the part of the student is irrelevant, and it is the teacher's responsibility to refrain from crossing sexual boundaries.

In 1984 the *Badgley Report* was tabled in Parliament. In its two volumes and 1,300 pages, it reviewed policy, law, and research on sexual offences against children and youth. It also provided recommendations for extensive revision of the criminal law based on the position that any adult sexual activity with children is harmful to them. Ultimately, this led to the enactment of Section 153(1) of the *Criminal Code*:

> 153. (1) Every person who is in a position of trust or authority towards a young person or is a person with whom the young person is in a relationship of dependency and who
>
> (a) for a sexual purpose, touches, directly or indirectly, with a part of the body or with an object, any part of the body of the young person, or
>
> (b) for a sexual purpose, invites, counsels or incites a young person to touch, directly or indirectly, with a part of the body or with an object, the body of any person, including the body of the person who so invites, counsels or incites and the body of the young person, is guilty of an indictable offence and liable to imprisonment for a term not exceeding five years or is guilty of an offence punishable on summary conviction.
>
> (2) In this section, "young person" means a person fourteen years of age or more but under the age of eighteen years.

The Supreme Court of Canada in *R. v. Audet* (1996) is the leading case in the application of this provision to teaching. During summer holidays, Audet, a twenty-two-year-old teacher, had gone to a bar with some adult friends, where he encountered by chance a fourteen-year-old former student. The student was accompanied by two cousins of legal drinking age, and Audet watched her consume three beers supplied by her cousins. The group then went to the cottage where Audet and his companions were staying. Audet left the group and lay down in a bedroom that had two beds. The student joined him shortly afterwards. Audet initiated sexual touching and mutual oral sex, to which the student consented. During the sex, the student became uncomfortable and asked Audet to stop, which he did immediately. He asked her not to say anything about the incident and suggested that they might see each other again before the next school year.

At the trial level, Audet was acquitted, for it was found that he had not been in a position of trust or authority at the time of the alleged offence. No consideration was given to the fact that Audet would return to the school in the fall, where he would potentially teach the victim again. The court ruled that because the student had consented and Audet was a young, inexperienced teacher, no exploitation had occurred.

The New Brunswick Court of Appeal affirmed the decision of the trial judge. The case then came to the Supreme Court of Canada. The Court found that under Section 153, Mr. Audet was in a position of trust by virtue of being the student's teacher and was therefore responsible to decline having sexual contact with the student. Thus, the student's apparent consent was irrelevant, and Audet was found guilty of sexual exploitation.

The Court declined to find that a teacher would always be in a position of trust or authority over a student, noting that theirs was a factual decision where the relative ages of the student and teacher, the evolution of the relationship, the status of the teacher in relation to the student, and so on, could all be considered. Having said that, the Court noted that common sense would lead one to conclude that in most cases, teachers would be in a position of trust or authority. This line of reasoning was affirmed in *R v. McLachlan* (2012).

Teachers are expected to use the authority and closeness they have with students in ways that are in the student's best interests. Because of the unequal balance of power and influence inherent in the teacher–student relationship, it is impossible for a student to give meaningful consent to any sexual involvement with a teacher. Therefore, student consent or apparent willingness to participate in a sexual relationship does not relieve teachers of their duties and responsibilities. The onus is on teachers to ensure that they do not encourage romantic or sexual feelings in their students or indicate in any way that they reciprocate such feelings.

WHAT THE CODES SAY

Avoid Conflict of Interest

A Member avoids involvement in a conflict of interest, recognizes that a privileged relationship with students exists and refrains from exploiting that relationship for material, ideological or other advantage.

—From the Manitoba Teachers' Society Code of Professional Practice

INTEGRITY IN RELATIONSHIPS

The maintenance of professional boundaries requires personal integrity of our feelings, thoughts, actions, and relationships. The absence of integrity is manifested in hypocrisy or insincerity at best, and betrayal or exploitation at worst. Both thinking and feeling are involved when we are confronted with ethical choices (see Chapter 2). If we have well-engrained preferences and lack integrity, it is far too easy to rationalize acting in a manner that is congruent with our predilections and incongruent with our ethical, professional, and legal obligations.

When faced with a situation in which the expectations of our professional role may be in conflict with those of another role, it would be wise to delay the decision and engage in a thorough ethical decision-making process (see Chapter 2). Paying attention to any uneasy feelings, doubts, or confusions and trying to figure out what is causing them will usually improve the ethicality of our decisions. Teachers for whom a boundary crossing turned sour often felt troubled in some way about the path they took but had failed to take it seriously, shrugged it off, or pushed it out of awareness for any number of reasons such as fatigue, stress, being in a hurry, or failing to appreciate the potential impact that boundary crossings have on students and teaching.

There may be times when you experience feelings of attraction to a student. If you want to remain professional and put the best interests of the student first, you should not act on those feelings. It is vital to acknowledge those feelings as soon as possible and take action to prevent the relationship from developing into a sexual one. Be alert to any signs that you may be starting to treat a particular student differently, such as ignoring established conventions that help maintain boundaries. These may include sharing personal problems with the student, offering to drive a student home, and socializing with the student outside of school hours, when no one else is around, or in nonschool settings. These high-risk situations should be avoided, and proper boundaries fastidiously guarded.

If you are struggling with sexual or romantic feelings toward a student, seek assistance as soon as possible. It can be helpful to talk to a trusted colleague or mentor, or to seek professional help from a qualified mental health practitioner. If it is the student who has been sexualizing the relationship, take steps to address the situation calmly yet firmly as soon as possible. Again, sharing concerns with a trusted colleague can be helpful. Even when it is the student who is attempting to sexualize the relationship, it is still the teacher's responsibility to maintain appropriate boundaries. One feature of student sexual attraction that makes dealing with it awkward is gender role expectations. Especially problematic is that males are assumed to be perpetually enthusiastic about sex and that women are expected to passively acquiesce. This can leave female teachers without a socially acceptable script for responding. Many report that they do not want to "hurt the student's feelings" or "harm the teacher–student relationship," for example.

The best way to maintain healthy boundaries in such situations is to acknowledge your own sexual desires, avoid ambiguity when discussing sexual topics, and be alert to the student's sexual attraction toward you. Feeling flattered by a student's attention is a particular warning sign. Proper professional boundaries should be made clearly and promptly with a degree of assertiveness proportional to the student's insistence.

False accusations of sexual misconduct against teachers can certainly occur. There are a variety of appropriate ways to use touch to communicate nurturing, understanding, and support, such as a pat on the back or shoulder, a handshake, or even a hug. However, this sort of touching can also be interpreted as sexual or intrusive, so sound professional judgment is required here. Teachers are expected to be cautious and respectful when any physical contact is initiated; they need to recognize the diversity of individual and cultural norms with respect to touching and be cognizant that such behaviour may be misinterpreted. Similarly, students may experience references to sexual matters very differently for a variety of reasons, including gender, sexual orientation, cultural and religious background, or personal trauma such as sexual abuse.

False allegations, whether they relate to teaching methods or to sexual misconduct, can have a devastating impact on the teacher's professional and personal life. Especially when sexual misconduct is alleged, the matter often receives widespread publicity and the teacher is "tried in the press" with little opportunity to respond. A review of the Canadian, English, and American literature finds that no statistics are available for false allegations. Having said that, in all three countries, teachers' associations have identified false allegations as one of their greatest concerns in this area. In Canada, many boards of education have addressed the problem of false allegations by publishing information circulars. For example, the New Brunswick Department of Education's Policy 701, *Policy for the Protection of Pupils* (2008), sets out that for a false allegation the penalties can be severe, including, in the case of students, suspensions, for teachers, dismissal, and for other adults or volunteers, banning them from the school premises in addition to bringing civil actions against them.

If the allegation has been made by a fellow teacher, then a complaint of professional misconduct will require an investigation to be undertaken, and some recourse may be achieved in this manner. In most cases, however, the allegation comes from a nonemployee such as a student or parent, and legal steps must be undertaken. If the allegations are ongoing, it may be appropriate to seek an injunction from the courts restraining the person from speaking on the matter, as was done, for example, in *Campbell v. Cartmell* (1999), where a disgruntled teacher was making false allegations against the school board officials, including sexual impropriety, forgery, and theft. However, such injunctions are often ignored or the damage has already been done, so that lodging a civil suit is appropriate.

In Canada the courts have awarded substantial damages in cases where the wrongful allegation was made maliciously against a teacher (*D.F. v. A.S.*, 2001) and the teacher's ability to fulfill his or her professional duty was maligned (*Kohuch v. Wilson*, 1988; *McKerron v. Marshall*, 1999). Without delving too deeply into this complicated area of the law, it should be pointed out that in the absence of malice, some otherwise defamatory statements may be protected by law, in particular under child welfare acts.

REFLECTING ON THE CHAPTER

Take some time to think about what you found most interesting or surprising or maybe even upsetting in this chapter. Perhaps you might go back and reread the parts that affected you the most. As you are doing so, you might want to think about why they had the effect on you that they did. Perhaps you might use this as an opportunity to reflect on how these issues might be important in your development and career as an ethical teacher.

■ SUMMARY

Effective teaching requires that teachers and students be in a relationship that is professional and thereby somewhat distant, yet also involves them personally and is therefore somewhat intimate. When a teacher has an additional personal or professional relationship with a student that includes additional expectations, either on the part of the teacher or the student, the primary teaching relationship can be put at risk. The concept of boundaries is used to distinguish between appropriate and inappropriate expectations in a professional relationship. In order to promote the development of students while also protecting them from harm, teachers must strike a balance between underinvolvement and overinvolvement within societal expectations of appropriate teacher–student boundaries. Sexual involvement with a student is the most obvious and blatant form of boundary violation and is always unethical and illegal because it is considered a breach of a teacher's authority and trust. The maintenance of professional boundaries requires personal integrity of our feelings, thoughts, actions, and relationships.

■ QUESTIONS FOR DISCUSSION

1. If you found yourself disliking a student intensely, how might you deal with the situation?
2. Is it ever possible to be completely objective in relation to a student? If not, at what point does subjectivity become a problem? If so, what is the role of your personal feelings toward a student? Can it be a problem if a teacher is scrupulously unbiased? Explain.
3. Returning to the scenario at the beginning of the chapter, have your thoughts changed? If so, in what way? If not, why not?

CASE STUDY

■ ENCHANTING STUDENT

You have developed a close relationship with an enchanting and bright student. At first the student came to you for extra help with her studies—nothing out of the ordinary. However, gradually she began asking you about minor problems in her life that were directly relevant to her ability to learn, such as being upset the day of a test. None of these conversations was in and of itself problematic, but the general tone of your role definitely moved from being purely that of teacher to include that of confidant. Finally, during one of your days off, the student left the class crying. The principal tried to help her but she was inconsolable and insisted on speaking to you. Upon your return the principal calls you in for a talk and expresses displeasure: "This girl needs professional help and not the meddling of a run of the mill teacher."

1. Do you think your principal is justified in being upset with you, or do you think your actions were appropriate? In either case, how would you respond to the principal?
2. Is there anything you might have done to clarify your role in the eyes of the student, or do you think a poor outcome was pretty much inevitable? Explain.
3. What do you think a reasonable parent would expect you to have done in this situation? Do you agree with these expectations? Why or why not?

CHAPTER 11

DIVERSITY AND EQUITY

CASE STUDY

LIMITED ATTENTION

One of the students in your class has a very limited attention span. When you direct your energies to the class as a whole, this student invariably ends up distracted and doing things that have little if anything to do with the curriculum. If you devote your individual attention to the student you can make steady albeit slow progress. Of course, in so doing you cannot help but take time away from the other students in your class, and you feel badly that you are short-changing their education. Alternatively, when you teach to the entire class, the student with the limited attention span clearly gains very little from the class. To make matters worse, the student then often becomes disruptive, further interrupting the learning of the other students. You share your dilemma with your principal, who tells you to cope as best you can.

1. To what extent do you think this is really your problem at all, versus the responsibility of the school's administration? Explain.
2. How would you go about deciding whose interests you place paramount—the student with the limited attention span or the other students?
3. What ethical and legal considerations factor into your decision about what to do? How do you weigh these considerations against each other?

There have always been students in classrooms who are different from "normal" students. That said, Canada's demographic mosaic is changing rapidly. If current immigration trends continue, people long considered minorities by virtue of having immigrated from countries other than those of Canada's founding peoples will be the numerical majority within a few decades. Assumptions that have been made for generations about the shared world view of Canadians—assumptions that were always shaky at best—will soon be quite invalid. And meanwhile, society is now requiring schools to be more accepting of characteristics long considered deviant. All of this means that teachers will increasingly have to teach students whose cultural backgrounds are quite different than their own and whose learning needs are quite different than the norm.

At the same time, teachers have fewer resources than in the recent past. Politicians are asking schools to streamline their operations for the sake of efficiency and fiscal prudence. This usually results in larger class sizes and less help. All in all, a situation has arisen in which teachers are often forced to ignore students' individuality. The result is more ethical and legal dilemmas with regard to diversity and equity in the classroom.

Equity issues are concerned with building community (see Chapter 1) by ensuring that all citizens have access to communal resources and are treated fairly, regardless of their social status or other irrelevant attributes. An equitable community is one in which citizens' autonomy is respected, honesty is the norm, and people are cared for, especially in terms of the fair distribution of resources. Equity and fairness have usually been viewed as the concern of policy planners and politicians. Yet teachers are in the "front line" of decisions involving the demand for educational opportunities. Society expects teachers to prepare students to be valuable members of the community through instruction and example (see Chapter 5). Given this central role that teachers play in society, diversity and equity are key to the professional identity of teaching.

Teachers have to make decisions about how to allocate their time among students based on need and merit. Typically, they are also the first nonfamilial adults that children encounter in a position of authority. Students learn from their teachers what to expect from society in terms of fairness and justice. Of course life is not always fair and just, and some suggest that unfair treatment in school will do children no harm and may even better prepare them for the real world. "A perfect teacher does not prepare a student for an imperfect world," the argument goes. While there is some truth to this, students who receive grossly unfair treatment at school are certainly less likely to build communities when they reach adulthood.

The cornerstone of equity, both ethical and legal, is that persons who are equal must be treated as equals. While fine in theory, this rarely helps much in practice because it is often difficult to discern which factors are the relevant ones when decisions are made regarding how to distribute resources. Canada has long decreed that everyone has the right to equitable access to an education. The framework for realizing this principle is that of *fair opportunity*. Fair opportunity says that no one should receive services on the basis of undeserved advantageous attributes (because no persons are responsible for having those attributes) and that no persons should be denied services on the basis of undeserved disadvantageous attributes (because they similarly are not responsible for having those attributes).

Imagine an educational system that offers a high-quality education to all children with basic abilities, regardless of attributes such as gender or minority status, but not to children with attributes that interfere with the realization of their basic abilities. Such a system would be unjust because children are not responsible for their disadvantageous attributes. This is why, when Canadian courts have been asked to decide these issues, they have used the fair opportunity rule to arrive at the conclusion that students should receive an education suitable to their needs and opportunities, even if it costs more.

But obviously, our society does not allocate unlimited monies to pay for schooling. So in the normal course of disbursing limited resources to education, the likelihood of success if the service were to be provided to the particular individual(s) is considered first, followed by "first come, first served" when the likelihood of success is roughly equal for eligible recipients.

Of course, many decisions about the distribution of resources are not made by individual teachers. As a consequence, teachers are often confronted with policies that run counter to their ethical and legal principles, which places them in a dilemma regarding whether and how to respond. To the extent that students without power are disadvantaged in our imperfect system, teachers are expected to use their knowledge and authority to contribute to change. Most teachers embrace the same broad goal, which is to improve our educational system for the benefit of students and all members of society. But there is much less agreement about the role teachers should actually play in bringing about those improvements. And the role an individual teacher might play in particular circumstances can generate outright dissension. Indeed, responding to inequity in particular cases involving individual students is very likely to give rise to ethical conflict.

It may be desirable for teachers to advocate collectively for social change, yet when individual teachers do so they are very likely to threaten community bonds. Thus, every teacher is expected to carefully balance the risks associated with advocacy for particular social changes against the missed opportunities for social betterment. Teachers are expected to work to ensure that their students are treated justly by the educational system. In doing so, they should be open about their motives and act in accordance with the core ethical values of the profession—particularly maintaining trust (see Chapter 1)—in all professional and many personal activities (see Chapter 5). When systems are unjust, the ethical teacher seeks change at the system level.

REFLECTIVE TASK

Personal Identity

Take some time to think about who you are in relation to groups you belong to. In what ways do you see yourself as typical? In what ways do you see yourself as unique? You might start by categorizing yourself along the dimensions of age, gender, sexual orientation, national origin, ethnicity, (dis)ability, religion, and social status. Feel free to consider any other attributes, identities, or groups that are important for you. Now take some time to reflect on which of these are a source of pride for you or give you an advantage, and which are a source of shame or cause you difficulties. How might your personal identity impact your teaching?

TEACHING ACROSS CULTURES

When we think of *culture,* we usually think of the shared language and customs that provide interpersonal norms for members of a group, such as how Canadians say "sorry" in situations where Americans would say "get off my foot." But it also applies to members of a niche within a society, such as how teenagers often prefer musical styles that annoy their elders. Culture is a social construction in that no one can be categorized as belonging to a cultural group in the same way that we can say one geometric shape is a triangle and another a rectangle. An individual cannot be identified as being of a particular culture based on some essential characteristic. Indeed, there are many ways in which people identify as members of a cultural group, such as ethnic heritage, nationality, and religion, and many ways in which people belong to a cultural group because others identify them as members, such as gender, sexual orientation, and physical abilities. That is, culture can be both chosen by us and imposed upon us, and effects are felt in either case.

Culture is often imposed and sometimes chosen based on some vague reference to race or genetics. Yet the search for a genetic basis for race has proved to be futile; all gene types are present in all populations, and there is vastly more genetic variation within racial groups than there is between them. More accurately, we can say that race reflects a myth about common bloodlines. We tend to see others in terms of race even though races do not exist in any tangible way. Race is a social construction that nonetheless has tangible effects.

Much more useful is the concept of *minority.* A minority is a socially defined group that has less access to power than the dominant cultural group within a community or society. Minorities are typically, though not necessarily, fewer in number than the dominant majority. Women, for example, even though there are more of them than men, are considered a minority because they do not have equal access to power in Canadian society. Although minority status is not a function of any essential attributes of individual members, it has real consequences. In particular, minority students tend to derive less benefit from educational services than their majority counterparts on almost every measure of success.

Cultural sensitivity in education requires teachers to accept that not everyone has equal access to power in our society. In particular, many groups have been subjected to oppression and mistreatment, and the prejudicial attitudes and behaviours that allow such violations to occur are far from extinct. One characteristic of Canadian culture is the myth that we are "race-less" and "racism-less." We Canadians tend to think we don't have a problem with oppression of minorities; we consider it rude to even discuss such matters. But we do have that problem. Differential access to power in our society affects us all, whether we are Aboriginal or European, immigrants or refugees, minority or majority members.

Even teachers, who as a group are fair and tolerant, can perpetuate practices that disadvantage minority students. This is because teachers, like everyone else in society, internalize behavioural norms. Those norms provide information not only about how to behave in order to remain a part of the group, but also about who is not a part of the group. Potentially harmful teaching practices can result from either of these two information sources.

Teachers tend to assume that their values and practices are applicable to everyone regardless of cultural background. This mistaken assumption can render a teacher ill-prepared to teach minority students effectively. When a student does not respond positively to teaching, for example, it is not uncommon to perceive the fault as residing in the student. At worst, the student is viewed as deficient. What is typically not considered is a mismatch between the world view embedded in the curriculum and that of the student's culture. Teachers who strive to treat everyone the same, therefore, risk harming students who require different approaches. Indeed, treating students differently is often necessary in order to provide meaningful access to an education, such as in the case of students with a learning disability or for whom English is a second language.

Cultural norms also define who is and who is not a member of the group. When we perceive another person as not of our group, we do not assume that they share the same values as we do and we turn to whatever knowledge we possess about the group as a whole. That is, teachers can fall into the trap of not paying attention to individual characteristics and seeing all students from a minority culture as different *in the same way* from students of one's own culture. Sometimes these expectations include that minority students are inferior (which is the root of discrimination), but benign assumptions can also cause harm. For example, gender stereotypes were found to be discriminatory in *Tillie v. Moose Jaw School Division No. 1* (1995), a case that involved girls being streamed into home economics and boys into industrial arts.

To teach minority students effectively, teachers are expected to focus on *openness, awareness, knowledge,* and *curricula.* Ethical teachers foster an attitude of *openness* toward other cultural world views and tolerate divergent standards of right and wrong. They accept that others will not have the same world view as they do and tolerate the discomfort they feel when students base decisions on different standards than their own.

Ethical teachers strive to become more *aware* of their own values, assumptions, and biases about human beings arising from the lessons they learned from their own culture. For example, because of the considerable academic hurdles they have overcome, many teachers endorse middle-class values such as upward social mobility. Indeed, some teachers tend to view students of low social status as disorganized, inarticulate, lazy, and unsuitable for high-status occupations. Attitudes like these interfere with good teaching, and teachers are expected to discard them.

Teachers are expected to gain *knowledge* of the values and assumptions arising from the various cultures in Canadian society. That knowledge is especially important when students are struggling with the expectations placed on them by their cultural world view that conflict with those of the Canadian majority culture. Obviously, it is not possible to become knowledgeable about all cultures of all the students one might ever teach. But teachers are expected to learn about the cultures of the students for which they are responsible.

Teachers are expected to strive to develop culturally sensitive *curricula.* Standard teaching methods may not sufficiently address the needs of minority students. In particular, teachers are expected to encourage students to take ownership of their personal cultural identity. This is not to say that curricula must be tailored to specific cultural groups. Rather, differences in cultural heritage can be honoured, varieties of values understood, and world views respected.

WHAT THE CODES SAY

Respect Dignity and Rights of All Persons

The teacher teaches in a manner that respects the dignity and rights of all persons without prejudice as to race, religious beliefs, colour, gender, sexual orientation, gender identity, physical characteristics, disability, marital status, family status, age, ancestry, place of origin, place of residence, socioeconomic background or linguistic background.

—From the Alberta Teachers' Association Code of Professional Conduct

SEXUAL MINORITY STUDENTS

It is difficult to know the exact percentage of students in a typical classroom who are gay, lesbian, bisexual, or transgendered, but the courts have acknowledged that sexual minority students are more likely to have poor educational outcomes and dramatically lower self-esteem. They are also more likely to be physically assaulted in school, to drop out of school, and to commit suicide. Some codes of conduct recognize explicitly that teaching ought to be done without prejudice to sexual orientation (e.g., the Alberta Teachers' Association's *Code of Professional Conduct*); many, however, are silent on sexual orientation though they refer in a general way to the need to recognize differences in students. The difficulty with codes that do not address sexual orientation directly is that they foster a tendency to assume that the issue is of little or no importance and is even to be avoided. Some school boards have taken steps to fill this void through programming, policy statements, and teaching resources for supporting sexual minority students.

In the case of public schools, the courts have found a positive duty to provide a safe and supportive learning environment for all students. This arises through provincial legislation and also through a broader view that the purpose of a school is to inculcate society's values and aspirations. As such, teachers are expected to be tolerant and impartial so that all students feel equally free to participate and learn.

A school board that fails to take adequate steps to provide such an environment can be found liable. The principles discussed in Chapter 9 with respect to "poisoned environments" arising from *Ross v. New Brunswick School District No. 15* (1996) apply equally to sexual minority students:

> In such situations it is not sufficient for a school board to take a passive role. A school board has a duty to maintain a positive school environment for all persons served by it and it must be ever vigilant of anything that might interfere with this duty.*

In *Trinity Western University v. British Columbia College of Teachers* (2001) (see Chapter 9), the Court held that the teacher education program had to be accredited unless there was proof that students graduating from the program posed a

*Ross v. New Brunswick School District No. 15 (1996)

greater risk of creating a classroom environment intolerant of sexual minority students. The Court was very careful to limit its finding to the public (i.e., nonsecular) school system. In applying *Ross*, it specifically restricted it to a teacher in a public school. More tellingly, it noted that while the requirement to sign the Community Standards pledge of the school would prevent gay, lesbian, and transgendered students and staff from applying, potential applicants would be aware that is was a religious-based school. Such schools are protected by the constitution as part of the historic compromise that made Confederation possible. So it is unlikely that the Supreme Court would find a religious school with a genuine belief against homosexuality to be acting contrary to the *Charter* even if the school, for example, indirectly excluded staff and students on that basis.

Having said that, the lower court decision in *Hall v. Powers* (2002) came to a different conclusion. Hall was a seventeen-year-old homosexual student who sought approval to bring his male date to the prom at his Catholic high school (students were required to have permission from the school to bring dates who were not members of the school). The school principal refused that permission on the basis that a prom as a romantic event was a form of sexual activity and that to grant permission would be to endorse homosexuality. The school board supported the principal on the basis that it upheld the doctrine of the Catholic faith.

The court granted an injunction requiring the school to allow Hall to bring his boyfriend to the prom on the basis that the school's position was contrary to the equality rights guaranteed by the *Charter*. The Court noted:

> The idea of equality speaks to the conscience of all humanity—the dignity and worth that is due each human being. Marc Hall is a Roman Catholic Canadian trying to be himself. He is gay. It is not an answer to his s. 15 Charter rights, on these facts, to deny him permission to attend his school's function with his classmates in order to celebrate his high school career. It is not an answer to him, on these facts, to suggest that he can exercise his freedom of disassociation and leave his school ... It is one of the distinguishing strengths of Canada as a nation that we value tolerance and respect for others. All of us have fundamental rights including expression, association, and religion ... For the reasons I have given, the principal and the Board have a duty to accord to Mr. Hall the respect that he is due as he attends the prom with his date, his classmates and their dates.*

A key issue in the case was whether the school board's decision was protected from the *Charter* by the religious freedoms for denominational schools enshrined in Section 93(1) of the *Constitution Act, 1867* (see Chapter 4). Considerable evidence was presented by the board, including from the bishop responsible for the region in which the school was located, as to the Catholic doctrine on homosexuality and how allowing Hall to attend the prom with his boyfriend would be contrary to that doctrine. The court rejected this evidence by not accepting that there is unanimity of belief in the Catholic Church.

---

*Hall (Litigation guardian of) v. Powers (2002).

The courts face a difficult challenge resolving the competing interests of those who are tolerant of sexual minority students and those who are not, especially in light of constitutionally guaranteed religious protections. Some religious groups have attempted to justify their stance by stating that they disapprove of the act, not the individual. However, the accepted view is that sexual orientation is not a choice and that therefore this distinction is not compelling. Both the public at large and the law are increasingly recognizing relationships that are different from the heterosexual norm. Even silence on the subject in the classroom is little better than open criticism—for sexual minority students, like all human beings, to be ignored is wounding.

■ REFLECTIVE TASK

Equity Audit

A very challenging task you may want to undertake is to review the practices, procedures, and policies in your school that deal with diversity, equity, and fairness in relation to minority groups. You could start with reflecting on what group in your school is invisible to common practice and standard procedures. Try to place yourself in the situation of students in your school who are unrepresented. What would it be like to be a student of gay parents, for example? Or to be lesbian? Or poor? Are such students able to see themselves in the curriculum? How might your school be more inclusive in its practices? Even if you don't take on a full audit, the experience of reflecting on the impact of being unrepresented can be a valuable one.

ABORIGINAL STUDENTS

Students of Aboriginal heritage have been at least as ill-served as other minorities in the education system, and probably more ill-served than most. The 1967 *Hawthorn Report* summarized their plight in this way:

> It is difficult to imagine how an Indian child attending an ordinary public school could develop anything but a negative self-image. First, there is nothing from his culture represented in the school or valued by it. Second, the Indian child often gains the impression that nothing he or other Indians do is right when compared to what non-Indian children are doing. Third, in both segregated and integrated schools, one of the main aims of teachers expressed with reference to Indians is "to help them improve their standard of living, or their general lot, or themselves," which is another way of saying that what they are and have now is not good enough; they must do and be other things.*

*Hawthorn, Harry B. (1967). A Survey of the Contemporary Indians of Canada: Economic, Political, Educational Needs and Policies.

Although the *Hawthorn Report* is almost half a century old, the problems it highlights remain disturbingly valid today. Contemporary data gathered by the Assembly of First Nations underline how the education of Aboriginal children continues to be a failure. The graduation rate is a dismal 36 percent, which is half the overall Canadian rate of 72 percent, and 61 percent of Aboriginal young adults aged aged twenty to twenty-four have not completed high school, compared to 13 percent of non-Aboriginal people. Aboriginal students are also overrepresented in special needs placements at a rate two to three times the national average. Aboriginal people aged fifteen and over have much lower educational attainment than their non-Aboriginal counterparts, with 44 percent not holding any certificate, diploma, or degree, compared to 23 percent for the Canadian population as a whole.

These tragic statistics highlight how all education is culture-based. Education provides students not only with factual understanding but also with linguistic and social ways of making sense of the world and the corresponding beliefs and values to interpret it. Aboriginal students are not educated in the beliefs and values of their cultural heritage or knowledge of the traditions of their nations. An education devoid of these, or that treats Aboriginal language and culture as something to be studied, tells Aboriginal students that their culture is unimportant and denies them opportunities to construct a culturally congruous identity. Since the *Hawthorn Report* there have been a number of commissions and reports that are remarkably similar in tenor. Most of their recommendations involve sweeping political change, including First Nations control over education, increased and more stable funding, and recognition of Aboriginal languages as official languages.

The fact that Aboriginal people are seriously underrepresented in the profession of teaching exacerbates these difficulties. Across Canada, Aboriginal people represent 4 percent of the population, but the percentage of Aboriginal teachers is one-third of that. Because of this low representation, it is important for non-Aboriginal teachers to educate themselves on Aboriginal culture. A number of teachers' professional organizations have taken valuable steps towards this goal and identified what teachers should be aware of in teaching about North America's First Nations. Even more imperative is the training of more teachers of Aboriginal heritage.

Even without, or prior to, these fundamental changes, teachers have a significant role to played. There is a need to recognize the history and culture of the First Nations and Métis. Besides empowering Aboriginal students by emphasizing the worth of their traditions, such a change in the curriculum would provide a more accurate and respectful view of the role of First Nations in Canada's history. Schools have been seen as paying little if any attention to Aboriginal cultures. Their efforts have been characterized as a "diets, dance, and dress" approach that furthers the myth that there was one First Nation as opposed to a large number of separate cultural groups living contiguously yet independently. Besides accessing local resources, many of the teaching federations have produced resource materials for teachers, and these should be consulted.

Standardized pedagogy also seems to work against the success of Aboriginal students. The typical teacher-centred direct instruction approach employed in most classrooms often fails to meet the needs of Aboriginal students. This is a widespread concern nationwide and among educators and researchers working with students from *all* ethnic and minority groups. An often-cited pedagogy to increase

Aboriginal student engagement is cooperative learning. This approach is organized around the values of cooperation, sharing, and harmony as well as the recognition that both students and teachers can contribute to the learning process. Cooperative learning seems to improve student satisfaction and achievement because it is congruent with many Aboriginal world views.

It is also the responsibility of teachers to recognize the challenges faced by their Aboriginal students. Many come from depressed socioeconomic circumstances or are hampered by parents who are unable to provide strong family support for a number of reasons, including the lasting impact of residential schooling (see Chapter 4). Among First Nations, there is a significant level of distrust of the school system; this has been seen as the reason why many Aboriginal parents are reluctant to visit schools. To preserve cultural identity and improve student outcomes, families and elders must be involved in their children's education when at all possible.

Perhaps most importantly, teachers should begin with the premise that Aboriginal children, like all children, can succeed. In defining success in education, however, there is a tendency for the majority to view their role as "raising up" the minority culture to the level of the dominant culture. But as we have seen, since at least the passing of the *Constitution Act, 1867* (see Chapter 4), and as affirmed by the Supreme Court of Canada, success in education means becoming a good member of society without having to sacrifice one's cultural identity.

WHAT THE CODES SAY

Respect the Traditions and Beliefs of Students

Members of the Association respect the individual rights, the ethnic traditions and the religious beliefs of their students and the parents of their students.

—From the North West Territories Teachers' Association Code of Ethics

STUDENTS WITH DISABILITIES

Historically, children were excluded from the school system if they were considered unable to benefit from instruction due to a mental or physical handicap. However, during the 1970s and 1980s, society began to value deinstitutionalization and the integration of these students into the school system. Many education acts were amended to reflect this change, typically with school representatives and the parents or guardians of the child determining whether the child could benefit from a regular classroom and what additional assistance was required. For example, Ontario's *Education Amendment Act* (1981) made it mandatory for all school boards to provide programs for exceptional students, with the goal of placing all students in the education mainstream to the extent that it benefited them.

The nature of how students ought to be integrated changed, somewhat, after the *Charter* became law; in particular, the equality rights afforded students with disabilities under Section 15 changed. In *Eaton v. Brant County Board of Education* (1997), the Supreme Court of Canada directly addressed the question of whether

Section 15 created a presumption that students with disabilities should be placed in regular classrooms. Eaton was a twelve-year-old girl with cerebral palsy who was unable to communicate through sign, speech, or other adaptive means, was largely confined to a wheelchair, and had significant cognitive difficulties. Although identified as an exceptional student from the outset, she began school in a regular classroom with the assistance of a full-time aide. This continued for three years until, after consultation with Emily's parents, the education authority determined that mainstreaming was not in Emily's best interests.

Her parents appealed this decision and were successful at the Court of Appeal based on Section 15's guarantee of equal benefit, which entitled students to be placed in a regular classroom. The Supreme Court of Canada overturned the Court of Appeal's reasoning, however, stating that the best interests of the child must be paramount. The Court accepted as reasonable the school's consideration of her special needs (including instruction in sign language), her safety (she was prone to placing objects in her mouth), and her degree of integration in the classroom (which was observed to be slight) in deciding to place her in a special class for disabled students.

The Supreme Court's decision required that "reasonable accommodation" must be made, following the leading case of *Eldridge v. British Columbia* (1997), in that a school board must be able to provide a reason for *not* providing accommodation. This reason (1) must be rationally connected to the failure to accommodate and (2) must minimally impair the student's rights; also, (3) the effect on the student of failing to accommodate must be proportional to the reason (the *Oakes* test; see Chapter 3). This is admittedly a difficult practice to apply. Consider, for example, a school board that denies entrance to a child with special needs who would benefit from a regular classroom, for the reason that the teaching staff has no experience with the disability. First, the fact of the staff's inexperience is unrelated to the fact that the child needs accommodation in order to benefit from a regular classroom. Second, not accommodating the child's needs would significantly impair the child's right to an education (see Chapter 6). Third, the inconvenience of providing training for the staff is disproportionately trivial when compared to denying the child's right to be educated.

However, equality claims under the *Charter* are also subject to "reasonable limits" such as cost, safety, and practical impact on operations. In *Bonnah v. Ottawa-Carleton District School Board* (2002), for example, the Ontario Court of Appeal found that, while a principal is required to consider students' special needs when deciding whether to remove him or her from school, the principal's primary duty is to maintain safety in the school. In that case, the principal was ruled to be justified in excluding a student whose challenging behaviour placed other students at risk of harm.

Just how much accommodation is expected of a school in order to allow meaningful access to an education was addressed in the landmark case *Moore v. British Columbia* (2012). Moore filed a complaint against the British Columbia Ministry of Education alleging that the public school system had discriminated against him by failing to provide the necessary supports for his severe dyslexia. When he was in grade two, a psychologist employed by the school district had recommended that since Moore could not get the remedial help he needed at his school, he should attend the local Diagnostic Centre. When the centre was closed by the school district in response to budget cuts, he transferred to a specialized private school to get the instruction he needed. Moore's parents mortgaged their home to pay for tuition at private schools for the remainder of his education.

A tribunal found that discrimination had occurred and ordered that Moore be reimbursed for tuition and some of the costs of transportation associated with the private schools he attended, as well as $10,000 in damages for injury to his dignity, feelings, and self-respect.

A judicial review, upheld by the British Columbia Court of Appeal, ruled that the tribunal should have compared Moore to other students with special needs, and not to the general student population, and set aside the tribunal's decision in its entirety. Moore then appealed to the Supreme Court of Canada.

The Supreme Court overturned the Court of Appeal and upheld the decision of the tribunal, ruling that the appropriate comparator group was all students in the school system, not just other special education students. The Court ruled that special education is the means by which students gain meaningful access to the general education services to which all students are entitled. It noted that the purpose of the province's *School Act* was to ensure that all students developed their individual potential in order to contribute to a democratic and pluralistic society. This was an acknowledgment by the government that the reason children are entitled to an education is that a healthy democracy requires their educated contribution and that special education is therefore "not a dispensable luxury." The Court noted that in spite of the one-on-one attention provided and the good qualifications of the teachers involved, the special education services provided to Moore were inadequate to support his meaningful access to education. The Court reinstated the remedies awarded by the tribunal.

REFLECTING ON THE CHAPTER

Take some time to think about what is most important in this chapter for you. Perhaps you might go back and reread the parts that resonated most for you. As you are doing so, you might want to reflect upon other parts of the chapter that parents and students and community members might think are most important. If these are different, take some time to consider how the different emphases might be important in your development and career as an ethical teacher.

SUMMARY

Challenges in teaching often arise around issues of diversity and equity. Diversity can be a function of gender, language, nationality, ethnicity, ancestry, age, social status, religion, disability, or sexual orientation. The significance is not the fact of diversity in itself, but that teachers may fail to recognize students' different world views or individuality, and as a result fail to teach effectively or actually cause harm. Teachers are cultural beings just like everyone else, but they are expected to address their students' needs by being sensitive to diversity. Ethical teachers are expected to cultivate an attitude of respect for students' individuality, make every effort to be aware of their own cultural world view, gain knowledge of their students' world views, and teach in a manner that is respectful of diversity. Schools and teachers are expected to ensure that all children have equal access to an education and that educational systems and pedagogical practices benefit all students.

QUESTIONS FOR DISCUSSION

1. In some societies the norms differ dramatically from what are considered universal human rights. For example, currently in some countries girls and women are denied education. Can teachers be respectful of students and families from such cultures and still honour those values? How?
2. Consider the core values of the profession described in Chapter 1 (autonomy, caring, trust, community). To what extent do you think they are culturally bound? Explain. Should some, or all, be modified to be less culturally bound? If so, how?
3. Do you think that education is fairly distributed among all Canadians? What do you think is the basic level of education that all members of society are entitled to? How would such a level be determined?

CASE STUDY

HEARING VOICES

Over the past year, a seventeen-year-old student of Aboriginal heritage in your class has become withdrawn and his academic performance has been declining rapidly. You have initiated an assessment by a psychologist to provide input into how to help engage the student in his schooling. When you meet with the student and his parents to discuss the psychologist's report, his parents say it is of little interest to them. You tell then that according to the report, their son is in the early stages of schizophrenia. His parents reject "these lies" and tell you that the voices their son is hearing are from his deceased grandfather, who was a powerful healer. When you ask him, the student says that he doesn't know what the voices mean, but they do upset him.

His parents say that if they accept a "white man's" understanding of their son, his connection with his ancestors will be lost.

1. Who do you think should have the final say in this situation? You, the parents, the student, or someone else? Explain.
2. How significant a role should your beliefs play in deciding what to do in this situation? What if you felt very strongly one way or another? Does there come a point when you shouldn't be the student's teacher? Explain.
3. If another teacher took exception to your decision—either with or against the parents—what ethical and legal principles would you draw upon to explain your reasoning?

CHAPTER 12

CONTROVERSY AND TEACHING

CASE STUDY

TEACHING EVOLUTION

You teach high school science in a community with a high percentage of people of a fundamentalist religious faith. So you are aware that the teaching of many science topics—evolution in particular—can be controversial. In an effort to respect the diversity of views on evolution, you put a lot of effort into the section. In class and on assignments, you describe evolution as a theory, albeit a well-established one, and make sure to clearly present the margins of error inherent in the evidence supporting it. However, one week into teaching the topic, a parent confronts you angrily as you leave for home. The parent accuses you of "pandering to narrow-minded religious zealots" and "failing to provide a proper education" to your students by not presenting evolution as "a scientific reality." The parent insists that you teach your students "the truth" and "stop walking on eggshells and tiptoeing around superstitions."

1. Is a modification of the curriculum such as this parent is demanding desirable? Why or why not? On what grounds?
2. What is the role of your own stance toward the issue of evolution versus, for example, creationism, if any? Explain.
3. Is there a right or a wrong way of presenting incompatible points of view in the classroom? If so, give a brief explanation of how you would do so. If not, why not?

Teaching inevitably involves controversy because there are inevitably controversial issues in the society for which students are being prepared. But how should teachers deal with controversy? Should controversial issues be avoided? If so, how? And if controversies are addressed in the curriculum, how are they to be taught properly?

As odd as it may appear, in order to discuss controversy in teaching we must first agree on what we mean by "controversy." The initial tendency is usually to think of issues that are likely to arouse strong feelings on the part of students, their parents, and perhaps other teachers. That is, we tend to think that controversy is a social fact as evidenced by significant groups offering conflicting explanations and solutions regarding an important issue.

The difficulty with this definition is that people are often, quite frankly, wrong or ignorant. Some people may strongly disagree about an issue for completely irrational reasons. People can argue all they want about whether the earth is flat, for example—at the end of the day, it isn't. Yet if all students are educated about the nature of reality, such as that the earth is spherical, many issues that appear to be controversial will remain.

What makes an issue truly controversial is when contrary views can be held without being contrary to reason, or, stated another way, when reasonable educated people can disagree. These views occasionally arise from insufficient facts to settle the issue, but more commonly they arise from disagreement about the relative value of known facts. The establishment of sufficient facts to support the theory of evolution or refute it, for example, may one day settle the controversy over whether human beings evolved from apes. Whether science or religion should be our ultimate guide to living a good life, however, will likely never be settled by mere evidence.

This is in part why the aim of education is more than the teaching of facts. An education is intended to prepare students to be contributing members of society. From the point of view of being a good citizen, controversy presents an opportunity to learn how people can hold different beliefs and still live together. The priority in handling controversial issues thus becomes fostering the development of students who are capable of envisioning and creating peaceful and cooperative communities.

The expectations for teaching controversial issues are therefore shaped by two fundamental aims. The first is to develop rationality by valuing evidence, logic, and the careful accounting of the arguments of others. Teachers are expected to give due regard to sound reasoning and to distinguish those matters that can be settled on rational grounds from those that are open to reasonable debate, and to instill such an attitude in their students. To teach as controversial something that is settled is misleading and contrary to rational principles; to teach as settled something that is controversial is indoctrination and is contrary to democratic principles. A properly functioning democracy requires a rationally educated populace that can appreciate controversy.

The second aim with regard to teaching controversial issues is to develop the knowledge, skills, and attitudes that enable students to work alongside other people despite fundamental differences in beliefs. This arises out of the foundational ethical expectation of building community (see Chapter 1). To teach only one perspective on a genuinely controversial issue alienates those who have a different perspective. Teachers are therefore expected to make a balanced presentation of opposing viewpoints on a controversial issue, without sacrificing rationality.

What makes this difficult for many teachers is that when they find an argument compelling, it is natural to assume that all reasonable people will also find it compelling. Yet our interests can never be completely separated from our beliefs. We all have a tendency to believe those things that are in our own self-interest, even if those interests are that the world make sense to us. The investment of personal identity that we make in our beliefs is such that it takes considerable effort to restrain ourselves from promoting them. The fact that we judge certain issues to be settled and true for everyone, therefore, should be tempered by the recognition that they may still be contestable by other rational people.

This stance with respect to controversy ultimately stakes its success on persuading students to take account of the needs of others despite their differences because the alternative of attempted domination and resultant conflict always turns out worse for everyone. That is, on showing students how no one benefits if we tear a community apart by fighting one another over controversial issues.

It also requires demonstrating how compromise is necessary for building communities. This can be difficult, given how compromise is often viewed as a lack of conviction or even hypocrisy. But compromise can be a positive decision to stand back from our beliefs in order to respect and consider the beliefs of others. It involves being willing to accept that the truth you personally hold dear is legitimately contestable by reasonable educated people.

Canadian society expects teachers to approach controversial issues with a commitment to reason and community building. This is manifested by expressing one's own beliefs and values in ways that respect and promote students' autonomy, and in showing tolerance and respect for the beliefs and values of others.

REFLECTIVE TASK

Experience with Controversy

Take some time to reflect on the last time you had a disagreement with someone over a controversial issue. Who was the person you disagreed with? What was the issue? How important is the issue to you? Was the intensity of the disagreement proportional to the importance of the issue to you? Was there an aspect of having to be "right" or having to "correct" the other person's (mistaken) position? As you reflect on the disagreement now, how do you feel and think about the issue? Did either of you shift your position? If so, how? If not, why not? Take as much time as you need to reflect on these and any other questions that occur to you.

WHAT NEED FOR CONTROVERSY?

Having determined what is controversial, we might also ask what role controversy plays in teaching. Consider the following quotation taken from the Supreme Court of Canada's 1996 decision in *Ross v. New Brunswick School District No. 15* (also discussed in Chapter 9):

> A school is a communication centre for a whole range of values and aspirations of a society. In large part, it defines the values that transcend society through the educational medium. The school is an arena for the exchange of ideas and must, therefore, be premised upon principles of tolerance and impartiality so that all persons within the school environment feel equally free to participate.*

If teachers are to educate in a manner that influences the values of tolerance and impartiality of students, then clearly sometimes it will be necessary to teach what is controversial. Also underlying this conception of the role of education is the notion that a teacher is expected to effect positive societal change, even if doing so involves upsetting the sensibilities of some people, be they students, parents, or other members of the school community. In reality, teachers are largely constrained as to what curriculum is taught, and school boards through approved resources largely dictate the techniques used. Thus, while it is easy to say that "a good teacher is one who instructs while a great teacher is one who reforms," in practice social reform is almost always controversial, as the decision of the Supreme Court of Canada in *Chamberlain v. Surrey School District No. 36* (2002) demonstrates.

In 1996 the Surrey School Board was approached by one of its kindergarten–grade one teachers for approval of three books dealing with same-sex parents to be used in his family life education course. In British Columbia at the time, the education minister specified the core curriculum materials, while school boards could select supplementary materials, subject to ministerial approval. The board refused the teacher's request, noting that the curriculum did not include same-sex parenting, that the controversial nature of the material was unlikely to be supported by the parents in the school district, and that there was a risk of "cognitive dissonance" arising out of the students being exposed to views at odds with those of their parents.

At trial level, the board was found to have acted improperly in that it was motivated by religious views of some of the parents and one of the board members. The matter ultimately made its way to the Supreme Court of Canada, who upheld the trial judge's decision. The Court noted that the school board was not wrong in considering the viewpoint of parents who had a religious objection to same-sex parenting. Religion forms an important part of many persons' lives and it is unreasonable to expect that it be left at the boardroom door. Where they erred was in allowing this viewpoint to override the rights of the minority, including in particular that of same-sex families.

The Court observed that families in Canada are diverse, with "traditional" family groupings, "single family" groupings, families with step-parents, interracial parents, foster and adopted families, and same-sex families all being represented.

---

*Ross v. New Brunswick School District No. 15 (1996)

If the school includes a curriculum that requires a wide spectrum of family ideals to be taught, the board cannot exclude certain lawful family constellations simply on the basis that some parents find them morally questionable. All families warrant equal respect and consideration in the school curriculum.

The Court also directly refuted the concern of "cognitive dissonance" between what students learned at home and what they were taught in school:

> Exposure to some cognitive dissonance is arguably necessary if children are to be taught what tolerance itself involves ... [T]he demand for tolerance cannot be interpreted as the demand to approve of another person's beliefs or practices. When we ask people to be tolerant of others, we do not ask them to abandon their personal convictions. We merely ask them to respect the rights, values and ways of being of those who may not share those convictions. The belief that others are entitled to equal respect depends, not on the belief that their values are right, but on the belief that they have a claim to equal respect regardless of whether they are right. Learning about tolerance is therefore learning that other people's entitlement to respect from us does not depend on whether their views accord with our own. Children cannot learn this unless they are exposed to views that differ from those they are taught at home.*

At the heart of the dispute in *Chamberlain* were various beliefs about the role of schools and teachers. Given that a teacher's authority arises *in loco parentis* (see Chapter 7), then the expectation of not undermining parental authority was a compelling argument in that case. Thus, if one accepted that a school's primary purpose was to indoctrinate students into their community's values, then a case could be made for the school board acting as it did in considering the particular views of the community in which the school was located. The Supreme Court did recognize the role of the school board's regulations, which presumably reflected the views of the community, and the larger purposes set out in the provincial *Act*. However, the Court also observed that while parental involvement is important and their concerns should be accommodated, they cannot override the requirement to teach tolerance. Teachers are expected to embrace some level of controversy if in so doing they are promoting the community's overriding value of tolerance.

So if one accepts that education involves promoting a free interplay of ideas as determined in *Ross* (1996), students ought to be presented with divergent viewpoints and given appropriate guidance so that they can decide for themselves the validity of the various positions. Instead of thinking of them as passive recipients of a consistent line of thought, teachers are expected to acknowledge students' natural tendency to actively consider and choose among diverse views. It is inevitable that students are exposed to differing views, whether in a class, through the media, or in personal encounters. The courts have recognized that the school, where students have the benefit of the teacher's objective guidance, is in fact the preferable arena for exposure to controversial issues.

---

*Chamberlain v. Surrey School District No. 36 (2002).

WHAT THE CODES SAY

Teach Controversy Objectively

A member keeps his or her teaching as objective as possible in discussing with his or her class controversial matters whether political, religious, or racial.

—*From the Nunavut Teachers Association Code of Ethics*

CONTROVERSIAL METHODS

In *Chamberlain* the controversy was about *what* was taught. However, sometimes controversy may be about *how* something is taught, as in the 2002 case of *Morin v. Regional Administrative Unit # 3 (P.E.I.)*. Mr. Morin, a junior high teacher responsible for a grade nine language arts program, recorded a television documentary (*Thy Kingdom Come, Thy Will Be Done*) critical of Christian fundamentalist religion. He showed part of the film as a component of a planned assignment titled "What Religion Means to Different People." The next day, several parents called the school to complain. In response the vice-principal asked Morin not to show the rest of the film without first discussing the matter with the principal. The principal determined that the material was not suitable because it could adversely affect the children of fundamentalist parents in the school, that it might not be age-appropriate, and that the project had not been well thought out.

A Curriculum Committee was established to review the matter, and it determined that the lesson plan was appropriate in terms of theme, topic, skills, and learning materials, but not in terms of preparation. They also criticized it for failing to meet the expectations of parents and students on a sensitive topic and for failing to provide an alternative assignment. On that basis, it was cancelled until amended to be acceptable to both the teacher and the principal. Morin was placed on paid leave until the end of the school year, at which time he was told that his contract would not be renewed.

A prolonged and convoluted series of court cases followed on a number of different issues. The substantive question, however, was whether Morin's academic freedom and freedom of speech had been infringed upon. The trial judge rejected Morin's claim of academic freedom, holding that the notion of academic freedom is based on tenure in universities and could not be extended to a teacher of students who were not adults.

This left the simple *Charter* Section 2(b) freedom of expression argument that Morin had an unrestrained right to say as he wished within the classroom. The trial judge also rejected this, stating:

> I hold that freedom of expression does not grant teachers at the elementary and secondary public school levels the right to teach whatever they like to their students as a captive audience. Administrators must have broad discretion in regulating what is taught as part of the school curriculum, and a school principal should be entitled to make such decisions, based on reasoned

> grounds, without fear of lawsuits from dissatisfied teachers who believe they know better than their superiors how to achieve the objectives of the curriculum. Teachers in an elementary or secondary public school have no constitutionally protected right to determine, based on their own personal views, how the aims of the curriculum are to be achieved over the informed judgment of school principals and school boards.*

It is important to understand, in legal terms, that the trial judge found that Morin, as a teacher, had *no* freedom of expression rights within the classroom. This is considerably different from saying that teachers have freedom of expression rights that are justifiably limited in some circumstances, as outlined in Section 1 of the *Charter*.

The matter was appealed on the basis of the freedom of expression aspect. The Court of Appeal disagreed with the trial judge's reasoning and found that the actions of the principal had restricted Morin's freedom of expression. The court noted that freedom of expression had been given an expansive definition by the courts—for example, it included the solicitations of a prostitute, advertising to children, the language of signs in Quebec, the hate propaganda of a teacher, airport regulations prohibiting soliciting on airport premises, and a municipal sign law. It was inconceivable, they concluded, that teachers during the course of their profession had no rights of expression while prostitutes and advertisers did.

The school authorities appealed the matter to the Supreme Court of Canada, which declined to hear the case without providing reasons. Thus, the Appeal Court's decision stands as a precedent. Morin was initially awarded $15,000 in damages but was not rehired. He appealed that award on the basis that the board's decision not to rehire him was a result of malice or bad faith. The court rejected his submission, although it did increase the damages for the infringement of his freedom of expression to $75,000 on the basis that the administration's actions had been arbitrary. As the court noted:

> The attitude of the respondent school board that there is no need for justification of such arbitrary action simply reinforces the importance of the Charter right. The principal's position was that showing the film after he said not to would be insubordination. Insubordination in such an employment context would have serious implications. What is being dealt with in this case is the freedom of teachers to carry out their mandate in a free and democratic society without fear that a whiff of controversy could spell the end of their careers—or result in suspension or other punishment. Is education not well served by a stimulating debate, discussion of different points of view, exposure to different perspectives? Should not teachers be encouraged to challenge their students, to raise topical issues, rather than be intimidated from raising anything that might be controversial?*

---

*Morin v. Regional Administrative Unit # 3 (P.E.I.).

Ultimately, the court noted that there is a need in a democratic society to protect teachers' freedom to teach in a manner that stimulates and encourages the exchange of opinions and ideas. The court clearly indicated that the administrative decision to ban the assignment based on little more than the principal's desire to maintain good relations with parents was arbitrary. Some type of justification explicitly or implicitly prescribed by law, such as a district policy, is needed in order to buttress any decision to place restrictions on how a teacher chooses to teach a subject. Even then, however, prohibitions that forbid teachers from teaching in a controversial manner would likely not survive a court challenge based on minimal impairment of rights. Suppose, for example, that a school board passed a regulation forbidding discussion of religious issues in junior high schools. The teacher's ability to teach would be impaired significantly by such a blanket prohibition, and alternative policies that interfere less are readily available.

It is also important to note that, unlike *Keegstra* (discussed in Chapter 6), Morin was not promoting hateful ideas; rather, he was asking students to undertake a fairly mainstream albeit controversial assignment. From a teacher's perspective, therefore, a major positive outcome of *Morin* is that indiscriminate restrictions on teaching methods will not stand up to legal challenge. However, it is still possible that future courts will find restrictions that can be considered prescribed by law to be justifiable.

■ REFLECTIVE TASK

Prepare For or Improve Society?

Consider the following two narratives:

a. For most of human history, too many people have suffered under harmful and oppressive social institutions. Teachers have an obligation to continually work to overcome unjust and repressive aspects of society by teaching children to do likewise.
b. Human history has been characterized by the accumulation of wisdom and essential values that have enabled the benefits we enjoy today. Teachers have an obligation to preserve these social institutions through teaching children to do likewise.

Which of these two narratives do you endorse more strongly? Can you imagine a reasonable person endorsing the other? How might your preferred narrative influence how you relate to controversy in your teaching?

ACADEMIC FREEDOM

Neither *Chamberlain* nor *Morin* fully resolve the issue of what limits can be placed on a teacher's freedom to teach as he or she sees fit in the classroom. Read together, the two cases suggest that the determination of curriculum is within the purview of first the province, then the provincial authorities, and finally the school boards acting, in part, as elected representatives of the local community. It seems that very little scope is available to the individual teacher to deviate from the approved curriculum. Although *Morin* suggests that a claim could be made on the basis of a teacher's *Charter* right to freedom of expression, it is unlikely that this right would prevail over the responsibility of the administration to control what is taught in the classroom.

On the other hand, the importance of exchanging and examining ideas in a democratic society is arguably the primary reason why we value freedom of expression. The need for critical discourse, and the very complexity of the teaching enterprise itself, rejects a simplistic understanding of teachers as technicians who transmit the fiats of societal authorities. Indeed, the Canadian Deans of Education describe the competent teacher as one who observes, discerns, critiques, assesses, and acts accordingly.

If teachers are expected to teach the kind of critical awareness and political engagement necessary for meaningful democratic citizenship, they must be granted the freedom to teach controversial ideas that extend beyond those that are popular. Teachers must be free to question orthodoxy and explore controversial issues with their students, colleagues, and administrators without explicit or implicit threats of recrimination.

Thus, while the power to set curriculum may be beyond that of the individual teacher, the authority of school boards does not encompass the power to restrict teachers to a verbatim script or an approved official position. Teachers determine how to present the material in the classroom, how to encourage or moderate discussion on it, and how to employ it. In the best instances, they do so as inspiration for free thought. While the content of what is taught may be regulated, teachers have substantial latitude in how it is presented. In other words, administrative control over material cannot totally rule out teachers' academic freedom.

Academic freedom is the right and the responsibility to present, interpret, and discuss all the relevant facts and ideas pertinent to the subject being taught. This freedom implies no limitations other than those that are imposed by generally accepted standards of scholarship and that are required to maintain a spirit of free inquiry, open-mindedness, and impartiality in the classroom. Such freedom is considered necessary for the discernment of truthful ideas and the development of students prepared to participate in a democratic society.

Thus teachers are expected to present their reasoning and the facts and values on which they have formed their opinions as a model for students to consider. After all, isn't this how noncontroversial curriculum is taught? Teachers are able to facilitate student discovery of established facts and conclusions, having already treaded the path and therefore able now to act as guides. Teachers necessarily have to make judgments about how information is presented, and even if they think they have presented matters as fairly as possible, others may still judge the presentation to be biased.

This is not to say that teachers should not have an opinion. Rather, the implication for teachers who hold a minority position in relation to a particular controversial issue is that they are expected to seek to persuade through effective reasoning and credible evidence, and not by persuasion from authority. Conversely, teachers who hold to the majority position are expected to remain open to counter-arguments and evidence on the grounds that paradigms can and will change.

A teacher's presentation of a controversial issue becomes problematic when the disputed facts or values of reasoned contrary views are not presented, or not presented fairly. In such a circumstance the student is lead to believe that this issue is not controversial, or that contrary views are not reasonable. A teacher who is trying to further students' educational growth will encourage students to develop a tolerance for uncertainty and an appreciation for the limits of knowledge, while still valuing informed and reasoned opinions.

There is considerable concern as to whether academic freedom is largely illusory. Unfortunately, there has been little judicial examination of what are the rights of a teacher to teach an approved subject in a controversial manner. However, some guidance is provided by the criminal case of *R. v. S.D.* (2002), in which a teacher was convicted of inviting sexual touching by a person under the age of fourteen.

The teacher, who was highly regarded within his elementary school community, arranged for a number of girls to suck on lollipops in a suggestive manner while he videotaped them. The existence of the video came to light after a complaint made by the Children's Aid Society to the school. In his defence, the teacher claimed that the video was part of a demonstration on advertising he was creating to be used to illustrate questionable techniques and exaggerated claims. At the time the provincial curriculum for grades one to eight did, in fact, include advertising and its presentation.

The court rejected this defence and gave some indication of which factors will be taken into account when considering academic freedom. First, is there a reasonable connection between the approved curriculum and the method chosen by the teacher? Second, has the teacher discussed the method with other teachers and the administration (as in *Chamberlain*, where the teacher approached the administration with the proposed books before using them in the classroom)? Third, is the controversial means of teaching part of a written lesson plan, rather than an *ad hoc* decision (as the court observed in *Morin*)?

Clearly, teachers are expected to intentionally support the development of citizens who are able to engage effectively with controversial issues. It is the development of an understanding of the nature of controversy and the ability to deal with it that is important—not developing students' understanding of some particular issue in isolation. Any academic freedom that teachers have is granted in order that they can help students explore how reasonable individuals can arrive at different perspectives on an issue. Introducing students to multiple perspectives is a necessary part of teaching about controversial issues and is acceptable if it is done as part of a teaching plan with the knowledge of the appropriate school administrator.

In this way teachers are mediators between the values of the community, the educational needs of the students, and the expectations of the administration in dealing with controversy in the curriculum. It is ideally a supportive role rather than an aggressive one, and progress is made less through grand gestures and more by subtle attitude. Indeed, teachers are expected to approach such issues by facilitating respectful discussion in a balanced and reasoned way, and not by imposing their beliefs on students or doing so behind the back of the principal.

WHAT THE CODES SAY

Model Social and Political Responsibilities

These are the ethical ideals for Saskatchewan teachers . . .

. . . To model the fulfillment of social and political responsibilities associated with membership in the community.

—*From the Saskatchewan Teachers' Federation Code of Professional Ethics*

TEACHERS' FREEDOM OF EXPRESSION

Controversy also surrounds the extent and limits of a teacher's freedom to express his or her beliefs and opinions outside the classroom but while still in the school, as opposed to in the community (see Chapter 9 for a discussion of a teacher's community role). A significant thread running through all Canadian freedom of expression case law is that open communication and debate is the hallmark of the free and democratic society the *Charter* is designed to protect. Under Section 1, however, expression can be reasonably limited in particular circumstances, including in schools. The leading case is *British Columbia Public School Employers' Association v. British Columbia Teachers' Federation* (2005), commonly referred to as *Munroe* (after the name of the arbitrator in the first decision).

The facts of the case are that during renewal of a BC teachers' collective agreement in 2001, the provincial government enacted legislation to remove class size and composition clauses and exclude them from collective bargaining. In response, the British Columbia Teachers' Federation (BCTF) launched a number of initiatives, including sending teachers flyers critical of the government's actions to be posted in their schools, as well as information cards detailing the effects of the government's actions on class size to be handed to parents during parent–teacher interviews. Administrators in several school districts removed the flyers from bulletin boards and directed teachers not to discuss class size issues or hand out BCTF materials to parents during parent–teacher interviews. The BCTF grieved the directives, citing Section 2(b) of the *Charter*.

The arbitrator ruled that the directives did restrict teachers' freedom of expression and that they were not justified. The case was taken to the BC Court of Appeal, which upheld the arbitrator's finding that teachers' political expression is protected by Section 2(b) of the *Charter*. The main issue before the Court of Appeal was whether the directives issued by the boards were justified pursuant to Section 1 of the *Charter*. The court found that the school boards had a legitimate interest in maintaining public confidence in the school system and ensuring that parent–teacher interviews met their purpose (reporting on the progress of a child to that child's parent), and that these interests may well justify placing some limit on teachers' freedom of expression. However, the school boards' absolute ban on discussion with parents on school property failed the minimal impairment-of-rights test under Section 1 by virtue of being too restrictive in light of the importance of a teacher's right to political expression. The court held that "School Boards cannot prevent teachers from expressing opinions just because they step onto school grounds. School grounds are public property where political expression must be valued and given its place." The Court did note that teachers' freedom of expression must be balanced against society's interest in effective education. However, teachers' political expression plays a valuable role in a democratic society and exposing children and parents to diverse opinions is an important part of their educational experience.

In *British Columbia Teachers' Federation v. British Columbia Public School Employers' Association* (2013), the BCTF appealed an arbitrator's decision that a school district's restriction of teachers' rights to freedom of expression under Section 2(b) of the *Charter* was a reasonable limit under Section 1. The question before the court was the extent to which the *Charter* protects teachers' expression of political views on education issues in public schools.

The particulars of this case are that in 2008 the BCTF launched a campaign critical of government policies regarding school closures, increased class sizes, and services for special needs students. Campaign materials, including posters and buttons, were circulated by the BCTF to teachers. The campaign was started prior to municipal elections, which included the election of school trustees, and the provincial election. In response, the school district sent an e-mail to all principals in the district advising them that political posters or information should not be displayed in school hallways, in classrooms, or on school grounds.

The local teachers' association disagreed with this directive and filed a grievance. The arbitrator denied the grievance, finding that the instructions to the teachers not to post political material were rationally connected to the pressing and substantial objective of insulating students from a source of actual or potential harm in the form of political discourse in the classroom and adjacent areas associated with it. The arbitrator concluded that the teachers' freedom of expression had been minimally restricted, that the measures were proportional to the objective, and that the effect on the intended audience of parents was modest at most.

On appeal, the BC Court of Appeal held unanimously that the arbitrator had misinterpreted and misapplied the *Munroe* (2005) decision, which was indistinguishable on the facts. There was no evidence before the court in *Munroe* of any actual or potential harm to students from being exposed to the materials about political issues, nor were there any facts from which an inference of harm could be drawn. On the contrary, Canadian jurisprudence, including *Munroe*, was found to stand for the principle of open communication and debate about political issues being a hallmark of a free and democratic society.

In the context of *Munroe*, the arbitrator was also found to have erred in inferring that the goal of insulating students generally from such messages was a pressing and substantial objective. The arbitrator had also misapplied the tests of minimal impairment and proportionality by failing to consider whether there were other, less restrictive means to limit the teachers' expression, and in considering proportionality had failed to identify any evidence or particulars of harm to students that could result from seeing the material. According to the Court of Appeal, the law supports teachers' exercise of their right of free expression in schools, as developed and applied in *Munroe*, and there was nothing about this case that would exclude it from that principle.

Again, the court noted that these rights are not unlimited, and that teachers' rights to free speech with regard to political issues must be balanced against the rights of their students to an education free from bias. Exposure to only one view of an issue about which there are legitimate competing views would represent a failure to uphold the principles of tolerance and impartiality that teachers are expected to promote and foster. However, overall teachers do have a right to freedom of expression within the school system. This freedom includes the right to take positions contrary to and critical of the educational administration and government. Attempts by school boards to control the learning environment impact this freedom and are bound by the *Charter*.

■ REFLECTING ON THE CHAPTER

By now you should have reflected on some eleven previous chapters and, so, should know what to do. If you haven't or don't know what to do, perhaps you might take some time to reflect on why not.

SUMMARY

The courts have curtailed the right of the individual teacher to determine what is taught on a number of grounds, including the need for consistency in education, and to avoid schools becoming the tools of teachers advancing their own agendas. While how curriculum is taught is left largely to the individual teacher, teachers are expected to foster rationality and tolerance in students. Although the courts have held that the *Charter* right of freedom of expression exists for teachers, it is likely that the administration will be justified in fettering such right in exercising its right of control. Ultimately, what is important is not so much what is taught to the students but rather the promotion of their ability to understand that controversies exist in life, so as to facilitate their acceptance of such while they validly support their own beliefs. Only in this way can students become contributing members of a healthy and vibrant democracy.

QUESTIONS FOR DISCUSSION

1. In *Chamberlain* would the result have been different had the students been older? If you think that age was relevant, do you accept that there may be a sliding scale for theories of education, such that the wishes of parents become less important than the benefits seen for open classroom education as the student ages? If age is irrelevant, why does age-based censorship end when a citizen reaches the age of majority?
2. As part of a junior high English assignment, a teacher provides a list of supplementary books, which includes J.D. Salinger's *A Catcher in the Rye.* A complaint is made that the book contains foul language (in fact, it is minimal) as well as conduct unsuitable for a young adult (there is a brief reference to homosexual relationships and a brief passage involving a prostitute). Did the teacher do anything wrong? Does it make a difference that the text is widely acknowledged as a modern classic? Would it make a difference if the book were available in the school library? Is there a difference if the teacher requires that the students read the book? Explain your answers.
3. Where does prescriptive socialization of students in order for them to be good members of society end, and autocratic indoctrination begin? Explain and give examples.

CASE STUDY

YOUNG PHILOSOPHERS CLUB

You are a new teacher at a high school and have inherited an extra-curricular "Young Philosophers Club" from a teacher who recently retired. During lunch one day, a subgroup calling themselves the "New Atheists" set up a "False Prophet Game Show" under the guise of the club. Using caricatures of religious figures on a game board, they asked participants questions that presented the world's major religions in the worst light possible. Two Muslim students confronted them for making images of their prophet—which that religion forbids—but the students from your club refused to discontinue the game. The Muslim students come to you demanding that something be done. By the time you speak to the "New Atheists," they are dismantling the game and are elated with their success. They tell you they have recruited new members to the club and share their anticipation with you about doing something even more provocative next week.

1. Do you experience any conflict about what to do in this situation? Or does one course of action seem obviously correct? Explain.
2. How compelling do you find the argument that students are free to express their opinions so long as they are not promoting hatred? Can you formulate a counter-argument?
3. What do you think the average person would expect a teacher to do in this situation? Do you agree with those expectations? If so, how would you present them in a persuasive manner to a fellow teacher struggling with what to do in this situation? If not, how would you persuasively correct an average person's expectations?

REFERENCES

LAWS

Alberta School Act, R.S.A. (2000) c. S-3.

Canadian Charter of Rights and Freedoms, Part 1 of the *Constitution Act, 1982*, being Schedule B to the *Canada Act 1982* (U.K.), 1982, c. 11, s. 32.

Convention on the Rights of the Child, U.N. Doc. A/RES/44/25 (1989).

Criminal Code of Canada, R.S.C. c.C–46 (1985).

Cyber-safety Act. SNS 2013, c 2; Bill No 61.

Education Act, 1974, S.O. 1974, c. 109, s. 34(1).

Education Amendment Act, 1980, S.O. 1980, c. 61.

Juvenile Delinquents Act, S.C. 1908, c. 40, s. 31.

Young Offenders Act, R.S.C. 1985.

Youth Criminal Justice Act, S.C. 2002, c. 1.

CASES

A.S. (Litigation Guardian of) v. Toronto District School Board, [2001] OJ. No. 3669 (Ont. S.C.J.).

Bain v. Calgary Board of Education, [1993] A.J. 952.

Bazley v. Curry [1999] 2 S.C.R. 534.

Boese v. Board of Education of St. Paul's Roman Catholic Separate School District No. 20, [1980] S.J. No. 211; aff'd [1979] S.J. No. 87.

Bonnah (Litigation Guardian of) v. Ottawa-Carleton District School Board, (2002) 1212, 44 *Admin. L.R. (3d) 25* (Ont. S.C.J.); affirmed 2003 64 O.R. (3d) 454, 170 O.A.C. 248 (C.A.).

British Columbia Public School Employers' Association v. British Columbia Teachers' Federation, [2005] BCCA 393, 44 B.C.L.R. (4th).

British Columbia Teachers' Federation v. British Columbia Public School Employers' Association, [2013] BCCA 241.

C.(J.S.) v. Wren [1987] 2 W.W.R. 669.

Caldwell v. Stuart [1984] 2 S.C.R. 603.

Campbell v. Cartmell [1999] O.J. No. 3553.

Canadian Civil Liberties Association v. Ontario (Minister of Education), (1990) 65 D.L.R. (4th) 1, 71 O.R. (2d) 341 (Ont. C.A.).

Canadian Foundation for Children, Youth and the Law v. Canada (Attorney General) [2004] S.C.J. No. 6.

Catherwood v. Heinrichs [1996] B.C.J. 1373.

Chamberlain v. Surrey School District No. 15 [2002] S.C.J. No. 87; revg. (2000), 191 D.L.R. (4th) 128; revg. [1998] B.C.J. No. 2933.

Cromer v. British Columbia Teachers' Federation, [1986] 29 D.L.R. (4th) 641 (BCCA).

Cropp v. Potashville School Unit 25 [1977] S.J. No. 328.

D.F. v. A.S. [2001] Q.J. No. 3273.

Doe v. Metropolitan Toronto (Municipality) Commissioners of Police, (1998), 39 O.R. (3d) 487.

Donohue v. Copiague Union Free School District, 418 N.Y.S. 2d 375, 47 N.Y. 2d 400 (1979).

Dziwnka v. The Queen in Right of Alberta, (1971), 25 D.L.R. (3d) 12.

E.B.J. (Litigation Guardian of) v. Upper Canada District School Board, [2001] O.J. No. 4174 (Ont. S.C.J.).

E.D.G. v. Hammer [2003] S.C.C. 52.

Eaton v. Brant County Board of Education [1997] 1 S.C.R. 241.

Edward Gianfrancesco and Jessica Gianfrancesco (by her litigation guardian, Edward Gianfrancesco) v. The Junior Academy Inc. [2003] O.J. No. 931.

Egan v. Canada, [1995] 2 S.C.R. 513.

Eggertson v. Alberta Teachers' Association [2003] A.J. No. 384.

Eldridge v. British Columbia (Attorney General) [1997] 3 S.C.R. 624.

Emily v. Brant County Board of Education [1997] 1 S.C.R. 241.

Essex County Roman Catholic Separate School Board v. Porter, (1978) 89 D.L.R. (2d) 445, 21 O.R. (2d) 255 (C.A.).

Essex County Roman Catholic Separate School Board v. Tremblay-Webster, (1984) 5 D.L.R. (4th) 665, 84 C.L.L.C. Para. 14,030, 45 O.R. (2d) 83 (C.A.).

Fraser v. Campbell River School District No. 72 [1988] B.C.J. No. 2453.

Freer v. Okanagon-Skaha School District No. 67 [2002] B.C.J. No. 2739.

G.(J.) v. Kawartha Pine Ridge District School Board, 2009 CFSRB 16.

George (Guardian ad litem of) v. Port Alberni School District 70, [1986] B.C.J. No. 1726.

Germschied v. Richardson [1987] B.C.J. No. 2250.

Gillick v. W. Norfolk and Wisbech Area Health Auth., 3 WLR 830 (1985).

Gould v. Regina (East) School Division No. 77, [1996] S.J. No. 843 (Sask. QB).

Gu (Litigation Guardian of) v. Friesen [2013] BCSC 607.

Haines v. Neudorf [1995] S.J. No. 314.

Hall (Litigation Guardian of) v. Powers, (2002) 59 O.R. (3d) 423.

Hamilton v. Delta School District No. 37 [2010] BCSC 712.

Hawreluik v. Shamrock School Division No. 38 [1987] S.J. No. 108.

Hopkins (Guardian ad litem of) v. Mission School District No. 75, [1998] B.C.J. No. 568 (BCSC).

Hoyt v. Hay [1978] N.B.J. No. 9.

Hozaima v. Perry et al. (2008) MBQB 199.

J.O. v. Strathcona-Tweedsmuir School (2010) ABQB 559.

Kawartha Pine Ridge District School Board v. Grant [2010] O.J. No. 1093.

Kempling v. British Columbia College of Teachers [2005] B.C.C.A. 327.

Kohuch v. Wilson [1988] S.J. No. 682.

Lutes (Litigation Guardian of) v. Prairie View School Division No. 74 [1992] S.J. 198.

M.B. v. BC, [2001] B.C.J. No 586 (BCCA).

MacCabe v. Westlock Roman Catholic Separate School, [1998] A.J. No. 1053.

Madsen v. Mission School District No. 75, [1999] B.C.J. No. 1716.

Mahe v. Alberta [1990] 1 S.C.R. 342.

McKay v. CDI Career Development Institutes Ltd. [1999] B.C.J. No. 561.

McKay v. Govan School Unit, (1967) 60 W.W.R. 513.

McKerron v. Marshall [1999] O.J. No. 4048.

Metropolitan Separate School Board v. Ontario English Catholic Teachers' Association, (1994) 41 L.A.C. (4th) 353.

Moddejonge v. Huron County Board of Education, [1972] 2 O.R. 437 (Ont. H.C.).

Moore v. British Columbia (Education) [2012] SCC 61.

Morin v. Regional Administrative Unit # 3 (P.E.I.), [2002] PESCAD 9.

Murdock v. Richards, (1954) 1 D.L.R. 766 (N.S.C.C.).

Myers v. Peel County Board of Education [1981] 2 S.C.R. 21.

North Vancouver School District No. 44 v. Jubran [2005] B.C.J. No. 733 (B.C.C.A.); revg. (2003), 9 B.C.L.R. (4th) 338; revg. [2002] B.C.H.R.T.D. No. 10.

Ontario College of Teachers v. G.W.D. [1999] O.C.T.D.D. No. 15.

Ontario College of Teachers v. H.J.R. [2001] O.C.T.D.D. No. 17.

Ontario College of Teachers v. Haines [1999] O.C.T.D.D. No. 12.

Ontario College of Teachers v. Hungerford [1999] O.C.T.D.D. No. 17.

Ontario College of Teachers v. J.L. [2001] O.C.T.D.D. No. 12.

Ontario College of Teachers v. King [2003] O.C.T.D.D. No. 59.

Ontario College of Teachers v. Knott [2000] O.C.T.D.D. No. 11.

Ontario College of Teachers v. Kuhn [1998] O.C.T.D.D. No. 10.

Ontario College of Teachers v. Markson [2001] O.C.T.D.D. No. 16.

Ontario College of Teachers v. Newton [1999] O.C.T.D.D. No. 10.

Ontario College of Teachers v. Raciot [2001] O.C.T.D.D. No. 5.

Peter W. v. San Francisco Unified School District, 60 Cal. App. 3d 814 (1976).

Phelps v. Hillingdon London Borough Council et al. [2000] HLJ No. 49; [2000] 4 All ER 504 [HL].

Plumb v. Cowichan School District No. 65 [1993] B.C.J. 1936.

R. v. Audet [1996] S.C.J. No. 61; [1996] 2 S.C.R. 171; revg. (1995), 155 N.B.R. (2d) 369; revg. (1993), 142 N.B.R. (2d) 382.

R. c. Caouette [2002] J.Q. no. 1055 (C.Q.).

R. v. Cole, [2012] S.C.C. 53 [2012] 3 S.C.R. 34.

R. v. Godin [1996] N.B.J. No. 148.

R. v. Haberstock, (1970) 1 C.C.C. (2d) 433.

R. v. Imbeault, (1977) 17 N.B.R. (2d) 234.

R. v. Jones, [1986] 2 S.C.R. 284 (S.C.C.).

R. v. Kanhai [1981] S.J. No. 1353.

R. v. Keegstra [1990] 3 S.C.R. 697.

R. v. Kind [1984] N.J. No. 243, 50 Nfld. & P.E.I.R. 332.

R. v. M.R.M., [1998] 3 S.C.R. 393; (1997), 159 N.S.R. (2d) 321.

R. v McLachlan [2012] SKCA 74.

R. v. Oakes [1986] 1 S.C.R. 103.

R. v. Ogg-Moss [1984] 2 S.C.R. 173.

R. v. Plourde [1993] N.B.J. No. 487 (Prov. Ct.).

R. v. Robinson [1899] 7 C.C.C. 52.

R. v. S.B. [1996] O.J. No. 4724.

R. v. S.D. [2002] O.J. No. 5141.

R. v. W.(J.J.) [1990] N.J. No. 73.

R. v. Wetmore [1996] N.B.J. No. 15 (Q.B.).

R.B. v. Keewatin-Patricia District School Board (2013) HRTO 1436.

R.T. v. Durham Catholic District School Board [2008] CFSRB 94.

Robinson v. Calgary School District 19, (1977) 5 A.R. 430.

Robinson v. Northmount School for Boys [2014] O.J. No. 2123 (Ont. S.C.J.).

Ross v. New Brunswick School District No. 15 [1996] 1 S.C.R. 825.

Schachter v. Canada et al., [1992] 2 S.C.R. 679.

Shewan and Shewan v. Abbotsford School District No. 34, (1987) 21 B.C.L.R. (2d) 93, 47 D.L.R. (4th) 106.

Smart v. College of the Rockies [2002] B.C.J. No. 3119.

Snell v. Farrell, [1990] 2 S.C.R. 311.

Stolen v. British Columbia College of Teachers [1995] B.C.J. No. 1980.

T.(G.) v. Griffiths [1999] 2 SCR 570.

Thiessen v. Winnipeg School Division 1 [1967] S.C.R. 413.

Thornton v. Prince George [1976] 5 W.W.R. 240; varied on other grounds [1978] 2 S.C.R. 267.

Tillie v. Moose Jaw School Division No. 1, (1995) 23 C.H.R.R. D/87.

Toronto District School Board v. Ontario Secondary School Teachers' Federation, (2011) ONSC 7018 (Div. Ct.).

Trinity Western University v. British Columbia College of Teachers [2001] 1 S.C.R. 772.

Vriend v. Alberta [1998] 1 S.C.R. 493.

W.R.B. v. Plint, [2001] B.C.J. No. 144.

Ward v. Blaine Lake School Board, [1971] 4 W.W.R. 161.

Williams v. Eady, (1893) 10 T.L.R. 41.

Young v. British Columbia College of Teachers [2001] B.C.J. No. 405.

Zylberberg v. Sudbury Board of Education (Director), (1988) 52 D.L.R. (4th) 577, 65 O.R. (2d) 64 (Ont. C.A.).

SOURCES

Alberta Teachers' Association. (2004). *Code of professional conduct.* Edmonton: Author.

Blackstone, W. (1765–1769). *Commentaries on the Laws of England.* Oxford, England: Clarendon Press.

British Columbia Teachers' Federation. (2003). *Code of ethics.* Vancouver: Author.

Dolmage, W.R. (1995). Accusations of teacher sexual abuse of students in Ontario schools: Some preliminary findings. *Alberta Journal of Educational Research, 41(2)*, 127–144.

Hawthorn, H. (1967). *A survey of contemporary Indians of Canada*, Volume II. Ottawa: Queen's Printer.

Jaffe, P., Straatman, A., Harris, B., Georges, A., Vink, K., & Reif, K. (2013). Emerging trends in teacher sexual misconduct in Ontario 2007–2012. *Education and Law Journal, 23*(1), 19–39.

Manitoba Teachers' Society. (2003). *Code of professional practice.* Winnipeg: Author.

Mill, J.S. (1896/1991). *On liberty.* Oxford: Oxford University Press.

Moulden, H. M., Firestone, P., Kingston, D. A., & Wexler, A. F. (2010). A description of sexual offending committed by Canadian teachers. *Journal of Child Sexual Abuse, 19*(4), 403–418.

New Brunswick Department of Education. (1998). *Information for parents and pupils about the policy for the protection of pupils in the public school system from misconduct by adults.* Fredericton: Author.

New Brunswick Teachers' Association. (2011). *Code of professional conduct.* Fredericton: Author.

Newfoundland and Labrador Teachers' Association. (1974). *Code of ethics.* St. John's: Author.

Nova Scotia Teachers Union. (2002). *Code of ethics.* Halifax: Author.

Nunavut Teachers Association. (2006). *Code of ethics.* Iqaluit: Author.

Ontario College of Teachers. (1999). *Standards of practice for the teaching profession.* Toronto: Author.

Ontario College of Teachers. (2000). *Ethical standards for the teaching profession.* Toronto: Author.

Prince Edward Island Teachers' Federation. (no date). *Code of ethics.* Charlottetown: Author.

Saskatchewan Teachers' Federation. (2000). *Code of professional ethics.* Saskatoon: Author.

Saskatchewan Teachers' Federation. (2008). *Code of professional competence.* Saskatoon: Author.

Tupper, C. (1896). Debates of the House of Commons, 6th Sess., 7th Parliament, 59 Vict. 1896, col. 2719, at 2724, March 3, 1896.

Winters, J., Clift, R.J.W., & Maloney, A. (2007). Adult-student sexual harassment in British Columbia high schools. *Journal of Emotional Abuse*, *4*(3–4), 177–196.

Yukon Teachers' Association. (2010). *Code of Ethics.* Whitehorse: Author.

INDEX

N

O

P

Q

R